II

Prepare for the Great Tribulation and the Era of Peace

Prepare for the Great Tribulation and the Era of Peace

Volume II:
July 1994 – June 1995

by John Leary

Queenship
PUBLISHING COMPANY
P.O Box 42028 Santa Barbara, CA 93140-2028
(800) 647-9882 • (805) 957-4893 • Fax: (805) 957-1631

The publisher recognizes and accepts that the final authority regarding these apparitions and messages rests with the Holy See of Rome, to whose judgement we willingly submit.

– The Publisher

Cover art by Josyp Terelya

Library of Congress Number # 96-68181

Published by:
Queenship Publishing
P.O. Box 42028
Santa Barbara, CA 93140-2028
(800) 647-9882 • (805) 957-4893 • Fax: (805) 957-1631

Printed in the United States of America

ISBN: 1-882972-72-4

Acknowledgments

It is in a spirit of deep gratitude that I would like to acknowledge first the Holy Trinity: Father, Jesus, and the Holy Spirit, the Blessed Virgin Mary and the many saints and angels who have made this book possible.

My wife, Carol, has been an invaluable partner. Her complete support of faith and prayers has allowed us to work as a team. This was especially true in the many hours of indexing and proofing of the manuscript. All of our family has been a source of care and support.

I am greatly indebted to Josyp Terelya for his very gracious offer to provide the art work for this publication. He has spent three months of work and prayer to provide us with a selection of many original pictures. He wanted very much to enhance the visions and messages with these beautiful and provocative works. You will experience some of them throughout these volumes.

A very special thank you goes to my spiritual director, Fr. Leo J. Klem, C.S.B. No matter what hour I called him, he was always there with his confident wisdom, guidance and discernment. His love, humility, deep faith and trust are a true inspiration.

My appreciation also goes to Father John V. Rosse, my good pastor at Holy Name of Jesus Church. He has been open, loving and supportive from the very beginning.

There are many friends and relatives whose interest, love and prayerful support have been a real gift from God. Our own Wednesday, Monday and First Saturday prayer groups deserve a special thank you for their loyalty and faithfulness.

Finally, I would like to thank Bob and Claire Schaefer of Queenship Publishing and their spiritual director, Fr. Luke Zimmer for providing the opportunity to bring this message of preparation, love and warnings to you the people of God.

John Leary, Jr.
January 1996

Dedication

To the Most Holy Trinity

God

The Father, Son and Holy Spirit

The Source of

All

Life, Love and Wisdom

Publisher's Foreword

John has, with some exceptions, been having visions twice a day since they began in July, 1993. The first vision of the day usually takes place during morning Mass immediately after he receives the Eucharist. If the name of the church is not mentioned, it is a local Rochester, NY, church. When out of town, the church name is included in the text. The second vision occurs in the evening either at Perpetual Adoration or at the prayer group that is held at John's home.

Various names appear in the text. Most of the time the names appear only once or twice. Their identity is not important to the message and their reason for being in the text is evident. First names have been used when requested by the individual. The name Maria E. which occurs quite often is the visionary Maria Esperanza Bianchini of Betania, Venezuela.

We are grateful to Josep Terelya for the cover art as well as the art throughout the book. Josyp is a well-known visionary and also the author of *Witness* and most recently *In the Kingdom of the Spirit.*

Volume I covers visions from July, 1993 through the end of June, 1994. This volume, Volume II, contains visions from July, 1994 through June, 1995. We expect to release Volume III in early summer, 1996.

The Publisher
April, 1996

Foreword

It was in July of 1993 that Almighty God, especially through Jesus, His Eternal Word, entered the life of John Leary in a most remarkable way. John is 53 years old and works as a chemist at Eastman Kodak Co., Rochester, New York. He lives in a modest house in the suburbs of Rochester with Carol, his wife of 30 years, and Catherine, his youngest daughter. His other two daughters, Jeanette and Donna, are married and have homes of their own. John has been going to daily Mass since he was 17 and has been conducting a weekly prayer group in his own home for 22 years. For a long time he has been saying 15 decades of the Rosary each day.

In April of 1993 he and his wife made a pilgrimage to Our Lady's shrine in Medjugorje, Yugoslavia. While there, he felt a special attraction to Jesus in the Blessed Sacrament. There he became aware that the Lord Jesus was asking him to change his way of life and to make Him his first priority. A month later in his home, Our Lord spoke to him and asked if he would give over his will to Him to bring about a very special mission. Without knowing clearly to what he was consenting, John, strong in faith and trust, agreed to all the Lord would ask.

On July 21, 1993 the Lord gave him an inkling of what would be involved in this new calling. He was returning home from Toronto in Canada where he had listened to a talk of Maria Esperanza (a visionary from Betania, Venezuela) and had visited Josyp Terelya. While in bed he had a mysterious interior vision of a newspaper headline that spelled "DISASTER." Thus began a series of daily and often twice daily interior visions along with messages, mostly from Jesus. Other messages were from God the Father, the Holy Spirit, the Blessed Virgin Mary, his guardian angel and many of the saints, especially St. Therese of Lisieux. These messages he recorded on his word processor. In the beginning they were quite short but they became more extensive as the weeks passed by. At the time of this writing he is still receiving visions and messages.

These daily spiritual experiences, which occur most often immediately following Communion, consist of a brief vision which becomes the basis of the message that follows. They range widely on a great variety of subjects, but one might group them under the following categories: warnings, teachings and love messages. Occasionally, there are personal confirmations of some special requests that he made to the Lord.

The interior visions contain an amazing number of different pictures, some quite startling, which hardly repeat themselves. In regard to the explicit messages that are inspired by each vision, they contain deep insights into the kind of relationship God wishes to establish with His human creatures. There also is an awareness of how much He loves us and yearns for our response. As a great saint once wrote: "Love is repaid only by love." On the other hand God is not a fool to be treated lightly. In fact, did not Jesus once say something about not casting pearls before the swine? Thus there are certain warnings addressed to those who shrug God off as if He did not exist or is not important in human life.

Along with such warnings, we become more conscious of the reality of Satan and the forces of evil "...which wander through the world seeking the ruin of souls." We used to recite this at the end of each low Mass. In His love and concern for us, Our Lord keeps constantly pointing out how frail we humans are in the face of such evil angelic powers. God is speaking of the necessity of daily prayer, of personal penance, and of turning away from atheistic and material enticements which are so much a part of our modern environment.

Perhaps the most controversial parts of the messages are those which deal with what we commonly call Apocalyptic. Unusual as these may be, in my judgment, they are not basically any different than what we find in the last book of the New Testament or in some of the writings of St. Paul. After a careful and prayerful reading of the hundreds of pages in this book, I have not found anything contrary to the authentic teaching authority of the Roman Catholic Church.

The 16th Century Spanish mystic, St. John of the Cross, gives us sound guidelines for discerning the authenticity of this sort of phenomenon involving visions, locutions, etc. According to him, there are three possible sources: the devil, some kind of self-imposed hypnosis or God. I have been John's spiritual confidant for over two years. I have tested him in various spiritual ways and I am most confident that all he has put into these messages is neither of the devil nor of some kind of mental illness. Rather, they are from the God who, in His love for us, wishes to reveal His own Divine mind and heart. He has used John for this. I know that John is quite ready to abide by any decision of proper ecclesiastical authority on what he has written in this book

Rev. Leo J. Klem, C.S.B.
January 4, 1996
Rochester, New York

Visions and messages of John Leary:

Friday, July 1, 1994: (First Friday 9:00 a.m. Mass)

After Communion, I saw the Ark of the Covenant which housed the Ten Commandments and it was located in a closet and then the light went out and the Ark was in darkness. Jesus said: ***"My people, listen closely to the prophet this day, for it is your message as well. In the days before the Babylonian exile My chosen people had taken up with the practices of the pagan gods around them. They had ceased listening to My prophets and were drawn to those things that pleased the senses. Today, you have a similar plight, since many of My faithful are also attracted to the little gods of materialism and self. You have made yourselves gods, since you do not depend on My help anymore. Many of My people believe they can depend on themselves for everything—they no longer seek My love. For this, My people, you also will experience a spiritual famine. For those who hold fast to My love in faith, I will protect you, but those who refuse Me and listen only to their ways, I will withdraw all My graces and leave them on their own to be tormented and abused by the demons. They will not taste a morsel of My dinner. Pray, My children, to keep strong in faith and ever ready to follow My will."***

Later, at the Carmelite Monastery with Adoration in Denver, I saw several nuns praying and then I saw a picture of the congregation at Mass. Jesus said: ***"Blessed are you, My child, for you are on holy ground here. This will be one of My refuges that I will protect from evil. There is a deep sense of prayer here in reparation for the many sins of the people. This is a life's calling which few find, but is beautiful to imitate. Just imagine yourself able to be in prayer with Me before My sacrament, able to pray for as long as you will. I am indeed calling all My people to pray as***

often as possible. Because in that moment you are united to Me in conversation. It is a sharing of My peace beyond which nothing else matters. When you can listen for My word to you, I can instill in you a way of life, beautiful and in conformance with My plan for your life. I want to be a part of every moment in your life. Open your heart to Me and give Me your many loving tears of love. You know I love you every minute of every day. Please return your love to Me and you will never regret any time you have given Me, for I will multiply the graces I give you by the measure of your fervor to please Me."

Later, at the Mother Cabrini Shrine in the top grotto near the springs (rain forced us down from the top) I had a vision of an angel and I could see the wings plainly. Then Mother Cabrini gave a message: ***"Thank you, John, for answering my plea to return to my springs. This also is holy ground and many souls have been brought back to Jesus here. My springs have also graced many pilgrims. Many of the people need Jesus in their lives. It is the holy faithful who now must help to bring souls back to Jesus. Pray much that these souls will find their way back. I will be with you in your prayer group for honoring Me here and with your thoughts of love for Jesus. I know you are strong in the faith but tell all your friends to stay close to our God for these will be perilous times. Give thanks to God also for the many gifts all you have received. Many times you are grateful for help but you sometimes forget to thank Jesus personally for your gifts. Concentrate in your prayers to be ever faithful to the Blessed Trinity."***

Saturday, July 2, 1994:

At St. Thomas More (7:30 a.m. Mass) after Communion, I saw a picture of an eagle flying and it soon was engaged in a fight and then it was dark. Jesus said: ***"I will send you many prophets like Amos to warn My people of the tribulation that will befall you. You have seen the eagle representing your country and its freedoms which will soon be in turmoil. My people, you will soon witness a change of life as you know it with your freedoms stripped from you. You have been drawn to see My refuges and safe havens, for many of My faithful will be threatened with persecution. For many years I have blessed you with abundance, but men have abused these gifts and the rich lord it over the rest.***

Your morals have reached a low ebb and your greed for money and position have blinded you from My love and following My commandments. As a consequence, you will face a purification which will demand a faith in Me. Look to Me for help—for you will not be able to overcome this evil on your own. It will be a test of your trust in Me to win this battle over evil. Let Me buoy you up in hope in My grace and love which will sustain those who believe in Me. Remember with Me all things are possible. Then you will see your reward I have prepared for you both in heaven and on earth."

Sunday, July 3, 1994:

After Communion, I saw an altar with an empty chair in the middle. Then I felt myself walking to the podium to recite the word of God. Jesus said: ***"Throughout the history of My people I have sent you many prophets to tell you of My word and how to follow it. Even now I tell you—all of you are prophets by your very Baptism. There are even more special gifts I have given certain of My faithful. Listen to their word if they be faithful servants of God, for I am beseeching all of My apostles at this time to go out and speak My message of love to all the people. I love all of you so much that I have given up My life on the cross for your sins. No man has a greater love for his friends than he give up his life for them. I tell you My message of love must be spread lovingly and not forced on anyone. For those who repent and accept Me, you will receive a prophets's reward. Keep a strong prayer life so that you will remain ever faithful to Me in all I ask of you. Give praise and honor to your God and you will never have want of anything either spiritually or physically. Thank you, My children, for listening to My word."***

Later, at St. Thomas More after Communion I saw a memorial piece before the altar. I then saw a picture of the flag of our country waving. Jesus said: ***"My people, how long must I warn you that many of you spiritually are headed down the wrong path to perdition? Your country was founded on many noble and holy principles of freedom, especially religious freedom, but now you are in moral decay. You fail to understand how gradually you have turned your face from Me and follow more the things of the world. For this evil, your country will have many destructions and hard-***

ships fall on you as your worldly things will be rendered useless. It is not lip service I am asking of you, but I want you to conform to My will. In doing so you will save your soul. Repenting of your sins and asking forgiveness of your weaknesses—this is My request of you. Once you have acquired a prayer life to ensure your own soul's protection, only then can you go out to seek other souls for salvation. No matter how much persecution you encounter, strive to complete the fight against evil. Then I will say, 'Well done My good and faithful servant. Enter into My everlasting banquet of love.'"

Monday, July 4, 1994:

At Adoration, I saw a picture of Our Lady and then I saw a bright flame of light burning. Jesus said: *"My people, come often to visit me in My Blessed Sacrament to give me your love and adoration. Also, pray your Rosary three times daily, if it be possible. It is this I ask so you may build up your spiritual strength to do My work. My friends, you are all a part of My Body and I am calling on all My faithful to witness to My love. You are seeing My flame which is a sign of vigilance for you. I am calling My prayer warriors to continue with your prayers of reparation. You are to maintain a constant vigil of prayer to Me. In doing so, your light of faith will be a beacon for others who are searching for Me in their lives. By seeing your faith, My faithful will understand more fully how I am asking each person to give up their will to Me. By seeking My forgiveness, they will be able to repent of their sins and come to Me. Tell everyone to reach out for me everyday in their lives. Then I will bless them with My peace and they will receive My graces through My loving generosity to My people."*

Tuesday, July 5, 1994:

At the Carmelite Monastery after Communion, I saw some 5 nuns praying. Then I saw a huge but narrow hall where all the faithful had gathered for a graduation to heaven. Jesus said: *"My people, I love you with an everlasting love and I implore you always to follow My will for you. You cannot go through life on your own, but ask for My help constantly in prayer. It is through a prayerful life that you will see how keeping your eyes fixed on Me is meant for you to follow Me. You must give up the things*

of this world so your goal in life will not be blinded by material things. I have given this message of following My will so often because it is the single most important request I ask of all My faithful. Also, I am asking you, as before, to be laborers in My harvest for souls. Time is growing short My children. You must encourage all who will listen, to answer My plea to return to your God before it too late. Now is the acceptable time to be saved. Now is the desperate hour to save as many souls as possible, for soon the evil hour will be upon you and your time to save souls will be almost impossible. Pray that you can convert all your friends and family."

Later, at Adoration, I saw a white door amidst the darkness and then I saw a picture of a grandfather clock. Jesus said: ***"Peace be with you. Fear is useless as I have advised you before. Many are apprehensive of the evil times to come, but I come to offer you a great sense of hope in me that I will protect you and watch over your spiritual welfare. My people I know you will be tested much, but for all that you will encounter I will offer you a doorway of opportunity to graces to withstand the battle. No matter what the demons will try, if you hold fast to My will, your soul will not be in danger. Do not fear, My little ones, for fear is from the evil one. I offer you hope to trust in Me and My word. Since I have promised you My protection, fear is not even to be in your mind. The time of this test will be shortened. With Me you will be able to accomplish miraculous feats, for I will ever be at your side leading you on to save your soul and those of your neighbors. Many of My prophets have been called forth now to advise My faithful, but most of all they shall lead you to hope in My victory despite any ploys of the devil. Faith in Me will conquer evil in all its forms."***

Wednesday, July 6, 1994: (St. Maria Goretti)

After Communion, I saw Our Lady and then I saw a mantle or veil being drawn over her. Jesus said: ***"My people, many souls are lost to sins of the flesh. You have a society which is full of lust in instant gratification of the senses. Gradually, over the years, you have seen a breakdown in the morals and virtues in the use of the body. Your movies and advertisements promote this debasing of the body to only animal instincts. I have created***

your bodies as a picture of beauty and innocence, but you have turned into a people of harlots and perversions. You must restore the former respect for the body. It is only in marriage that these activities come from the love of the spouses. At the same time, you must preserve the marriage bond which is also being abused. If you would follow the example of the holy family, you would see how even earthly life can be beautiful. It is when you follow My will for how you are to live that makes every act proper in My sight. If you would lead chaste lives, you would please me greatly. Pray constantly to keep My commandments and you will be led to your eternal reward."

Later, at Adoration, I saw a large red maroon velvet tapestry covering the tabernacle as a kingly robe for the Lord. Then I saw people in the streets enjoying themselves. Jesus said: ***"My people, I am very pleased with those who visit me in the Blessed Sacrament. Those that come to visit Me are like the one cured leper who returned to give Me thanks. The other nine who also were cured failed to see the importance in giving me thanks. I tell you, those who visit Me I give many graces because this is done freely without any obligation as Sunday Mass. The few that come to Me, make up for all those who do not. I love all of you so dearly and it warms My heart when My faithful share that love with Me. Whether you come out of love, for thanks, for petitions or other reasons—I revel in that opportunity to pour out My graces on you. Those that come, know how special it is to converse with Me. Please share the knowledge of My peace and joy with your friends so that they too may come and worship Me. If you had a good friend or a lover, you would try to see that person as often as possible. Now, My people, your Divine Lord awaits you. This should be even a more compelling reason to share My love."***

Thursday, July 7, 1994:

After Communion, I saw many lights circling around me as if I was inside a kaleidoscope. Then these lights appeared to speed up and I sensed another vision of the warning. Jesus said: ***"I am indeed a gracious God. I have told you many times how I love you and wait for you to return to Me. Again, I have told you no matter how ugly a sinner you are, I would always be there to receive you. Even so, every soul will be tested and will be judged***

at the end times. You are given many opportunities to choose Me over anything else, but you will in fact be judged on whether or not you repent of your sins and receive Me as your Savior. I am showing you My graciousness even more explicitly when I bring My warning as a supernatural event to everyone alive at that time. You will be shown all the sins of your life and how you have hurt me individually on the cross."

Later, at St. Mary's Church before the Blessed Sacrament in Grand Island, Nebraska, I saw a statue of Our Lady and then I saw a long hall with many statues of the saints. Jesus said: ***"On your travels you have sought Me out and you knew to find Me in the tabernacle of the nearest church. My people, everyone is on a spiritual pilgrimage through life. You know that you can find your strength in Me wherever My presence can be found. I am here held prisoner in My tabernacle until you come to release My graces on you. You will see when you put your trust in Me and My graces, that your life will run easier with My help. Also, if you listen for My word to you, you will see how you can follow My will for your life. Once you have this love of Me in the tabernacle, shout it from the roof tops so all who want to listen will be led here as well. I await anyone who wants My graces and especially I, wait for those who seek repentance in confession. It is being humble in asking forgiveness that I look for in the heart of every penitent. Keep close to Me in My sacraments and continue your daily prayers to withstand the evil one."***

Friday, July 8, 1994:

At St. Mary's Church in Grand Island, Nebraska, I at first saw Marie E. And she said: ***"Praise Him this day."*** I then saw a church and a dark window opened up. Then I saw a dove at the top of the window and He came in. The Holy Spirit said: ***"I am the Spirit of Love. My people, I come among you and you are overly concerned with the problems and anxieties of life. You are too glum with your lot and have lost that radiant feeling of love in your faith. If you had but the faith of a mustard seed, you would bloom into joy. I tell you I am bringing My grace and love to you to awaken your original love for God. Renew your love and have joy in your heart, for with the Lord everything is new and glorious in His sight. You must put on My virtues and shine your smile and vigor***

of faith on all those around you. When they see faith burning with love in you, it will be contagious to them and they will be uplifted with My love as well. My glory is a splendor to behold. Keep in prayer and carry forth your faith to all that they may know and serve God as beautifully as you do."

Later, at Chicago in Naperville, Ill. at the Excel Inn after watching "A Date with an Angel" and saying my Rosary, I asked Jesus' permission for my guardian angel, Mark, to give me a message. Mark said: ***"You have seen a poor earthly imitation of what angels are like, but it is good for the thought to ask me to give you a message. Many of you ignore our help. but guardian angels are sent by God to assist you in all you do. If you would but pray with us each day, you would see how much more intimately we could help you. Even when you ask God for protection from the evil one, you can also call on me for help as well. When you show your love for Jesus, you can also show love for me and I will intercede for you. We love bringing God's people closer to Jesus in any way we can help you. But you must first seek my help and I will be there guiding your every action and advising you of the proper things our Lord wants of you. Yes, we angels are always at your side just as Jesus, ready to help you. Have faith in Jesus and me and we will help lead you to your eternal salvation."***

Saturday, July 9, 1994:

At Sts. Peter and Paul's Church in Naperville, Ill. after Communion, I saw some standing water and then I saw a Nativity scene with a star above. Jesus said: ***"I have known all of you since you were in your mother's womb. Your mother brought you forth and then if you were fortunate, you were baptized into the faith. I am asking you to remember the vows that were spoken for you at that time, especially how you renounced Satan and all his allurements on this earth. You were then made clean and innocent in My sight as you were brought into the faith. As you grew older you have become choked many times by the cares of this world. Remember I have given you My Sacrament of Penance that you may come before the priest to renew yourself and forgive your sins. Then you will be a beautiful innocent soul before Me again. You will again be radiant as angels with My grace and pleasing in My sight. My children keep close to Me and innocent as chil-***

dren by being humble before Me. Keep close to Me in prayer as I love to be with you in love. I just want to embrace you with My arms of love and hold you tight. It is a joy to have you give Me praise and thanks."

Later, at St. Dormitilla Church in Hillside, Ill. after Communion, I saw an abyss or hole in the ground as a well. Then it began to circle and it grew very dark. Jesus then appeared in light to dispel the darkness. Jesus said: ***"Do not be deceived by the evil one. Be on the watch for his deceptions. Be attentive to My word and close to Me in prayer and in that way you shall not be drawn to sins of the flesh nor allow yourself to be controlled by money. Even beware of distractions of your own liking which uses your time away from My plan for you. My people, I have told you before and I am reinforcing it now. Those things, except for caring for bodily needs, are not necessary. I am the one who draws you to Me. Spend as much time as possible before My Blessed Sacrament and in prayer. I love you, My people, and I long to be with you whenever you can open your heart to Me. I am always waiting for you. It is your decision how much you wish to share with Me and how many graces you want Me to bestow on you. Ask and you will receive all in My will for you. Give example of your adoring love for Me to others and your witness will draw them to Me."***

Sunday, July 10, 1994:

At St. Dormitilla Church in Hillside, Ill. after Communion, I saw a beautiful deep blue pillow. Then I saw the blue gradually disappear. Again I saw what looked like Our Lady coming and her face faded so I could only see her mantle and dress. She said: ***"My children, I come to you as a Mother ready to shed on you my Son's graces. I am here to lift up your spirits for this is another glorious day in the Lord. I see your beautiful tears of joy at my coming. I am blessing you, my son, and all my people since you will indeed need my help to see your way through the coming test. Satan is strong right now but his strength will be on the wane as I come in my triumph. I am giving everyone hope in the present and your future for I am the herald of my Son's coming again. I have shown you many times how I will not be with you much longer. My messages of love and warning have fallen on some deaf ears, but it is like the seed cast over all the people.***

You, my people, my faithful remnant, I am confident you will take my messages to heart and continue your preparation for my Son in your prayer and fasting. Keep close to my Son and have trust in His word and you will have hope that will carry you to your eternal salvation."

Later, at the cemetery with Joseph R., I saw a vision of Our Lady dressed in blue and white. Then I saw a pillar of flame and it seemed to come closer and finally I could see into the middle of the flame and Jesus was there. Mary said: ***"I am well pleased with my children praying sincerely as I asked here. This indeed is holy ground and I have brought the angels to guard it from the demons. My people are doing good work here, where many blessings and graces are flowing out to my children. All who come here are given my personal blessings. My son (John), you are seeing a foretaste of the purification with the flame of my Son (Jesus). He is all loving but His justice must be meted out, for man has refused in many places to repent of his (man) sin. You will see some have so given themselves over to the world that even miracles and the warning will not persuade them. These hardened hearts require the most prayers to be saved. Even so, they must at one time accept Jesus or they cannot enter into heaven. Pray constantly as I have requested. It will take great spiritual courage and stamina of faith to achieve keeping close to my Son. He is your salvation 'follow Him'."***

Monday, July 11, 1994:

After Communion, I saw a crocodile, the Nile River and then the river turned blood red. I sensed there would be plagues sent against the earth much like in the Exodus story. Jesus said: ***"My people, how long must I endure your sins and rejection? I have called you many times to Me through My prophets and My Mother. Even though you have been told many times, you are still far from My heart. I tell you a judgement is coming which you least expect but which has been foretold for ages. You will see a separation of the goats on My left and My sheep on the right. You have read of the plagues I visited on the Egyptians in the Bible. Even now I tell you those who continue to sin and reject Me will also experience such plagues as before. Those who defy My glory will at that time wish they had not been born, for there will come***

such a purification as yet to be seen in all of history. It is about to begin soon, so I tell all those in sin to repent now while there is still time. My love is ever waiting for your conversion. But those who refuse Me will be lost forever in the fires of Gehenna."

Later, at Holy Trinity in Webster with Eileen George, I saw Our Lord carrying His cross and He had fallen on His knees. Jesus said: ***"My people, I love you with an all-embracing love which means I love you all completely for each individual. While I was carrying My cross to Calvary, I fell three times for you. You should realize that along life's pilgrimage you may falter many times to sin, but with My death on the cross I am reaching out My hand to you to help you spiritually to your feet again. No matter how serious the sin, I am here for you in My Sacrament of Penance ready to heal your sins. All you need do is be sincerely sorry for your sins and I will forgive them. This is a lesson in spiritual humility, to admit your faults and ask for forgiveness. I want you to be close to Me always, so do not let sin keep any barriers between us. When you go to confession, you will seem fully refreshed in My love and graces. It is this peace that I give to all My people. All you need to do is reach out for My helping hand. Show others by your going to confession that My love waits in My sacraments for everyone. I will be among you forever."***

Tuesday, July 12, 1994:

After Communion, I could see a priest at the altar and there was a bright light around the consecrated Host. There were angels on either side. Our Lord in the Gospel was condemning the towns for their disbelief. Jesus said: ***"I have performed many miracles in the towns about Jerusalem, but still many of the people failed to believe in My words. I tell you this evil age seeks a sign but none will be given it except the sign of Jonah, for you have a greater than Jonah here. Faith is a gift I freely bestow on My people. For those that believe, hold it close and dear to your heart. Every day, at the Mass, I give you a miracle in faith by coming to you personally in the Host. Be thankful, My people, and give Me praise for I seek love from you and trust in My word. For those that believe, live My messages in the Gospel and reform your lives, so at the Last Judgement you will have your white robes washed and be ready to receive Me. If you indeed are ready, then you will see the***

greatest miracle of all when you are allowed into My Kingdom. Live each day in My honor, then you will see your faith is richer than even those who saw My miracles, but did not accept Me."

Wednesday, July 13, 1994:

After Communion, I saw a monkey and sensed the thought of how we have failed to advance spiritually as we try to learn of secular things. Jesus said: ***"My people pride themselves on the advances of science in their day. If you only were able to tap into the knowledge of just your own earth, you would understand how you have only scratched the surface of knowing anything. So do not be filled with any such pride, for it is too easy to show you how little you actually are aware of. In the spiritual realm, My people, you are even in worse shape, for unless you come to Me as little children, you will block any advance to know of Me. Spiritual awareness begins with simple humility and a childlike trust in your God. The saints have come to know Me through this channel of giving over their will to Me. You must allow Me to run your life if you expect to advance spiritually. for it is not knowledge you need, but putting into action what you have learned of love for Me and your neighbor. By living a lifestyle I have shown you in the Scriptures, you then are on the right path to salvation. By losing your life to Me, you will gain all that is needed for eternal life. Come to Me, My children, I wait to give you all the graces for a true spirit-filled life."***

Later, at the prayer group I saw a little baby like Christina. Jesus said: ***"Life is too precious to waste or snuff out. Take every care to preserve life in all its forms, for each person and creature I have given a plan for its life. Do not thwart that plan by jeopardizing or killing any of My creatures, especially My human family."*** I then saw a mother bending over her child. Our Lady said: ***"Many mothers take pride in their children and are caring for their every need. I too am not only proud of my Son, our spirits are as one. I am always taking care of my children and I watch over your spiritual welfare as well. In all I do, I continue to bring you to my Son who has the words of eternal life."*** I then saw a young rabbit playing. Jesus said: ***"All young in the animal world are innocent and fearless in the beginning, but as they grow older, they rely on animal instincts for survival. You, My people, are***

spiritual beings as well. Do not let animal instincts lead you but come to me as innocent children. Do not let fears and anxieties run your life, but put your trust in me and I will lead you to heaven." I then saw a fetus of a human being. Jesus said: ***"Take a lesson from nature in how most species protect their young and would not think of killing them. You, My people, are killing your babies in the womb which shows even how this is contrary to nature. Follow My commandments and preserve these future lives for I have planned their way."*** I then saw Our Lady come with a Rosary and all the beads sparkled as gems giving off a glow to each of them. Mary said: ***"This is my rosary and it is the vehicle by which you can come to know and love my Jesus, for through your humble prayers and attention to pleasing my Son, He will bring you eternal life—a life in the spirit beyond your wildest dreams of love."*** I then saw someone holding some branches of a tree. Jesus said: ***"I am the vine and you are the branches. You all are a part of My one Mystical Body. You draw your life from Me and apart from Me you are nothing, so praise your God for your very life here and in the life hereafter which is always dependent on Me."*** I finally saw Our Lord standing in His bright glory and He presented a veil with His face on it as to Veronica. Jesus said: ***"You are all made to My image and likeness. Look for Me in all humanity and give each person respect. Honor My presence in all of creation, for everyone is glorious and wonderfully made. Give praise and glory to your God for all that you have been blessed with."***

Friday, July 15, 1994:

After Communion, I saw a spectacular heavenly display as a comet was seen circling into the planet Jupiter and a flash occurred. Jesus said: ***"My people, there are many ominous portents in the skies which will be given you at the end times as a sign of My coming again. As you have read in the Scriptures how I allowed the sun to move back ten steps, know that I have control over the stars and the planets. Nothing occurs without My desiring it so, for this is to show you that indeed I am God and you will see Me coming on a cloud in glory and wonder to judge all of humanity. Prepare and be watchful for you will not know the time nor the hour when the Son of Man will do these things. As in the Gospel,***

listen to My words, it is mercy I desire and not sacrifice. Have mercy on all those around you. Do not be judgmental. For the measure you use on others will be the same measure for yourself. Understand the meaning of the words in the Our Father."

Later, at the Mapledale Party House for the 10th Anniversary of Mt. Carmel House Hospice after Communion, I saw a long line of beds and a brief picture of Rose and Raoul. Jesus said: ***"These are My favored people, for you are blessed for doing My corporal acts of mercy. Your reward in heaven will be great since you gave of yourselves to help Me in your patients. When they ask, when did we see you helpless and in need, I will tell them 'when you help the least in My Kingdom, you are helping Me.' Continue to help your neighbor lovingly and freely since through them you will achieve your salvation. If you keep your roots based in faith in Me, your works will continue to be fruitful. Continue your devotion to My Mother in your namesake through the rosary and we will be very pleased with My faithful. I am giving you all My blessing through the Holy Spirit. Give praise to your Lord and God."***

Saturday, July 16, 1994;

After Communion, I saw a butterfly with a varied design on its wings. Jesus said: ***"My people, you are so caught up in the web of confusion in your lives; you do not let My graces keep you on the road to following My will. Do not lose sight of Me during your day. If you are busy, you can say little love messages as — 'I love you, Jesus.' Do not crowd your lives into a corner so that you do not give Me any of your time. You must prioritize your life better, so that you leave some time for meditation. If not, you will be no better than the pagans who only concern themselves with the world. Remember you are a spiritual being made to adore Me. Do not let the evil one so distract you from Me that you no longer follow My will. You must be as the butterfly and shed your old life so you can live and prosper as sons and daughters of your one true God."***

Later, at Nocturnal Adoration, I saw a cross leading in a huge number of people and I sensed this was during the triumph after the tribulation. Jesus said: ***"My people, your efforts to please Me to gain heaven are not in vain. If you follow My commandments and do My will, you will be protected during the tribulation. As I mentioned before it is saving souls which is most important at*** *this time. Some will be martyred for the faith, but saving the body will be for only those I have chosen. Be most concerned with saving your soul. This testing time will be severe and will test your trust in Me, but keep focused on Me through the tribulation and you will have nothing to fear. Prayer will help you remain faithful. Be vigilant and you will be saved."*

Sunday, July 17, 1994:

After Communion, I saw Jesus holding some sheep. Then a little later I saw an eagle in flight. Jesus said: ***"Come to Me those of you who are heavily burdened and I will refresh you. Many of you are wearied and hassled by the plight of daily life. You need to take time away from your busy life and visit Me, so I can settle down your spiritual lives from all life's distractions. It is good to keep your life in perspective toward your ultimate goal in heaven. Do not lose sight of your path and give your time freely, without Me asking, so you can nurture your faith. For without Me in your life, your fruits will turn empty toward only a humanistic goal. You must be steadfast in your prayer life and adjust your priorities accordingly. With your eternal life at stake, it is not much to put more emphasis on your soul than on just bodily needs. Once refreshed with My love, you will be ready to continue your goal to evangelize souls for My Kingdom."***

Later, at Adoration, I at first saw a cross with a silhouette in darkness with light around it. I then saw a stadium with markings of dragons to indicate it was run by Anti-Christ. This was the place where the Christians would again be tortured as with the Romans. Jesus said: ***"The days of tribulation are almost upon you. Know that I have gone before you and have suffered pain and death for you. Some of My faithful also will be tested with torture and martyrdom. I tell you to flee your cities if you want to spare your lives, for the evil one will dominate the people most in the cities. Thus far you have seen evil inspired men, but you have yet to see evil incarnate as will happen in the end times. This evil will require My help and your guardian angels to protect your souls from the demons. You must have full faith and trust in Me to weather this battle of good and evil. Those who endure it though, will receive a reward, even while still on earth, as I come in glory to purify this evil. No matter how powerful Satan may appear, he will be dis-***

patched at My coming. While he is in power, they will taunt you with, 'where is your Lord's power now?' You must endure this evil for awhile, much like I suffered the jeers while I was on the cross. In the end, though, you will be freed of this evil and all those who follow the evil one will be cast with him into the eternal hell fires. Be vigilant and faithful, My people, and you will have your reward with Me in heaven as the good thief on the cross."

Monday, July 18, 1994:

After Communion, I saw some lines on a planet like Jupiter. Jesus said: ***"While I was on earth, I worked many miracles and cures before My chosen people. Still they continued to ask for signs of who I was. I referred them many times to the Scriptures about the prophecies of My coming. I even told them that the reign of God was upon them in My presence and still many did not want to believe in Me. Now today, again people go through life wondering if God is present in their lives. I tell you many signs are around you in the planets, in wars and in many earthquakes. Even in the face of these events, man still does not see the signs of My Second Coming. Believe Me, My people, a time is coming shortly when all evil will be put aside and judgment time will arrive. There will no longer be time for decision making. I will find that you are either with Me or with the world and the devil. Pray, My people, that you be with Me or you will meet a fate worse than death in eternal hell."***

Later, at church, I saw a demonic looking face which had eyes which sparkled with green rays emanating from them. This was a picture of the Anti-Christ. I then saw a very clear brilliant white cross come signifying Jesus' victory over him. The demonic face became one of fright as I saw a deep pit and he was thrown into the abyss. Jesus said: ***"You, My people, are almost at the time of the Anti-Christ as foretold in the Scriptures, for he will have an appointed time in history which I will allow. This will not be a time for the weak of faith. Once the evil one comes to power, many will be drawn to him because of his seeming miraculous powers. My faithful must seek My protection at this time in My Eucharist where it can be found, My Mother's rosary, and help from your guardian angels. This will truly be a test of your will to choose Me and trust in My word, for there will ensue a great battle of good and***

evil at Armageddon. All the people of the earth will be drawn into this conflict between Anti-Christ and My warriors. At that time, the Anti-Christ will be defeated and a great cataclysm will occur that will wipe out his forces. I will enter to claim the victory over him and he will be dashed with all who are evil in My sight into the fires prepared for Satan and his angels. At this time, I will renew the earth and there will be My Mother's triumph as she promised. This will be an era of peace free from corruption where all My faithful will live in love and adoration of Me. It will be as heaven on earth. Pray My people that you will be vigilant in prayer and you will see Me just as I have promised you."

Tuesday, July 19, 1994;

After Communion, I saw a cross in a casket. Then I saw a bright light as the cross rose up into the air above the casket. Jesus said: ***"My people, as I carried My cross to Calvary, you too must walk in My footsteps and carry your own crosses. You will stumble and fall many times, but with humility, come to Me in Confession to forgive your sins. As stated in the Scriptures, I delight in receiving any sinner who seeks forgiveness. As you have heard, all in heaven rejoices over one repentant sinner. If you follow My way for you in love, at your death you will win your prize of salvation. On that day you will rise with Me to heaven and your joy will know no bounds when you see My day I have promised all of you. Be faithful to the end and keep vigilant in prayer and in grace."***

Later, I saw the moon had an orange corona around it. I saw Jesus in a monstrance radiating out His light. Then I saw some buildings with strange markings and I felt they were international in scope. Jesus said: ***"You need My strength in My Eucharist. That is why you are drawn to Me, for the future trials that will come, will require great faith in Me. You indeed can see events in the world as things gradually take shape for a one world order. I tell you it is not long that you will see My warning and the Anti-Christ soon to follow. He will assume power very quickly since he has been preparing for this time for many years. When he comes to power, find a way to avoid him at all costs since his power will be almost angelic. Pray constantly during this time for the way I will direct you how to live. You will be apart from the mainstream*** *for My name's sake, but do not be afraid that you will be persecuted, for I will be at your side protecting you. Those who witness to Me will be tested, but you also will be given the graces to withstand any attacks. I am giving you hope now for this evil time. Do not fear, My faithful will keep their souls protected. Later, you will witness My victory which will make all your suffering more than worth any pain you might endure."*

Wednesday, July 20, 1994:

After Communion, I saw a figure which from a distance looked like Jesus wanting me to come to Him. Then I saw a very ornate stairway leading up to an entrance door as if to heaven. Jesus said: ***"My people, My arms are stretched forward reaching out to you to welcome you home as the Father welcomed the prodigal son. You are always welcome no matter where you have come from, for I will give you My peace and your rest. It is with Me that all you ever wanted lies. For I have the words of eternal life. It is with Me that everyone of you should strive. With Me is your home that beckons to you. Please, My children, see how a loving Father loves you and is calling you home. Heaven is within reach of everyone. All I ask is that you prepare yourself properly and wear your clean white robes which My faithful receive from My graces of confession. If you follow My will and My commandments, your future will be glorious in My presence. Come to My wedding feast My people, and you will enjoy My supper as you receive the Bread of Life."***

Later, at the prayer group I saw a monstrance and Jesus said: ***"I am always inviting you to visit Me in My tabernacle or where I am exposed in exposition. When you are before Me, you can receive My graces which radiate out to all present. It would be good to have a little monstrance in your house to remember Me by when you cannot make it to see Me in person."*** I saw a multicolored fan moving like a blur. Jesus said: ***"I have told you before how events will occur so fast it will seem many of them are simultaneous. What is happening is a convergence of things coming together in concert right up to these end times. This is a time for the crucial battle of good and evil."*** I then saw a nun under the shadow of her habit and it was St. Therese the Little Flower. She said: ***"My faithful children, you must be humble in all you do and offer your gifts up to the glory of God. Forget your pride and do whatever you can to please your Lord. Give Him your love and your all and follow His commands."*** I saw Our Lady in a very intense deep azure blue mantle which seemed to have a special significance. She said: ***"My little ones in faith, thank you for continuing to be vigilant in praying my Rosary. Many prayers are needed to combat the evil in this time. I will continue to protect you with my mantle from the evil one's attacks. Pray often and I will be at your side."*** I then saw a single lit candle burning brightly. Jesus said: ***"I am the Light in your life to follow. I light your spiritual path so it will guide you to Me. It is a light of love which warms even the coldest of hearts who give Me even a small opening. This is a love which permeates all creation and makes it one. Stay close to Me in love and you will have all your heart desires."*** I saw a group praying. They were huddled in a circle as if for protection from evil. Jesus said: ***"You will find strength spiritually and much consolation in your prayer groups, for where two or more are gathered, I am in your midst. With My help you will overcome evil and no longer fear it, for when you have Me, you have everything."*** I saw a large crucifix and it was placed in the woods. Jesus said: ***"My cross is the symbol of your salvation. It keeps showing you how much I love you that I would die for you. Keep My likeness in the cross in your house and a crucifix on your person. It will be a protection for you during the evil times."***

Thursday, July 21, 1994:

After Communion, I at first saw Maria E. and she said: ***"Keep focused on Him."*** I then saw Jesus standing close by and He said: ***"I have visited you for a year now. Can you take stock of how your spiritual life has grown? You must live My messages and give good example to My people. This is indeed a grace and you are one of many who are bringing My word to My people. It is important that My messengers stay extra close to Me in prayer, for your lives are to be changed to closely follow Me. The times ahead are significant in the life of My Church. There will be great testing ahead. It is important that all My people are prepared for these events but even more spiritually than physically.***

Many souls are at stake in this battle. This is the real treasure which I am seeking—to help bring souls to Myself through all means possible while still honoring your God given free will."

Friday, July 22, 1994:

After Communion, I saw a narrow slice in space as a picture of our own galaxy. There was an explosion or collision and a fragment came forward. A big hunk of rock was directed toward me and the earth. Jesus said: ***"My people, you have witnessed My sign of a comet hitting Jupiter. I have now already put on track a comet of My judgment which will strike the Earth. No matter what your scientists will do, My justice will come with swift fury, for My people have allowed evil to choke their lives with too much care for worldly things. You are made to My image to adore Me, but you do not want to accept Me as My chosen people rejected Me also. Those faithful who know and love Me will be protected from My purification, but woe to those who blaspheme Me and utter all abominations, for they will taste of My wrath instead of My dinner."***

Later, at the Adoration Chapel at the Marian Conference I saw an unborn baby and there was a broad light at one side and narrowing to a small band to the left. The unborn baby was in the middle of the band of light. (There was a baby crying in the background in reality at the time of the vision. Otherwise, it was quiet.) Jesus said: ***"I have given you many messages on abortion since it is the sin I suffer for most on the cross for your world. I am all loving as you know, but how long do you think I will allow you to frustrate My plans for these future human beings? This destruction of life is the devil's most vicious attack against humanity whom he hates. He has found many accommodating souls to push his lies and deceptions on abortion. You, My people, cannot stand idle and do nothing. Along with prayers and donations you must struggle to do what you can to fight this heresy against Me. By your actions and motivations of your heart, I will see your attempts and bless you. If you do nothing, it will be the same as condoning these acts. Reach out to these women to help those both before and after any abortion. You must love the sinner even as I plead with all sinners for forgiveness of their sins. Seek con-***

fession regularly and pray especially for this intention, so one day My Mother's promise to remove abortion can be achieved."

Saturday, July 23, 1994:

After Communion at the Marian Conference downtown, I saw people at Mass and then I saw some stained glass windows. Jesus said: ***"My people, it is incumbent upon you to listen to My words of Scripture, for many times I have told you these are the words of eternal life. Many of you have indeed lost your initial fervor for My word. It will be commonplace for you if you do not live what is being read. I love you, My people, but do not be drawn in by modernism in the Church. My word is not to be comfortable only in your hearing. It is meant to uplift you and make you desire to serve and follow your God, so read My Scriptures often and meditate on the word. It will always bring you to Me because I am the living word and the direction for your life. Pray to Me often and visit Me in My Blessed Sacrament and you will be led to My peace. Listen to My faithful prophets—those only whose fruits lead you to Me. My prophets have led My people to Me throughout history. Their message many times asks repentance and humility in asking you to seek My forgiveness of your sins. When you follow My word, I will be waiting for you at the close of your life to receive you into eternal peace in heaven."***

At the Adoration Chapel at the Marian Conference, I saw a monstrance and there were circular rays going out like waves. Inside the center was a blue circle and then I could gradually see Our Lady. She said: ***"My son you are always drawn to my Son, Jesus, and it is good you are close to Him. Where you see my Son, Jesus, I am always present as well, for we are inseparable. Your conference will bring many graces to your city. There are many trials here, but you have seen how heaven has its way despite Satan's attacks. In the future you will see many good effects from this effort. Your bishop, in time, will even be affected. With my graces present, good will always see hearts opened to me and my Son. Continue your Rosaries and your fasting my children, for there is a great need of your prayers said slowly and from the heart to make up for so much evil in your world. Much prayer is needed to atone for those rejecting my Jesus. When you pray, you are***

bringing some souls closer to their salvation. You need to change your priorities and continue to make time for your three Rosaries a day, since there is such little time left."

Sunday, July 24, 1994:

After Communion, I saw Our Lady dressed as a Queen and then I saw Jesus on the cross. Again I saw a picture of a Host. Jesus said: ***"This is a glorious day since all of My body is witnessed together around Me in the breaking of the bread. I am giving myself to you in the Blessed Sacrament in Communion. I have promised that I would always be with you and this is the means of My presence to you. Through My Body and Blood we are united as one, so I can share your joys and your pains. In Me you find eternal life. In My Sacrament you are given the grace to carry on each day. I am truly your daily bread for your spiritual survival. In the future you may even require My manna for your bodily survival. Live in Me always by your prayers and caring for what pleases Me—by your love for Me and your neighbor."***

Later, after Communion at the Marian Conference Mass, I saw different statues of Our Lady at various levels going up a hill representing the various apparition sites. Then I saw a beautiful sight of prayerful people coming in crowds to a mountain where Our Lady appeared. This seemed a picture of her triumph. Mary said: ***"My children, you are so beautiful before me. I have been coming among you all day long as you have smelled my rose scent. I have been blessing you all with my graces for your devotion to me and my Son. We both love you very much. If you had the faith of a mustard seed as my Son said, you would believe that you will be protected with my mantle throughout the tribulation. Have hope in me, since my Son will fulfill my promise of a triumph over evil. Then, my people, you will enjoy the beauty of my Son's peace as an era of peace will reign on the earth. Continue to be faithful and keep up your barrage of prayers to fight the evil in your world."***

Monday, July 25, 1994: (St. James)

After Communion, I saw an older nun in a small enclosure welcoming me to a service. It appeared to be a representation of an underground Church. Jesus said: ***"I have told you to prepare for***

the evil days ahead. You have been blessed in America with religious freedom for many years. You have been protected from persecution as seen in other countries. There is a time, My people, though when you will face persecution for My name's sake. There will be a tribulation of evil days over your land. It will be a test of your faith. You have been too affluent and not always appreciative of your many gifts I have given you. Now you will see the true value of your faith when you are threatened with persecution for that belief. Pray for strength from Me during that time so you can endure it. I will see by your fervor and your intentions in your heart how much you really care for Me when put to the test. It is through a meditative prayer life that will bring you closer to Me. It will allow Me to help you to be constantly faithful until you await your crown of eternal life in heaven."

At church, I saw Our Lady and she held a rose close to her face. I saw several monks praying. Then I saw many flowers enveloped around Our Lady. She said: ***"My children, you are seeing me prepare for my moment of triumph. It will be glorious indeed and it is not far off. My children, you have seen how prayerful my daughters were at the Carmelite Monastery. (Denver) You too must pray much, for there is only a short time that you will be able to pray for sinners to soften their hearts. If you can evangelize fallen away faithful, it would be most helpful and a blessing, but you must come close to my Jesus now in prayer. By being united with Him and myself, you will be strengthened to endure your trial. I need many prayer warriors to help me in this plight of evil in your world. Without enough prayers, many souls will be lost and not be able to return to my Son. So, I am pleading for more prayers, especially from my faithful who know how serious this situation is. My family of loving children, look to your Jesus more than ever. Stay close to Him in front of His Blessed Sacrament and you will receive His graces."***

Tuesday, July 26, 1994: (Sts. Joachim and Anne—parents of Mary)

After Communion, I saw Our Lady in a beautiful blue mantle and dress—the color lingered as one to remember. Mary gave the message: ***"My children, you all are rich in your gift of faith which comes to you through God and most often through the instruments of your parents. Many times we take for granted our reli-***

gious upbringing. You should thank your parents for bringing you the instruction in the faith and your visits to Mass. This is indeed your heritage in the one body of my Son. It is also part of your own responsibility to bring your own children up in the faith. Each person must choose God for themselves, but it is important you teach your children in the early years how to know and love God. It is also important to bring them to the sacraments and even, if possible, encourage vocations. Bringing souls to my Son is paramount in all your missions on earth, but your own children, for sure, are your first obligations."

Later, at Adoration, I saw a man standing with his arms stretched out against a wall as he was being tortured in a stockade. I then saw a rustic cross in the woods. Jesus said: ***"My people, you are worried about many things in this world, but I tell you if you have hope in Me and trust in My promises, you will no longer have any fears. I love you dearly and I draw you close to Me since there are few in My faithful ready to give Me full attention as I desire. My faithful remnant, I am depending on you to carry the day for the prayers that are needed. Pray often that you will be united with Me throughout the day. It is walking in My footsteps each day that requires a leap of faith to understand the significance of My presence in your lives."***

Wednesday, July 27, 1994:

After Communion, I saw Jesus in a boat. The boat was on a stage as the stage of life. Jesus said: ***"Many times My people you are buffeted with the winds of life and its trials. Think of Me as the apostles did when in the boat on the Sea of Galilee a storm was swamping the boat. I am ever present with you. Call on Me, My children, and I will help you with whatever problem besets you, for I will give you My peace so that you will have a strong faith and not be worried over things in life. You must reach out to Me and take a leap of faith as I asked Peter to walk to Me on the water. Life can be so beautiful if you walk through it with Me guiding your every step. Give your will over to Me and you will not have to ask what shall I do for the Lord."***

Later, at the prayer group I saw a white and magenta porcelain flower holder. The view changed to an icon of an Orthodox Church. Again there was a picture of Our Lady's icon weeping. Mary said:

"I am reaching out to join the Church of the East and the West. You all should be one in adoring my Jesus. I am weeping for the many souls who have rejected my Son. My signs of my presence are being shown you to help send more prayers, so these souls may be brought back to my Son." I then had a vision of Jesus superimposed on a chandelier in a dining room. Jesus said: ***"I am present in your homes ready to preserve the unity in your families. I am greeting you in your homes and I am asking you to make a home for Me with you. When you make yourself open to receive Me, I will rest with you as you join Me in prayer."*** I saw a picture of a gold amulet in the shape of a heart. It is the kind which contains a little picture. Jesus said: ***"I want to have you close to My heart so you can feel the love I am pouring out to you. Hold your head close to My heart so you can hear it beating out a constant love message to you. At the same time, hold Me close to your heart so I can be a part of your life. Our hearts can be joined in love as My Mother is already joined in My oneness of spirit."*** I then saw a picture of stars of the universe and I saw a presiding picture of God the Father reigning over it all. He said: ***"Look to the skies, My people, for you will see many signs of the end times as they draw near. In My signs there is hope that you will see the fulfillment of Scripture in my Son's Second Coming—listen to Him."*** I saw a lighted sign of the word LOVE with a big L and at the top was a red rose. Mary said: ***"My children, I come to you as a loving Mother always watching over your spiritual welfare. I am constantly reminding you to pray much to my Son to save souls. Be especially attentive to praying for your relatives and friends. You have the most influence on keeping them close to my Son."*** I then saw a dark picture and a man I believe was Anti-Christ standing. He had a grotesque face like a demon and it soon changed to that of a human. Jesus said: ***"Beware of the time of Anti-Christ, for he will lead many astray from Me. Satan will use this instrument to destroy as much of humanity as he can. This is why you must stay close to Me in prayer."*** Finally, I saw Pope John Paul II in a picture. Jesus said: ***"My pope John Paul II will suffer much for the world. he is being tortured by those around him and is offering his physical pain up for others. Pray sincerely for his strength for he is My witness for you leading into the end times."***

Thursday, July 28, 1994:

After Communion, I saw Maria E. and she said: ***"Prepare for the dark days ahead."*** Then I saw a rock and then a dark cave for protection. Jesus said: ***"My people, you are fortunate that you are being forewarned of your future persecution. Many of My prophets that have gone before Me were treated much like I was with disdain and disbelief. Even so, the message eventually came to reality in due season. So, today, My messengers are again preparing you to repent and pray because of the evil age you are in. You have seen in the Scriptures how many times My chosen people wandered from Me and had to be put back on track; sometimes with harsh treatment. I tell you your age is in no less condition that cries out for judgment. So listen to My messengers in the prophets for an evil age demands a sign. You are being given many signs to reform your lives and be on watch for My Second Coming."***

Friday, July 29, 1994: (St. Martha)

After Communion, I saw a woman carrying water and she was dressed as in the time of Jesus. Jesus said: ***"It is good to pay attention to the household chores, but the better portion of your lives lies with prayer and good works. The cares of the worldly things are not to be made an end in themselves—they are there only so far as your bodily needs are required. Most of all you should be concerned with your personal prayer and adoration of your Lord. Helping your neighbor both spiritually and physically is also important. For your guide ask whether you are doing something for Me or your own selfish interests. You will see your perfection lies in doing things to please Me and not in your own agenda. So seek first the things of heaven and all else will be given you."***

Later, at church, I was looking at the earth from a satellite and I saw dark clouds over all the earth blotting out the sun. Jesus said: ***"My people, I have warned you many times to prepare for the tribulation. You must have your soul freed from sin in Confession ready to receive My protection. The purification will not last long, but the three days of darkness will seem endless. You will need your blessed candles to have light. The evil ones will be purged and life will be renewed in My love. You will be fortunate to live through the persecution and suffering that will occur. Pray*** *to Me always for strength and guidance through this time. You will not survive without Me. You must have faith in Me and I will bring you through it all. For nothing is impossible with Me. This moment will bring a joy ultimately that My people could not believe possible on earth. Give honor and glory to your King always and you will be rewarded well."*

Saturday, July 30, 1994:

After Communion, I saw a doorway entrance and inside it again looked like a cave that went a ways back. Jesus said: ***"Many of My prophets have been persecuted and even put to death for bringing My message of judgment to the people. They do not want to be reminded of their sins which were done in darkness and in secret. Their consciences are telling them to repent, but their deeds show how they reject Me and anyone I send them. Even today, be watchful My own people, for I continue to send prophets to warn you of the impending days of evil about to descend on you. Take care that you listen to My word, if the prophets are faithful—for they will lead you and give you hope even amidst trials. Many of My faithful will be persecuted for believing in Me, but the prophets, as yourself, may be tortured and sought out even more severely by the demon inspired people."***

Later, at church, I saw a snake on a post like the one Moses lifted up to heal those with snakebites. Then I saw a cross of Jesus being lifted up. Jesus said: ***"Lift high My cross so all the people may see Me and remember how I died on the cross to save everyone from their sins. If you would accept Me as your Savior, surely you will be with Me in heaven. Let the people know that when they sin, I still suffer for them on the cross for each new sin. My people, you must learn to accept My peace and not be anxious over the things of this world. For everything here is fleeting by and will soon be no more. So practice patience and cool your pride when you are frustrated that you cannot do everything which may not be in your power to perform perfectly. When you see how futile it is to seek justice in this world among sinners, do not despair in such things. For everyone answers to My justice, do not be concerned that all is not perfect. Practice living peacefully in all you do and you will see how I lived in love and peace. With My peace you will not have distress nor hatred but will enjoy life*** *more fully. Keep up your prayer life and you will be closer to My rest. With Me guiding you, you do not have to worry how things will turn out. I will always protect you from evil if you stay close to Me. The more you converse with Me, the more you will desire heaven and My glory as soon as possible. It is living in My love and being one with My will that will bring you home safe to My banquet table."*

Sunday, July 31, 1994:

After Communion, I saw a big Host and then one in a monstrance. Jesus said: ***"My people, come to Me for I am the Bread of Life. You shall know Me in the breaking of the bread when you receive Me in Communion. For I give you spiritual food to nourish your soul and your body. If you truly had faith in My words, you could live on Communion alone. It is true I have fed My people both during the Old Testament and when I was on earth, but I have not forgotten your physical needs and especially during the coming tribulation when famines and control of food will be a problem for many. Remember, My people, I have told you, those faithful to Me will be protected. During the Anti-Christ's time, I again will be forced to feed My people the manna from heaven. Know, My people, that the spiritual bread is the most important, for you have Me with you more intimately. With Me you have My love and peace and not worrying about the survival of the body. Concern yourself more about the survival of the soul coming to life in heaven."***

Later, at church, I saw a jet plane with passengers and it looked like it had crashed. (A real crash occurred 9-8-94 in Pittsburg with 131 killed.) I then saw a propeller going around. Jesus said: ***"Many events will be happening which you cannot control. Do not worry about those things you can do nothing about. I love you, My people, and you need to understand and prepare for the times you are living in. You must be concerned most with following My will for you. I will tell each of you what you are to do, if you would pray to Me in meditative prayer listening for My direction for your life. It is one of prayer and adoration of your God first. Pray also, to help your neighbor in his need. Once these are fulfilled, you may tend to the rest of your bodily needs. Raise your*** *goals to seeking those thoughts of how to please Me in everything you do. If you allow the spiritual goals to run your life, you will not be lacking in what to do. You must love Me and one another and you will not be far from heaven."*

Monday, August 1, 1994:

After Communion, I saw seats and a stage. There was a bright light on the stage and there was some steam or smoke. Jesus said: ***"Dear people, you have not understood My light and how it should affect your lives. Look to your actions and the intentions in your heart. These are the things that will gain you merits in heaven. Life is full of many good intentions, but it is what you do with your life that counts. Do not be hesitant to do good works of mercy for your neighbor. Many times helping your own relatives and friends is what you are most called to do. When you help anyone, you are helping Me, but do not be lazy and do nothing, for you will have less treasure in heaven at the judgment. The next best thing is to pray for those who need spiritual help."***

Later, at church, I saw a bright flame burning as a sanctuary light for what looked like the Ark of the Covenant holding the tablets of the Ten Commandments. Jesus said: ***"My people, I draw your attention to My first covenant in the Ten Commandments. I have given you, My people, the principles by which you are to live. For those who desire perfection, follow My statutes out of love only, instead of obligation and you will be closer to Me. Those that live My commandments will be an inspiration for all of how to live a good holy life. My second covenant that I have left you lies in My gift of the Holy Eucharist. In this sacrament I will be present to you till the end of time. Know, My friends, that I have poured out My love to you so that you may partake of it and have My peace rest in your soul. Even the angels are jealous of this intimate union I offer you in My Bread of Life. My people, you would best honor and adore Me freely of your own accord as indeed My Body and Blood deserve your reverence. Visit Me often so I can be a blessed part of your life. You will never have enough of My love which I wish to continue giving you. Keep prayerful and close to Me always through Confession. I wish you to be holy always so you are more perfectly pleasing to Me."***

Tuesday, August 2, 1994:

After Communion, I saw myself facing a kneeler before a casket. Jesus said: ***"My people, your life is a long journey of faith with heaven as its goal. You must put your life in spiritual perspective for your time on earth is but a brief time compared to eternity. Lift up your thoughts to Me daily as each day brings you one step closer to your Redeemer. Once you have seen some time pass you wonder how quickly it had passed. So, My people, take care that you use your time wisely to benefit your soul and its spiritual welfare, for as you visit other people's passing away, you should be preparing and be watchful for this same fate, but you should not be fearful of death. Instead, if you are faithful, it will be the beginning of a new and glorious life with Me. Look forward to that day when you can be with Me in eternal peace."***

Later, at church, I saw a huge pole and at the top there was a great ball of light as a beacon shining out to the world. I then looked up and it seemed like the whole sky had circling colors. Lastly, I saw an evil grotesque eye looking to the left and then the view came around to show an ugly demon I could not stand to watch. Jesus said: ***"My people, you are seeing My announcement of the warning. The pole you saw is like a radio station sending this message to everyone on earth. As you saw the circling colors, this represents everyone able to view their whole life as seen by Me. This will be a revelation to many who did not believe in God and to those who knew of God but have become lukewarm. It will be a time where everyone will understand that they will have one last chance to choose Me or the devil in the world. There will be no misunderstanding or any excuse for everyone not to know. Some will have the fear of God awaken their soul and return to Confession, while others will reject it as just a dream. All will see themselves in the light of their own sins and have to answer to Me and their consciences. After this event you will see the entrance of the Anti-Christ as he will come to power. Know My people that no power is above Me. He knows his place and time but he will not be allowed to control the free will of My faithful for I will protect you. Do not fear this time, but rejoice in your suffering for you will soon see My glory come upon the earth as Satan will be vanquished in all his attempts to harm man. My people, you must continue in constant prayer to ask My help to endure this time."***

Wednesday, August 3, 1994:

After Communion, I saw someone carrying a plastic bag with what looked like their only possessions. Jesus said: ***"My people, you indeed carry too much excess baggage of the world. You are tied down by your pride in knowing how to do things. Again you have surrounded yourself with possessions of this world which will not last, but you trust them for your well-being. Still further, you have piled up wealth sometimes more than you will need instead of sharing it with the less fortunate. All of this I mention because these are the things many put their trust in before trusting in Me. I am asking you to put your full trust in Me and I will lead you safely through life. To follow Me in faith means giving up all your dependence on the things of this earth. Once you have control over your life, you can offer it up to Me so you will follow My will for you unencumbered with the trust in man or the things of earth. This kind of faith must be nurtured with prayer and a continuing trust in Me. For I offer you the hope of eternal life, if you would listen to My words and live them out in your life."***

Later, at the prayer group I first saw a picture looking out of a window and there were birds singing. Jesus said: ***"All creation gives Me glory which you can see even in the animals. Take a lesson from nature which recognizes its creator. You too, My people, must recognize how small you are on a speck in the universe. I love you and ask your thanks for all I have given you."*** I then saw someone laughing and Jesus said: ***"It is good, My faithful, that you be joyful. Even though you are approaching the end times, do not be glum and downcast. For My glory should fill you with a joy of heavenly expectation. You can witness your joy in My faith when you keep a smile and are friendly to all you meet."*** I then saw a cowboy indicating the West and some huge flames behind him. I was reminded of an earlier vision of flames along a hill. Jesus said: ***"The fires you are seeing in the western states are another sign to you of the end times, much as the floods were on the Mississippi. Know that you are being chastised for your many sins, especially abortion. Pray and make reparation for the sins of your country that My justice will be lessened."*** I then saw a picture of the Infant of Prague as we saw it over in Czechoslovakia. Jesus said: ***"I am calling you to come to Me as children in faith that you will keep your innocence and humility. You are***

seeing Me again displayed in majesty as King of the Universe. Give praise and glory to your God for He is rich in mercy and compassion." I then saw some white flags with insignias and they were being paraded through the streets much like they used to celebrate red flags on May 1st in Russia. Jesus said: ***"This is a glimpse of how the people will honor the Anti-Christ as he comes into power. Many will treat him as a powerful ruler over all the earth and will seek his peace and words."*** I then saw a bright light which shone all around an angel. I asked Jesus permission for My guardian angel, Mark to speak. He said: ***"You are being advised to be close to your guardian angels for we will help you through the tribulation. At that time, you need to pray to Jesus for His help to protect yourselves through Him. Ask Jesus for permission and with faith anyone can converse with their angel."*** I then saw Our Lady come with her beautiful face dressed in the brown habit of Mt. Carmel. Then I saw a bright light representing the woman dressed with the sun. Mary said: ***"My children, you are seeing great signs in the skies and nature which should indicate more to you that my Son's Second Coming is near. I come to prepare the way for Him by asking you to pray much and get ready to receive Him. Keep yourself holy through Confession so your soul will be ready to present yourself to Him."***

Thursday, August 4, 1994: (St. John Vianney)

After Communion, I saw Maria E. as she was receiving Communion and she said: ***"Receive your Lord."*** I then saw a serpent coming up a tree and Jesus said: ***"You are seeing the evil one who had caused Eve to sin. In your concupiscence after the fall, it was My covenant that released sinners at last from their bonds of sin. No longer does sin keep Me from you, for you have the means through Confession and My death on the cross to be forgiven of your sins. It is important that you take advantage of this great opportunity to always stay in My graces. If you falter, you now have Me in the priest to forgive you. It is you who must make the first movement to want and ask for My forgiveness. You must be sincere in wanting to please Me and I will bestow My graces and peace among you. You now have no excuse. You should be close to Me always. Pray in faith, My people, to ever follow My commands and never cease trying to please Me."***

Friday, August 5, 1994:

After Communion, I saw a band of colors as a blur of events that wrapped itself around the earth. I then saw a large number of dense dark clouds around the earth. There was a beam of light that shone down on the earth. This was definitely a supernatural event which was being beamed down to each individual soul. Jesus said: ***"My people, this is the warning and you will know that you are the creatures and that I am your creator. You will see all the events in your life both good and bad as I have told you, but even more fearful for some, you will see the current status of your soul at the time—whether you are headed for heaven or to hell. You will know if you have rejected Me, that this is your last chance to choose Me or not. After this event your soul's destiny will lie completely with your free will, but you will have also a brief view of your destination at the time."*** I then asked if the warning was close. Jesus said: ***"Yes, it is close."***

Later, in Penfield at a birthday Mass for Our Lady after Communion, I saw Our Lady dressed in white with a blue mantle and she was in a pose much like at Fatima. Mary said: ***"Thank you, my children, for gathering to celebrate my birthday. It is beautiful to see all your lovely faces shining with a glorious faith. As the priest was witnessing to being an uncle, I am so joyous to be your Mother watching over all of you. As you greet me, you greet my Son also in Communion. He is such an integral part of your life, you should pray much to please Him and keep close to Him. Join us always in praying for the conversion of souls. This is a trying time to be holy, but with the graces from my Son and myself, we will always lead you to your heavenly goal of being with us eternally. Continue, my children, to praise and adore my Son always and He will take care of your every need if you just ask Him."***

Saturday, August 6, 1994: (Feast of the Transfiguration)

After Communion, I saw Jesus with a sword and then a cross of light came over the sword as it was taken away. Another image came of Jesus carrying a lamb as the sheepgate. Jesus said: ***"I am your Master. Take heart, My people, this is a trying time, but I am always here, My love, waiting for you to return to Me. My people are ever anxious that I should start My judgment on their schedule, but know that it is My plan of how events will unfold. It is not*** *for you to know the exact time of events but instead concern yourself with accepting My will and time for you. As for wars, you are seeing Me taking away the sword. I have died for men to take away their sin and their feelings of hate. Those who live by the sword, will die by the sword. Win people over with love and compassion. Do not try to force your will and ways on others for your own self-righteous justice. I am coming to settle accounts with everyone. You are My sheep—follow Me as I have asked you many times and listen to My words in the Scriptures. If you live My word, that will be enough for you. Then on My direction, you will see My glory as I come on My cloud at the judgment."*

Later, during exposition I saw a bright long column of light coming down from heaven to a mountain. I then saw a picture of a priest placing the monstrance in a rustic church. Jesus said: *"You have seen many wonderful faith experiences. During these times you have been granted many graces. These are to be treasured as your mountain top blessings for helping you through more difficult times. When later you are beset by some daily trials, think back to the time you received My graces and dwell on those thoughts to get you through. You will be tested many times in your life to see how much you depend on Me and trust in Me. These are mostly little tests and sometimes greater tests of your faith. It is easy to love and think about Me during good times. The real blessing is being able to weather more troubled times. I will give you hope and grace to get through any situation. Pray and ask My help for I am always at your beckon call, but do not wait until troubles to visit Me and think of Me. Keep Me always in your heart and mind throughout every day. If I am before you in spirit, it will seem as a constant transfiguration to you through all life at all times."*

Sunday, August 7, 1994:

After Communion, I could see many lines of angels and then a procession of angels escorting the Bread of Christ from heaven to earth. Jesus said: *"I am the Bread of Life come down from heaven. You are most fortunate to be able to receive Me into your own body and soul, for I am really present in the bread and wine. I come to you, My people, to strengthen you as the prophet Elijah so that you may endure your faith pilgrimage through life. I only ask My people that you prepare yourselves properly before you receive Me. This includes frequent Confession, especially in cases of mortal sin. It would be an insult to Me if you committed sacrilege in receiving Me. I am all-loving and I long to be with you, but it is good to have your houses in your soul tidy and neat for My entrance. If you would receive a King as I am, would you not go to great lengths of preparation? Even if you receive daily, treat each reception as special for I am the most honored guest possible to greet you."*

Later, at church, I saw some bright lights and some black circles. Then I could see men dressed in black with white helmets on. Jesus said: *"My people, you need to prepare spiritually and where possible physically since the one world government is slowly moving into place. They will not be allowed full control until after My warning, but know that after the warning, Satan will not lose time to move the Anti-Christ and his co-worker in the Vatican to power over the world. I have warned you much in advance of these happenings. Soon your money, your government, your food and communications will quickly come under the Anti-Christ's control. You will have to take what you can carry and go underground away from the authorities. Remember to keep your sacramentals as Rosaries, statues, scapulars and Bibles ready. You will be a people in hiding, trusting in Me to help you through this time. It will indeed be a test for you, but remember winning souls for Me and leading My people will be your primary responsibility. There will be much chaos, but pray constantly to Me and you will have peace in your soul. I love you, My people, and Satan will be frustrated in trying to destroy you. I will conquer him in the end and his power will be no more, shortly."*

Monday, August 8, 1994:

After Communion, I saw the planets moving around and then I saw a comet headed for the earth. Various rockets were sent up to destroy it, but the angels deflected them. God's justice was about to purify the earth. Jesus said: *"Listen to your Lord this day. Know that I have a plan for you and it will not be changed by man. Satan will have a short span of time to tempt man, but in the end his plans will be thwarted as well as man's. I will purify the earth of all evil, since it is an abomination in My sight. You are indeed*

seeing My instrument of destruction, as well as how futile man's attempts will be. Know that I am God and ruler of the universe. All things will conform to My will or they will be no more. I love all of My creatures, but your free will will determine your destiny. If you seek My love and peace, you will be rewarded with eternal bliss. If you seek yourself or the world's ways, then you will go with the demons to eternal hell fire. It is your choice. Then you will see Me coming on a cloud for the last judgment in all My glory."

Later, at church, I saw at first the Host in a monstrance and then it disappeared. I then saw the remains of a church with a hole in the ground where it had been. Finally, I saw a very smooth flowing river going down a hill. Jesus said: ***"My people, soon you will approach the tribulation which will indeed be a battle of good and evil. It will be a time when the demons and the warriors of Christ will both be fighting over souls. You will no longer be able to find Me in the churches since the evil one's agents will attack them. If you are fortunate, you may find Me in underground Masses. If you can preserve a Host in a holder, you can protect My presence from desecration. You may then carry Me around in hiding to give hope and joy to the faithful. But you can call on Me in prayer also and I will come to you with My help and My peace. For you will need My strength during those days when evil will lurk everywhere. Pray and I will protect you, My children. In the short time I ask you to endure, I will conquer evil and your joy will be complete when My love surrounds you. My splendor then will have been worth the wait and the suffering. Trust in Me and you will win your salvation."***

Tuesday, August 9, 1994: (Ezekiel being called)

After Communion, I saw a blue kite that was flying in the air. This turned into a parchment and gradually I could see a Bible. Jesus said: ***"You, My son, I have gifted with My word. You must go out and proclaim My word among My people for them to hear My message of love. At the same time, do not be afraid to tell people of My Second Coming. My people need to hear My words of consolation as well as a warning to prepare for the tribulation. Some of these messages people may not want to hear, but it is your duty to tell them anyway. Once My people have been warned***

and comforted with My words of love and care, they will see that even allowing messengers to come among them is a gift of Myself as well. Heed My words of life and put them into practice."

Later, at church, I saw several pairs of arms reaching out but without bodies. Jesus said: ***"My people, I am calling on you at this time to reach out to My faithful with My words of wisdom. To those who are willing to receive you, share with them My Word in your messages. It will uplift their faith to see how warmly I am embracing them with My love. Share the sincerity and peace I have gifted you with your faith so it may enrich the lives of those around you. My people, all of you are potential healers. This is a ministry I gave to My apostles. If you have strong faith and believe in My power, you will indeed be able to heal people by praying over them in the Holy Spirit. So do not hide your gifts under a bushel basket, but be ready to share your gifts with others. In the end you all will be fulfilling My plan as I act through My chosen instruments. So go out as I have asked and evangelize, teach, and heal My faithful. For as some are given many gifts, more responsibility is on them to perform as well."***

Wednesday, August 10, 1994:

After Communion, I saw several piles of gambling chips. Jesus said: ***"My people, throughout life you are making many decisions. There are many risks in life you have to take if you want to move forward. One concern I ask of you in your decision making is to concern yourselves with what motivates your heart's desire. You should direct your lives to those things which please Me and not just your earthly appetites. For many times you will fail in the things of life, but money should not be an end in itself. If you put your trust in My love and those things I ask you, you will never be let down or disappointed. For those who aspire to heavenly things will receive their reward. You may have to suffer some trials to prove yourselves and you may fall into sin occasionally, but I am here in Confession to forgive you and console you as you pick yourself up again. For it is in your weaknesses that you lose your life and find new life in following Me. Rejoice, My people, for when you choose Me, all risk of your eternal life will be assured as I accept you into My Kingdom."***

Later, at the prayer group, I was looking down on the floor and I saw a footstool. Jesus said: ***"I am constantly asking you to be My servants in bringing souls to Me. You are the instruments I use to spread the faith of My Gospels. Please answer My call for help and you will have My peace and love to console your soul."*** I then saw a picture of a big clock and Jesus said: ***"Time is short. You must make the best use of your time in prayer and fasting. These are your means to grow closer to Me. You should always be prepared for you know not the time when I will come for you. At that time, all accounts will be settled and it will be too late to do anything else. So pray now for the reparation of your past sins and you will be more ready for heaven."*** I saw outside some leaves on trees with the sun on them. Then further I could see a large woods. Jesus said: ***"Some of My people will be led to live in the woods in hiding and worshiping together as a community. You will have strength in numbers to help each other. There I will be in your midst giving you My joy of faith and peace."*** I then saw a gold robot and the word ***"Simulator"*** came to me. Jesus said: ***"This will be one of the tools of the evil one. They will be able to manipulate images on the TV to make those who watch believe anything they want you to do. At this time, get rid of your cable and TV or you will come under their control."*** I saw some wash hung on several lines inside a room. Jesus said: ***"During the trial, many will not be able to buy electricity. You will have to go back to an old style of life without your current conveniences. This again will test your faith and trust in Me to help you. Ask anything in My name and you will see how I provide."*** I could see several images of flowers. Jesus said: ***"Even Solomon was not arrayed as beautifully as the lilies of the field. So I tell you, My people, do not be anxious about what you are to wear or what you will eat. For if I care for the lilies of the field and the birds of the air, do you not think I will care for you even during the tribulation?"*** Finally, I saw Jesus walking towards me and there was a bright light reflecting off His hair. Jesus said: ***"I welcome you, My people, at all times to share in My love. It is you who must choose to return My love. For I have loved you so much since your conception. Please receive Me into your hearts so I can be with you and lead you through your life. I have an abundance of heavenly***

gifts ready to disperse on you if you would ask Me to give you some. When you give your life over to Me, you will seem to be living in heaven on earth. I desire you to strive to perfect your spiritual lives. Keep close to Me."

Thursday, August 11, 1994:

After Communion, I saw Maria E. with her eyes closed praying and she said: ***"The Lord be with you."*** I then saw a large cave opening and Jesus said: ***"In many ways I have asked you to withdraw from the ways of the world. The tribulation time will be your opportunity to witness to the strength of the love in Me. If you ask My help, I will lead you to a safe haven, so you will be protected from the onslaught of the demons. I will provide for you at that time much as I provided for My people during the Exodus. For I am a loving and caring God who will not let His faithful be orphaned. I will not leave you alone. Just pray to Me and I will be at your side through all your troubles. Have faith and trust in Me and you will see My day of glory."***

Friday, August 12, 1994:

After Communion, I could see into a hallway and people were walking up and down very fast. Then I could see a bright light come from up above. Jesus said: ***"Do not be taken up so much with the fast pace your society is living. Slow yourselves down so you can plan a place for Me in your lives. I should indeed be a part of your life because I am your creator. You were created to honor and adore Me. If you are not paying attention to Me, what will happen when I come to take you home and you are not ready? In a word you should always be in a state of grace ready to receive Me for you do not know the hour of your visitation. Take time each day to pray to Me for help and ask Me to walk through your day with you. You need to stop following your own way and follow My plan for you. I will care for your every need if you put your trust in Me. I love you with an endearing love and I do not want to see you bury all your time in your own pursuits. I am a jealous God and I want you to recognize your place in relationship to Me. I have given you free will but not freedom to forget Me completely. If you do not listen to My word then expect a***

miserable despair in hell the rest of eternity. So wake up and see the real thing that is important—the destiny in eternity of your God given soul. Prepare your soul with Confession frequently."

Later, (Terry West - 25th Anniversary) after Communion, I saw a heart shape and then a priest wearing a dalmatic. Jesus said: ***"All people are led to a certain vocation in life—marriage, priesthood or single life. Once you have committed yourself by vows made to God, you should do your utmost to be faithful to that promise. When you give your word on something, your faithfulness in carrying it out is a sign of your moral character—barring any unusual circumstances. In marriage it means doing things lovingly for your spouse without necessarily any reward. This is why I have likened My relationship with My Church as a bride because of the faithfulness of the love bond, but faithfulness is required of both for a successful union. You and I have a love union which can be blocked by sin. As for the priesthood, My priest-sons are especially endeared to Me, but again the priest who does not watch his prayer life and keep up his communication with Me will tire of his responsibilities. In a word all vocations require a certain honesty of purpose in what they are about. Wrapped in all vocations, also, is My hand in these vows to give you grace through the sacraments. This care and grace does not stop after the ceremony but continues throughout your life. So if you are having difficulties with your vocation in life, call on Me to further bless you and help you through whatever troubles you are having. Above all, do not give up your vows just for creature comforts but remember your bonds are joined in heaven as well."***

Saturday, August 13, 1994:

After Communion, I saw what looked like a Bible looking down on it. Jesus said: ***"My people, I want you to look for My word in your Bibles. If you truly love Me, you will seek out what the prophets said about Me, but most of all, if you want to lead good lives, look to the Gospels for My teachings of life and what you should value most. By constantly taking time to read My Holy Word, you will begin to understand My ways truly are better than your ways. The way I have shown you with My life should be a carbon copy of how you should lead your life. You may suffer for My sake but know I have gone before you and was also rejected, but you must***

be holy and perfect as My Father desires. So continue to read and drink in a full measure of My spirit. I will be with you always."

Later, at church, I saw a man standing next to a cross with a bright light shining down on him. Jesus said: ***"Many times people ask Me for signs or what they are to do. My answer to you is not to worry about worldly gains for these are not what you should be striving for. When I answer prayers, it is in My time and for what will be best for that soul's spiritual benefit. You will face many trials in life, some of your own making, but know the most important thing your soul is seeking is My peace. Until you understand I am your goal, you will have much unrest and disappointment. I desire you to come to Me for help and I will show you the way to live. If you try to give Me some space in your life, you will see things will fall into place since your desires for worldly things will be second to Me. Also, you are not alone. Forget your pride in difficulties and do not be ashamed to ask for help from your friends and relatives. They would be only too happy to help someone in need if you would just ask. I am the same. If you ask for My graces, I would only be too anxious to bestow them upon you. In the end ask and you shall receive more than your heart desires, but most of all keep Me in your thoughts throughout the day and you will have My peace to put your mind at ease in My loving arms."***

Sunday, August 14, 1994:

After Communion, I saw a picture of a wedding with the bride in a white gown. I received the word ***"Life"***. Jesus said: ***"With each person I bring into the world I make a covenant of love. My people, you should know that life and your existence is the greatest gift I can give you all. The next most important is your gift of faith. Do not take either of these lightly. Life can be used for good or evil. It is up to your free will and your religious training to choose to follow My ways. Through the gift of faith by Baptism you are led to be a daughter or son of God. I have a plan for each of you to follow for your salvation. Listen to Me often in My word of Scripture at Mass and pray to Me for discernment in how to live your life. If you strive to please Me as a rule in your actions, you will not be far from My Kingdom."***

Later, at church, I saw a cross with a corpus on the floor. Then there was a multiplication of crosses so they kept piling high past the ceiling. Jesus said: ***"My people, you should realize that I died on the cross for each and every one of your souls—even for the souls I know in the future who will be placed in hell. For I am a loving God who gives you every opportunity for salvation. It is yourselves in the long run who will reject Me. I will never reject you for forgiveness. It is you who must keep coming back to Me in Confession. As you live your life, you may understand how much I love you by considering how I humbled Myself to become a man even though I am of divine nature. Even more humbling was allowing men to crucify Me to death. I have paid this price for each and every one of you not expecting any repayment. I have given you this freely of My own will, thus enabling your entry into heaven. So when you have difficulties, think of how much I suffered as well. I have gone through your pains and know what you experience. So ask My help to get through your trials and thank Me for all I have given you. Your acceptance of My will, will be enough for Me."***

Monday, August 15, 1994: (Feast of the Assumption)

After Communion, I at first saw Our Lady in a statue wearing a crown. Then in a dark alcove I could see her standing with a light that shone over her head. Mary said: ***"You, my children, are witnessing the glory of my triumph over death. I was resurrected by my Son as you will be at the end. You will receive a glorified body then just as my Son intended it before the fall. I give honor to my Son for all the graces of the Immaculate Conception I received. He has raised me to high places so that I may lead you, my children, back to my Son. I show you the way back to Him through My mediatrix of graces and through my Rosary. It is prayer, my beloved ones, that will keep you humble and in communication with Jesus. Let Him lead you home to heaven and you will enjoy the great peace and love found there."***

Later, at church, I was walking through a small hallway with beautiful arches. Gradually, the scene came to the resting place of Our Lady before she was assumed into heaven. Mary said: ***"My children, you should not be fearful of death, since my Son is the life and the resurrection for all. Heed His words and keep in His grace at all times. If you find yourself in sin, go to Confession at once to again be in grace—always in preparation to receive my***

Son. You know not the hour He will call, so go to Confession at least once a month. My children another preparation is to take time often to give Jesus praise and adoration. Picture the peace in heaven with no earthly distractions. In heaven my Son's love so possesses you that you will melt into His oneness. So give thanks to Him for all He has given you as well. Once you dispose yourself more to adoring your Savior, you will constantly seek that hour when you can be with Him face to face. You can be with Him before the Blessed Sacrament as well. This is the closest to heaven you can experience as well as receiving Him in Communion. For when you are one with my Son nothing of this earth will matter."

Tuesday, August 16, 1994:

After Communion, I could look down and see my foot stepping forward. Jesus said: ***"My people, as you go through life ask for My help and I will guide your every footstep. I will not force Myself and My love on you for I am a gentleman, but at the same time, I am a gracious friend always standing at your side waiting for your invitation. Once you accept Me, I will shower you with graces beyond your understanding. For those who have faith and trust in Me, you will receive an abundance of My love and peace. Life will seem almost effortless with My help. You will desire then to always want to be in My company once you have tasted of My fruits of the Spirit. For My love is like a divine wine which is never totally consumed—it is ever present continuing to flow with My graciousness. My children, I love you so much and I wish to forever share My love with you. Keep faithful to Me in prayer and you will enjoy My countenance."***

Later, at church, I saw modern images on a TV screen being manipulated. Then I saw a huge machine with the top looking like an Egyptian sphinx. Finally, I saw the light turn grey and misty darkness set in. Jesus said: ***"You are at first seeing how the Anti-Christ will use all the technology available to his advantage via your TV. He will come to power and most of the people will give him homage except My faithful remnant. You will be protected from his wiles as I have promised you, but know not long thereafter his kingdom will come to ruin as My chastisement of judgment will overthrow him. I will then establish an era of peace you***

have not known since the time of the fall of Adam. You will live and desire this time to be so intimately in love with Me. It will seem like you have been loving Me forever and you will not imagine how you lived without Me at times. Once you have truly visited My love and grace of heaven or the era of peace on earth, it will seem to you a life that you never thought possible. Being in My light of full knowledge, you will understand My divinity fully and desire never to leave My presence. You cannot understand constant adoration of Me but you will live for it. Even now if you could stay in My presence before the Blessed Sacrament in prayer for a long time, it would give you some idea of the sharing of My oneness with you."

Wednesday, August 17, 1994:

After Communion, I saw some waves and then some swollen rivers in a flood. Jesus said: ***"My people, you are not changing your ways as I have requested many times. Sin is still running rampant in your society. What do you expect Me to do? I tell you that My chastisements of the elements will continue. Many have not seen the connection between your sin and the latest ravages in your country, but until you come around to My plans, you will continue to be visited with such happenings. So do not say I did not warn you of this continuing devastation. You have brought this on yourselves by your rejection of My laws. Pray constantly to atone for this increase in sin or further calamities will be forthcoming."***

Later, at the prayer group I saw a young girl wearing a white shirt with a picture on the front. Jesus said: ***"I am warning you, My children, do not be misled by the New-Age or One-World movement. You will find it entangled with the occult, drugs and modern music all of which have been promoted by Satan. You are called to be holy in prayer not just to celebrate earthly pleasures."*** I then saw a seaplane with pontoons taking off from the water. Jesus said: ***"Your faith life was launched by your Baptism into My own body—the Church. You should remember to renew your vows by renouncing Satan and his works. You are also called to be an apostle and share your faith with others."*** Again, I saw a vision of old cars (1930's) in the street. Jesus said: ***"In earlier years, My people, you were much more conscious of helping your neighbor.***

Today, your "Me generation" disgusts Me. You are now centered around yourselves and your own independence. I call on you to go back to your old ways of helping each other and forget your pride and your selfish tendencies." I now saw a simulation by computer on a TV screen which looked like the use of ***"virtual reality"***. Jesus said: ***"The Anti-Christ will exploit the use of virtual reality over the TV using it for mind control with earthly "High" feelings. As I have told you, avoid this on your TV and probably get rid of them at that time for they will only be serving evil purposes."*** I then saw a dark river with a serpent slithering on the surface. I could see an evil demon face later in the darkness. Jesus said: ***"You should know, My people, that Satan and his demons are loose roaming the earth to capture souls. This is a heightened evil time and will grow worse. This is why I am asking you to say the St. Michael prayer often for his help to fight the demons."*** I saw a beautiful gold empty altar in a Church. Jesus said: ***"Why have you taken Me off the altar and now hide Me elsewhere in the Church? Are you ashamed of Me or are you praising other gods? In reality you are praising yourselves and your earthly possessions more than Me. You have moved Me aside to take Me out of your mind to enjoy your own earthly fantasies. I tell you to stop this madness. Wake up to the fact that I am the one most worthy of praise. You are worthless wretches which I still love despite you and you need to come into My light of understanding. It is only through prayer that you will realize who should be glorified—Me only as in My commandments."*** I finally saw Our Lady rising in splendor and light into heaven which appeared as the Assumption. I then saw her crying profusely. Mary said: ***"You are witnessing my Assumption as my Lord has seen to call me blessed, but, my dear children, you are breaking my heart with your sins. I am crying real tears for you because many are on their way to hell and they will not listen to my message of praying my Rosary. You must help me with your prayers to pray for the conversion of sinners before it will be too late to save their souls."***

Thursday, August 18, 1994:

After Communion, I saw Maria E. as myself kneeling with her hands over her face in prayer. She said: ***"Prepare for Him."*** I then saw a bunch of large rocks in a rock house with a fire on the floor.

Jesus said: ***"My people, many times your faith is tested and you are sometimes found wanting due to your weak faith. Your faith in Me needs to have deep roots for such times to be strong. You need a "rock solid" foundation based on Me in the Scriptures. When trials come your way, know that you can reach out to Me for help. You are strong only in the depth that you love. If your faith is shallow, it will not stand the test of time. So plant deep roots in Me where I am so involved in your life that your trust in Me will override any of your troubles. Then your love for Me will be so strong that My love will surround you with all manner of protection."***

Friday, August 19, 1994:

After Communion, I saw what looked like a great ball of exploding energy, but as the vision continued there was no mushroom cloud. This seemed to be an ever expanding energy of Divine nature which seemed to spread over the whole earth as it was being renewed. Jesus said: ***"This renewal of the earth will come after the tribulation and the devil and his people have been purified from the earth. I will restore the earth to its once pristine beauty at the time of Adam. It will be free from man's pollution and destruction of the animal species. Everything will once again live in harmony. You will see that this will be a time of hope for all to enjoy at My command. Just as the prophets enkindled the dead bones back to life, I will restore the earth and all My faithful will return who died in the tribulation. Then there will be an era of peace, which will be like heaven on earth since I will communicate with man much as I did with Adam and Eve. You will no longer fear death or sickness. Food will be abundant without having to work. This will be My first reward to all those who remained faithful to Me during the trial. Knowing this message should heighten your faith and trust in My word that I will protect and watch over you always. All I ask is that you pray and keep Me in your thoughts at all times."***

Saturday, August 20, 1994:

At St. Bernard's Church on his feast day in Easton, Pa. after Communion, I saw Mass being celebrated by a bishop. I received a message from St. Bernard and he said: ***"My son, it is good to be a man of prayer. Prayer should be first in your life because it is***

the best way to be united with your Lord. He is always beckoning for us to come to Him in prayer. It is through prayer that He distributes His blessings and gives knowledge of Himself to us. If you listen for Him in contemplation, He will gladly show you how He wants you to lead your life. Jesus wants you to show your love by helping people in their need. It is by good example both in prayer and deed that you show your faithfulness to your Savior. Visit Him often in the Blessed Sacrament and follow His words in the Scriptures."

Later, at the Blue Army in Washington, N.J. I saw a rolling hill with many crosses with martyrs going up and down on each side of the hill. (Inside the House of Loretto model) Mary gave the message: ***"My little ones, I want to thank you for coming here to my shrine. It is my Son you should work to please the most. We are in need of as many footsoldiers as possible for my army. The sin of the world is calling for reparation which my prayer warriors hold the key. Those of you who are close to my heart and that of my Son, we need your prayers most desperately. You, more than anyone, know the great need for prayers. So please keep to your practice of my three Rosaries each day for sinners. Many will go to hell, if there are not enough people praying for them. This house is also meant to promote devotion to the Holy Family. There is a great need for unity in the family today as many evils are attacking the family. Pray therefore, for peace in the families to thwart divorce and abortion. With peace in the families, this will be a step closer to stopping the wars going on. Continue to stay close to my Son through His sacraments and keep in daily prayer so you can keep on the narrow road to heaven."***

Sunday, August 21, 1994: (Spanish Mass)

At Easton, Pa. in St. Bernard's after Communion, I saw a lot of people in a church but the altar area was dark and enclosed as in an Orthodox Church. Jesus said: ***"My people, you are understanding how wide My Church is all over the world. Many people praise Me in all languages. You have seen even in South America how true My faithful are even if they do not have much in this world. You, My people, are My stewards of the faith and servants to the rest. It is up to My faithful to keep My love burning in the souls of the people. You who are strong in the faith and close to Me, need*** *to be examples in your living to My people. They look to you for inspiration. So be faithful to your prayer life and do not drift away from Me. If you make Me the most important in your life, you will continue to be My instruments of faith for the rest. I love you all and continue with your good efforts of evangelization."*

Monday, August 22, 1994: (Queenship of Mary)

In Easton, Pa. at St. Bernard's after Communion, I saw a casket and then the vision flashed to heaven where I saw Our Lady crowned in awesome splendor as she was beside her Son on His thrown. There was a blue tinted bright light which shone all about. Mary said: ***"My children, you have seen the celebration of my Queenship. My Son has graced me with His blessing in granting me Queenship over His people. We were joined two hearts together, during life, but in heaven it took on even more splendor. I am indeed grateful to Jesus for making me Mother of you all as well. It is this concern for you as a Mother that I look after you for your spiritual welfare. I have sent many messages to you through various visionaries on how to lead your lives to be more holy and closer to my Son, but you see my statues and icons crying because I am sad you are not living my messages as I requested. Some are and they are saving souls, but most are not praying and fasting enough. This is a serious battle with evil. You must not tarry any longer and do my bidding for you do not have much more time to save souls. Go out, my children, and live my messages to the fullest. Then one day you can share in my Son's banquet of love."***

Later, at Hazelton, Pa. in the National Sacred Heart Shrine in front of St. Margaret Mary's relic, I saw Jesus showing His Heart and there was a lot of darkness around Him. Jesus said: ***"My children, thank you for coming to My shrine here. I have come for Margaret Mary as much as I come for you. Please see I am greeting you with My heart of love. For I long to caress each soul who comes to Me out of respect and honor for Me. I am always waiting for you, My people, to ask for My graces and blessings. When you understand your weaknesses, it is coming on your knees for help that I will indeed answer your prayers. You must continue to value heavenly gifts more than those things of the world. Everything I give you, including Myself in Communion, is given for***

your salvation. Live for My gifts and you will have all that is necessary. Do not keep My love a secret, but spread it among your friends and relatives. Help them to burn with My love as much as it means to you. When more of the human family loves and adores Me, peace will be more forthcoming. Go now in My love and spread this message."

At night, at church, I saw a blue light on Mary's face with a crown of twelve stars around her head. There was a bright intense light that shone all about her. Finally, I saw a slithering snake crushed by her foot. Mary said: ***"My children, you are blessed to see my coming glory which will be radiant and glorious to behold. For my Son has blessed me with many gifts which are a result of my commitment to say yes as He did on the cross. This is a message of hope to you, my children, that you will experience the Lord's day of victory. He has dressed me with the sun and will provide me my triumph over Satan as I will crush his head as foretold in the Scriptures. At Satan's conquest, the earth will be purified and the triumph I have been promised will be fulfilled. I am revealing to you that I am the second Eve about to give birth to the second Garden of Eden which will be your heaven on earth. So keep faithful, my children, with your daily prayers and fasting and you will witness our glory in heaven and on earth."***

Tuesday, August 23, 1994:

After Communion, I saw some people standing on a bus while we were traveling. Jesus said: ***"You are seeing My faithful on their journey through life. All people are appointed to the plan I have for them to one day join with Me in heaven. There will be a destination for each of you depending on what you have done on earth as to which stop you each will get off. I pray, My people, that you have learned from your experiences that people and love should be most important in your life. Keep My love most in your thoughts for it is to Me that you must answer to at the end of your life. If I am to judge you, make sure we are not strangers but friends through each and every day. By reading about Me in the Scriptures and practicing what I have preached, you will be led to your salvation."***

Later, at church, I saw a black helicopter and some brown colored jet planes with no national markings on them. In another vision I kept seeing people receive the mark of the beast in their hand with a chip implant. Jesus said: ***"You are indeed seeing the preparations being made by Anti-Christ's agents for world take-over by the UN. Many forces of different nations will be secretly in your country under the auspices of the UN. You will soon see a call for all people to receive this computer chip so they can be registered with the world computer the "Beast". This will be hailed as a means for more efficient buying and selling, but in actuality it will be the Anti-Christ's means to control the people. When you see people applying for this chip, know that it is the time to go into hiding in some safe haven or refuge. After an initial grace period to sign up voluntarily, the agents will then come looking for those who did not sign up and force them to take this chip. This is the mark of the beast you should avoid at all costs. Refuse this even under pain of death or you will not be written in the Book of Life. It will be at this time you will need a heavy trust in Me to take care of you. I will do it, if you ask My help in prayer since I told you I would protect your soul. The warning will come before a transition of power so you will truly know that you will be choosing either Me or Satan. Keep together for safety in numbers and I will watch over you."***

Wednesday, August 24, 1994:

After Communion, I saw a sled with someone on it, which was being pulled along the ground without any one pulling it. Jesus said: ***"My son, you and other visionaries are being led and brought on the scene at this time to help My people through this transition time between now and the tribulation. This is a preparation time more spiritually than physically. If you save your body from destruction, of what value is that to your life in eternity? I tell you, fear most the one who can mislead souls to hell, for indeed, it is the concern for the soul's destination that is the most important issue at this time. You will see an ever increasing evil time as the demons attempt to control men more than ever. That is why I tell you now to prepare your soul with frequent Confession. Get your sacramentals as Rosaries, scapulars and Bibles ready to take with you where I will lead you. I will provide for you, so do not be as concerned for the body but direct your attention most to the soul."***

Later, at the prayer group I first saw a trumpet being played. Jesus said: ***"The time of the trumpets of the angels announcing the purification is drawing near. Read Revelation concerning these events and you will be prepared."*** I then saw just a jet engine on a plane. Jesus said: ***"As I have told you previously, you will see events start to occur very rapidly as the end times draw near. See this as a time to be ever ready spiritually, for you know not the hour."*** I then saw a bright light from a dove representing the Holy Spirit rain down on all of us. The Holy Spirit said: ***"I am blessing all of you tonight with My gift of discernment so you will know how to follow My will for you during these coming trials."*** I saw a man turning a wheel of a gate to a big dam. Jesus said: ***"It is in your hands to loose the floodgates of My love for you. I am always ready to pour out My graces on you. It is you who limit My graces by your distractions or thinking I will not be so generous. But open each of your own gates and you will see how I can come into your lives with great love and direction."*** I then saw someone tightening their belt. Jesus said: ***"My people, you will be a people in haste much like those in My Exodus who should be ready to move into the desert of the unknown in the tribulation. Keep a strong faith and trust in Me as Moses did for his people. Be on guard to keep holy."*** I saw burning flames with souls of people in it representing hell. Jesus said: ***"My people do not all realize how serious hell is and how many souls are going there since they do not make even an effort to love Me. Lose your self love in My love, My friends, or you may meet the same fate for all eternity."*** I finally saw a picture of men working in a mine. Jesus said: ***"During the tribulation some will be martyred and most who are captured will be tortured as slaves to do the bidding of Satan's agents. If they cannot win your souls, they will keep you alive with torture to try and change your mind. Keep in prayer even though you may be seriously tested."***

Thursday, August 25, 1994:

After Communion, I saw Maria E. greeting me at her porch and she asked me to: ***"Greet Jesus and love Him as I do with your whole heart."*** I then saw some flowers and sensed we are to take care of things for the Lord. Jesus said: ***"I have given each of you a measure of My gifts at the outset of your life. To those who*** *have been given much, more will be expected of you. I have given you these graces to be used to support and run My Kingdom, but it is for witnessing to souls your faith that is most important. You have been given many gifts of this world, but see to it that you use them to share with others. You must see yourselves as both a spiritual and earthly accountant ever responsible to your Master. Be thankful for My gifts, but most of all use them as they were intended to promote the growth of My Kingdom on earth. So do not be selfish but be outgoing to all so that by your example and faith others will be drawn to Me through you as My instrument. Be ever ready to help and console souls in their spiritual need. Be loving to all as I have been to you. In a word, do not hold anything back but freely give of yourself in helping My faithful in their need."*

Friday, August 26, 1994:

After Communion, I saw Our Lady in a mantle with outstretched arms but I could not see her face. Mary said: ***"My dear little children, this is your Mother pleading with you to listen to my messages of prayer and reparation. Be like the wise virgins in the Gospel and prepare yourselves with many Rosaries. There is not much time left to pray for sinners' souls. You have seen already how I have ceased coming to some of my favored visionaries. As in your vision, I will not be coming much longer. Many have failed to live my messages. How many times do you expect me to repeat myself to deaf ears? Already I have tried more than the number of Hail Marys you have recited. My mission was to be as St. John the Baptist in heralding my Son's Second Coming, but many of the people think life will continue on and are not ready to receive my Son. You must put aside your sinful ways and forget your earthly desires. These things will not win heaven for your soul. Instead make acts of self-denial through fasting and prayer and receive my Son into your hearts. He is the one to please, not yourselves. Pray with much fervor from the heart since soon the trials of the end times will be upon you."***

Later, at church, I looked up in the sky and there were at least seven levels of clouds of different sizes and colors. Jesus said: ***"I love you, My people, more than you know. I am constantly seeking you out to be with Me as much as possible. To be with My***

beloved faithful is My constant desire. I am showing you the seven levels in heaven since I told you I go to prepare a place for you. I am especially trying to raise your level of achieving all the perfection which you are capable of with My help. So do not be just satisfied with doing a minimum amount of prayer just to do your duty to Me. Think more of Me with a loving heart as if you are trying to show the most love possible to your lover. I am here always willing for you to reach the maximum level possible in heaven. Each level demands a little more depth in your love for Me. The more you can lose yourself in My oneness, the deeper in love you will be with Me. Put the thoughts of this world only in the direction which brings you closest to Me. See Me in every minute of your day standing by your side encouraging you to be the best you can be by prayer, fasting and good works. By pleasing Me as your sole direction in life, you can strive to gain the closest love with Me in the higher levels of heaven. Think of Me often and you will fill your cup of love to overflowing. At the end you will see My reward for your love will be beyond your comprehension."

Saturday, August 27, 1994: (St. Monica)

After Communion, I saw a castle tower. Jesus said: ***"My people, many of you are concerned with the looks of your homes. I tell you that you should be most concerned with the looks of your interior home in your soul, for this is the dwelling place of the Holy Spirit. It is also your home where you invite Me in to join with you. You must prepare your soul and protect it from the attacks of the devil. Use your spiritual arms of Rosary, daily Mass and Communion, visits to My Blessed Sacrament and frequent Confession. You must build the house of your soul on solid ground with faith as its foundation. By being holy you will have the necessary protection to achieve your salvation and win your battle of life. Once you have armed yourself with My protection, you can help other souls to do the same. Be persistent in prayer as My St. Monica was faithful."*** Note. This had a striking similarity to the *"Interior Castle"* of St. Theresa of Avila.

Later, at church, I saw a planet with rings around it. Then I saw what looked like earth from out in space. Jesus said: ***"You, My people, are a blessed planet. Since the fall of Adam, sin has corrupted My human family. Several times I have chastised you with*** *floods and fire. I could have left you in your sin until you all were lost to Satan. Instead, I love My human family too much to leave you on your own. I have come down to earth and have died for your sins making the supreme sacrifice from your perspective in offering you the possibility for salvation. I still have entrusted you with your freedom to choose Me or not. You have been given My message of love in the inspired word of My Scriptures. It is up to you now to see and understand My glory through My creation. You all must ask yourselves why you were put here with immortal souls and where you are going? I have led the way in showing you My resurrection and how you must suffer as I did to gain your crown in heaven. Believe My promises and deepen your faith and hope in Me. Many will reject Me saying they did not see Me or because the ways of the world are more to their liking. Those who fail to even acknowledge Me or My love, they leave Me no choice but to condemn them. I am asking your sincere prayers to guard My faithful and bring back to Me those who have fallen away from Me. Some need prayer to warm their hearts, while the rest will never see Me again. It is hard to believe how some refuse My love. But Satan has turned their hearts from Me with all his lies. Wake up, My people, before it is too late."*

Sunday, August 28, 1994:

After Communion, I saw a picture of the sun with a halo around it and then a picture of a priest at the altar. The next scene showed a bright light shining down from heaven to the altar with the bread and wine consecrated. Jesus said: ***"I am showing you My loving presence as it rains down to you in Communion. Know that I am really present in the Host and give Me honor and respect as you receive Me and at the Consecration. There is much sin about and it does come from within as in the Gospel. But I reach out to receive you and forgive your sin if you are sincerely sorry. This is why confession should be frequent, so you can personally share your contrite contrition of being forgiven. Being humble in Confession is the first step in admitting you are a sinner. You can call on Me to help you. Just ask Me and you will see. Keep close to Me in daily prayer."***

Later, at church, I saw several rows of white crosses in the ground and I felt like I moved behind one of them. There was a brilliant light above, which shone down and the image was of the Trinity with God the Father, Jesus and the Holy Spirit as a dove. Jesus said: ***"You are seeing how I will separate the evil men from the faithful during the three days of darkness. All My faithful will be marked with a cross on their foreheads, while those evil men and women will be marked with the sign of the beast. I will send My angels to mark My faithful to be protected so that they will be passed over for purification much like the Hebrews were protected with the lamb's blood on their lintel. The devil and his angels will be allowed to take those unprotected souls. At that time, all unworthy souls and the demons will be sent to hell to purify the earth. Then all the living souls and those faithful who died during the tribulation will be sent to a safe place. I will renew the earth. Then those worthy will be brought back to the heaven on earth to enjoy the fruits of My Mother's triumph for an era of peace. This will give hope to all My faithful to pray and keep close to Me since your reward is not far off."***

Monday, August 29, 1994: (Beheading of St. John the Baptist)

After Communion, I saw a huge banquet table dressed in white. There were many people present. Jesus said: ***"It is a blessing to be called to be a prophet. All those asked to speak in My name of My word to people have been picked especially by Me. Indeed, it is a grace and honor to proclaim My Gospel and at times words of reprimand to My people. The people need to hear when I am displeased with the sin of their age. It is necessary that the people be told to reform their lives as society's morals decay. If those that hear My word do not believe and take it to heart, they will condemn themselves by their own inaction. Otherwise, if they heed the prophet's instructions, they will truly be saved by My mercy in forgiving their sin. Woe unto you those who defile and torture and martyr My prophets for your sin will be avenged by My angels. My prophets must be ready to accept abuse though for throughout history they have not been well-received, but rest assured that if you must suffer, you will receive a prophets's reward for your service in My love. Therefore, if a prophet be just and true to My word through discernment, listen to him for he has the words of eternal life with Me."***

Later, at church, I saw a thick grayish-blue cloud circling into a vortex. It gave the appearance of a whirlpool or a black hole. Jesus said: ***"My people, I am giving you a visual image of how to avoid hell. The devil in his cunning is always laying snares for unsuspecting souls. Be on guard, My faithful, for his subtle attacks. For he uses the cares of the world and the weakness of your spirituality to lure you into his web. At the outer edge of a whirlpool it is calm and unsuspecting, but if you allow yourself to think only in worldly terms, your heart will grow increasingly cold to My love. If you do not make a conscious effort each day to pray and give honor to Me, you will lose that love I inspired in you at Baptism. The way to hell is made by procrastination of prayer and forgetting your death as something far off. Do not let yourself be drawn into Satan's pool of ease and evil. Once you fall into that trap, it will be very hard to break out of your bondage of sin unless a miracle or someone's prayers will save you. Remember, hell in eternity is serious business and loving Me is one way to avoid it. If necessary, your fear of My wrath and burning there can also inspire you to be saved."***

Tuesday, August 30, 1994:

After Communion, I saw a large dark floor with some design as in an altar. Later, I could see Mass proceeding. Jesus said: ***"My people, treasure your churches and the Mass while you still have them. There will come a day when My churches will be used for other purposes. This will be near and during the tribulation when the Mass will have to be offered underground in private homes and possibly in the woods. Men will so detest Me with demon influences, they will try to remove anything holy from sight. This will be why you will be in hiding since My faithful will be sought out for persecution. It will be much as the treatment of the Jews during the Second World War. Satan and his agents will seem in control but you must know he is only doing what I have allowed him to do. I am and have always been in control of events. I have allowed this test to really see whether men love Me or the things of earth. Since evil has heightened to its last moment, know that My purification of the earth will start shortly. I have allowed Satan a span of time after which he, his angels and all the souls who follow him will be banished from earth into hell. This will be a*** *glorious time of My justice when My people will see Me face to face."*

Later, at church, I saw some hills and there was terraced strip mining going on with many working there. Jesus said: ***"You are seeing future mines which will use My faithful as slaves of torture. They will be mining for metals used in war-making as Satan and his minions are preparing their weapons for the final battle. This Battle of Armageddon will be fought for the control of the people. Many angels will be in the battle led by St. Michael. It will represent the turning point in Satan's reign and his power over the earth. Those of My faithful who live during this time, do not despair for evil's reign will last but a twinkling of an eye in time. You are My favored people and I will protect your souls. Do not worry so much about the body, but ask for My help to keep you holy during this evil time. You may suffer some hardships, but your reward with My new heaven on earth will be well worth the wait and your trust in Me. Prepare always with prayer for you will need a great strength of character and My help to win the battle over evil."***

Wednesday, August 31, 1994:

After Communion, I saw the pews of a church and I looked up toward the altar. Above it I saw a large vision of Jesus illuminated in light. He was beckoning me to come forward. Jesus said: ***"Come to Me you who are burdened and I will refresh you, for My yoke is easy and My burden light. But I invite you to a land of milk and honey, a future life with My peace where no one will disturb you. If you live and follow My ways, your reward will be great. Even during this life I offer you My abundant love in My daily bread for you in My daily Eucharist. I am here both to refresh you and help you to carry on with your life. I reach out to receive you always into My heart. When our hearts are joined, you can experience a taste of My peace and all embracing love. Live on in My grace and you will be able to fulfill My plan I have destined for you."***

At the prayer group I could see into dark space over the earth and it was covered with many demons. Jesus said: ***"Be on guard, My faithful, and call on Me and your guardian angels to protect you through these evil times. Leading into the tribulation, much***

evil will abound. The demons will be loosed to torture those not under My protection." I then saw a Bible closed on a table and in the background a football game was on the TV. Jesus said: ***"My people do not be taken with the many distractions of earthly things. Instead take time to read My Scriptures and learn from the lessons of life in the Gospel. Then you will see how to spend your precious little time left pleasing Me by following My example."*** I saw some water drops very vividly falling from the top of the inside of a cave. Jesus said: ***"Some of you will be called to hide in caves for protection from the future religious persecution. Be prudent and ask My help to survive in these trying times. Do not be fearful for I will provide for your spiritual needs and your bodily needs. Have trust in My promises."*** I could see some horror movies on TV. Jesus said: ***"My people have slowly been led to a heightened sense of awareness in order to be impressed with TV programming and movies. These directors have increased the violence, sex and have changed lifestyles by their suggestions in these films. This evil has become so accepted that men have lost their awareness of what is sinful. It would be well for you not to watch TV or these movies. I am most displeased with all of it."*** I then saw some events in the sky concerning the stars. Jesus said: ***"You should be aware that there will be a celestial event in the heavens that will announce the coming into power of the Anti-Christ. When you witness this event, be on guard with your spiritual weapons and ask Me to protect you."*** I could see some large light globes on a stand. There were many stairs and it looked like it went up to heaven. Jesus said: ***"You are being called to work your way each day toward your heavenly goal of being with Me. Each day brings you a step closer to My glory. Offer up the trials of each day that it will bring you merits that will be stored up for you in heaven on your arrival. Strive for storing these heavenly savings and forget any material gains in your earthly life."*** I saw finally, Our Lady coming with a Rosary in her hand. Mary said: ***"I offer you all these beads of my most powerful weapon against the evil one. I encourage you to pray the Rosary together as a family. The family is coming under increasing attacks. If you are to keep peace and unity in your families, you must pray the family Rosary. With this you can gain back your harmony and love which Satan is trying to destroy."***

Thursday, September 1, 1994:

After Communion, I saw a very weak image of Maria E. and she said: ***"Help me. Pray for me."*** I then saw an image of a tomb area and my guardian angel was there. Mark said: ***"I have come to calm your fears of what lies ahead as demons have their hour. You are to remain steadfast with your Lord Jesus, for He is in command at all times. The demons will hurl their temptations and curses at you, but I and the Lord will defend you. I ask you to pray and keep close to Jesus and there will be nothing to fear. Many of the faithful will be put to the test, but in the end your heroic faith will be your salvation."***

Friday, September 2, 1994:

After Communion, I saw an empty chair and Jesus said: ***"I am addressing all of you today on leadership. I have placed each of you in charge as a steward over your station in life. You have been given a plan by Me to carry out your life so that you can be a living example of a good Christian life. Use the things of this life to help others and provide for your family. Remember, you are only given gifts to watch over, you are not the true owner. So do not squander what I have given you with your talents or be selfish in keeping everything for yourself. To properly use what I have given you in talent and this world's goods is a training in life on which will be based the outcome of your judgment. For if you loved Me and your neighbor through life, I will treat you as the man who doubled what was given him and I said 'you have done well in a small matter. Come and enjoy your Master's table in heaven.' But if you tarry and do not do My will, I will treat you as the man who buried My treasure and I said 'you worthless lazy lout, take the money from him and give it to the rest and you will be bound and cast into the darkness to wail and grind your teeth."***

Later, at church, I saw a woman by a window as she was opening it. Jesus said: ***"I am calling out to the souls who are not listening to My message of love. I am asking you as in the vision to open the window of your heart to Me so I can fill you with My peace and love. This is a difficult time for My people to be faithful. Many have turned away from Me because of their pride in their selfishness and their lust for the flesh. If you center your*** *lives around the pleasures of this life, you will never be at peace. You will always have cravings for sensuality, but you will never really be satisfied since you will always want more than you can obtain. If you put your trust and faith in Me, your love will be returned many times and you will be fulfilled in My peace. You must look beyond the realm of your own lives to help others. Do not be satisfied with yourself until you can share your love and worldly things with others. In giving of yourself you will receive back many more blessings and favors in return. Do not seek what you can get out of life but be willing to give all you have to those around you. Then you will truly be pleasing Me and you will be rewarded in heaven."*

Saturday, September 3, 1994:

After Communion, I saw a vision of looking out of a cave. In another scene I was looking out of a hole in the earth from an underground tunnel. Jesus said: ***"Many wise in the ways of the world do not want to know Me because the pride of their wisdom will not allow it. If they have to lower their image of self-esteem to have faith in Me, it is too much to ask of them in their minds. To follow Me unquestionably demands an allegiance many are not willing to commit themselves. You see having faith in Me might mean giving up their wealth or their pleasures in life. It is not always comfortable to be a Christian. Some would say it is foolishness to believe in God, but My ways are not your ways. Those who give up looking smart in this world for Me are in reality the wisest men of all because they are preparing themselves for Me in eternity. So do not be fearful of how you will be persecuted or abused. Loving Me and following My ways are the way to follow the narrow road to heaven, but it is much more desirable than the broad road to hell which the world and the evil one calls you to."***

Later, I saw inside a church and there was a bride and groom and a bright cross of light above them. There were many people in the pews. Jesus said: ***"My people, you are seeing Me as the groom and you, My Church, are the bride. I come before you in many ways: in Communion, in Exposition, in the people around you and in creation. You were made in My image to honor, adore, and serve Me. Yet I look down on you today and there are very few following My requests. Why are you more content to wallow in the*** *pleasures of this world? The devil has taunted you with so many distractions, so many curiosities, that you live from day to day more interested in the news than in adoring Me. Why is it so difficult for you to pray and take time to tell Me your troubles and ask My help? I am here for you always as a faithful groom, ever faithful to filling your ears and heart with My love, but you are the harlot, always going to town more interested in a good time than to be before My Blessed Sacrament drinking in My graces. Come in to Me out of the confusion of the world and seek My peace, for as a spiritual being your soul yearns for Me. Give your soul its rest by coming back to Me. Then you will see the real pleasure in life is to enjoy My countenance and the joy of My peace."*

Sunday, September 4, 1994:

After Communion, I saw a cross on a blank wall and space open by the altar. Jesus said: ***"My people, are you ashamed to have My presence in the Blessed Sacrament not prominent to be seen in My churches? There are increasing abuses of where the tabernacles are being placed in My churches. The priests or others do not have the right to hide Me from My people. The Church was made to honor Me and not men or the congregation. You have your understanding of these matters completely confused by the devil. If My tabernacle is hidden, as in today's Gospel, open your mouth in righteous criticism. If these people do not take action, then continue on to higher authorities. I tell you that in a short time you will no longer have use of your churches, since you do not even reverence Me there now. Worship Me now My friends while you can, for the devil and His agents will only grow stronger in evil for a while."***

Later, at church, I saw the outline of an altar and it was set up outside in the open. Jesus said: ***"My people, you are becoming too fearful of how it will be during the tribulation. I bring you a message of hope to all those faithful to My word. Many are asking for more specific details than I intend to reveal at this time. The ones that should fear most are those the devil has enticed on the road to hell. These are the souls who will ultimately be tortured the most and even more so in hell. This trial is a test for all. It will be as with Job. I will strip away all the things of this world from you, those things on which you have depended for your survival.***

You will indeed have to trust Me day to day for your sustenance. It will be a time when your prayers will mean the most to you, since by doing so I will help and lead you. Once you fully depend on Me, you will later wonder why you did not do it sooner. By understanding this training, you will be ready to accept your life with Me in the era of peace and in heaven. It is following My will for you which is most important. Pray to Me during your trial to have more of an understanding of My ways. The saints have seen this light even while it was harder. But you will be greatly assisted to see this light of knowledge. Then you will understand how My plan works in your life. Pray for understanding."

Monday, September 5, 1994: (Labor Day)

After Communion, I saw some bread in a sandwich. Jesus said: ***"My people since the fall of Adam I have given you to work by the sweat of your brow to provide a living for yourselves. Work is a means for you to have fulfillment in the skills and talents I have given you. It is a way you can help each other in providing for your needs, but remember, man does not live by bread alone of this world. It is the heavenly food I give you during the Mass that is the living bread which will provide for your eternity with Me in heaven. This Eucharist is your life in Me here on earth. Without your eating it you will not have eternal life. So keep the heavenly gifts and their importance in perspective to the things you look to for survival in this earthly life."***

Later, at church, I saw a big shiny car coming towards Me. Jesus said: ***"I am trying to show you by example and by life's experiences how futile it is to seek glory and possession of the things of earth. You have an earthly body which craves to be famous and respected by others. Much as you try to impress others, they only turn to envy and despise you for doing well. So any earthly awards are soon forgotten and when you pass on they are thought of even less. When you seek the things of this world, it is only the anticipation of possessing it that drives you. Once you have acquired what you wanted, your brief joy quickly turns to despair as it no longer means that much. When you aspire to riches, even they turn into a non-entity since it does not really satisfy you. Compare this to when you do a good deed for someone and how good you feel about it. Also, when you struggle to***

help someone spiritually, it lifts the spirit. Even in earthly terms you can see spiritual good works are more rewarding than your earthly good fortunes. This should prove to you that your spiritual being is more important and should follow why I created you so. So strive more to please Me and seek heaven since you will have more peace and satisfaction with Me—more than the world could ever offer you."

Tuesday, September 6, 1994:

After Communion, I saw a bright sun shining through the trees and I moved out from under the trees into the sunlight. Jesus said: ***"My people, I welcome you always into the light. I am the Light of the World. So do not hide yourself from Me, but come to Me. I will give you My light of understanding, My light of grace and***

most of all My light of love. Since it is truly My love for all of you that attracts Me the most, I welcome even the most wretched of sinners. I await you to give you My forgiveness. All you need do is ask for it and I will bring you back into My good graces. For it is truly sad for those of you who do not want to enter into My light since without it, you can never be fully mature spiritually. Pray for those sinners who do not feel worthy to come to Me."

Later, at church, I saw a flat table and on it was a cup with a bunch of grapes in it. Jesus said: *"You are seeing the great harvest of the pressing of the grapes at vintage time. The judgment time is coming and you better be on guard lest you are not prepared spiritually for it. At that time you will see the volume of your works and the quality or intention of them as well. You will be judged first whether you are worthy of heaven or hell. Your individual measures will then be judged at which level of hell or heaven you will reside in. If you are not worthy of hell or heaven, then again your life will determine the level of purgatory you will enter. Only in purgatory can you change levels, but not in heaven or hell. I am showing you this so you can pray all the more for the poor souls in purgatory, so one day they can graduate from the last level into heaven. As fall arrives or you contemplate how you are spiritually, think how you can better yourself so you can rise higher in the glory of heaven one day. Be steadfast in your love for Me and do good works for your neighbor."*

Wednesday, September 7, 1994:

After Communion, I saw a house built into the side of a hill. Then I felt like I was moving past the surface of the hill and felt it was a home inside the ground. I then saw snakes and scorpions outside and felt the home underground was protection. Jesus said: *"My children, seek your protection underground both for protection from evil men and the plagues I will send to the earth to torment man. I will direct you at the proper time where to be and what to do. Do not fear, My faithful, for I have promised to take care of you. You must have full trust in Me and ask for My help. This coming trial will be hard on all those who live through it. But My faithful remnant must stay true to My commands and give Me your love and adoration."*

Later, at the prayer group I first saw a birthday cake and I saw a vision of Our Lady of Fatima coming. Mary said: ***"My dear children, it is a joy to be with you this evening. Your Rosaries are the most beautiful birthday gift I could receive. Thank you for being faithful to my request for prayer and fasting. Continue your Rosaries each day, for much reparation is needed for the sins of the world."*** I then saw a small clock on the table and its hands were moving around. Jesus said: ***"Time as you know it is slowly diminishing as the end times draw near. Be ever ready and prepared for the time when you are to come to Me at the end of your life. As you prepare things for winter, also think to recollect yourself often and make your soul ready to receive your Savior."*** I saw a school chair and thought of kids returning to school. Jesus said: ***"As you have educated yourselves in the secular life, think also of how you could advance yourself in spiritual knowledge. Read My Scriptures and you will see how the various people were taught to be faithful to Me. My Gospels show you vividly how I desire you to lead your lives."*** I then saw the evening as it grew dark and thought of how the nights were getting longer. Jesus said: ***"As the darkness increases each night, know that evil in your world is advancing as well. How long do you think I will allow man's sins to continue? Sin abounds so much that it cries out loudly for My justice, so prepare My people for My Second Coming since it is not far off."*** I saw a pyramid with shimmering glass faces with many colors as it was rotating. There was a huge eye at the top of the pyramid. Jesus said: ***"The Masons and the One-World people are rapidly preparing the world for the advent of the Anti-Christ. Many plans are secretly being crafted to combine world control into the hands of a few of the devil's agents. Look for the signs; many abound as evil will have its hour."*** I then could see signs of Egypt and a picture of the Pope as the Cairo Conference came to mind. Jesus said: ***"This meeting is another use of the UN as a puppet to spread the blasphemies of the evil one. You must remember that all sins of the flesh are serious mortal sins and require Confession to be forgiven. They are abortion, contraception, pre-marital sex, fornication and adultery. Avoid these sins under pain of loss of My grace."*** I finally received the word ***"Confession."*** Jesus said: ***"I will preach to you on Confession or Rec-***

onciliation since you hear little of it from your pulpits. People are still committing sin even though they do not think so. I ask you to make a monthly habit of going to Confession to receive My grace of the sacrament but most of all to ask My forgiveness of your sins. Without being sorry for your sin and admitting how it offends Me, you cannot be My disciple. Your will must come into conformity with mine if you choose to want Me in heaven."

Thursday, September 8, 1994: (Birth of Mary)

After Communion, I saw Maria E. lying down and she said: ***"Continue to pray for me my children."*** Then I saw Mary with outstretched arms and she said: ***"This is a moment for joy and celebration. Remember, I am at your side ever willing to give your prayer requests to my Son. I am always leading you to Jesus in everything I do. I praise Him especially since He has blessed me by allowing me to be His Mother. His birth overshadows all birthdays for this was His announcement of our salvation. He is always with you as well. Welcome Him into your hearts and your joy will be like a birthday celebration every day. Continue to pray my Rosary and keep close to my Son."***

Friday, September 9, 1994: (St. Peter Claver, baby)

After Communion, I saw a fetus in a womb being lifted up to Jesus above, with a bright light around Him. Jesus said: ***"See to it, My people, that you strive to protect every life I gift to you on earth. Life is a special gift I bestow on you as the Creator. No one can give life without with My approval, and no one can take a life for the same reason. I have given each life a plan in My infinite wisdom. This life is called for a special duty unique to that person. This is why an abortionist or any murderer is thwarting My plans for this individual. Anyone who does such a thing will be liable to judgment. I will forgive such persons if they are sincerely sorry, but there will be much reparation required for this sin. When you violate life, it is the most serious sin you can commit. See to it therefore, that you protect life from this endangerment at all costs."***

Saturday, September 10, 1994:

After Communion, I saw some large monuments of some men. Jesus said: ***"My people worship many idols during the week and*** *sometimes begrudge Me even one hour on Sunday. If you place money, material things or yourself before Me, you are in essence making gods or idols out of these. If you trust in yourself or your money instead of Me, how will you have room for Me in your hearts? If you think you have received these things only through your own efforts, you are badly mistaken. I have provided for you and you are only stewards of your possessions. Do not make your possessions ends in themselves; they will not save your soul. And do not think you have done everything alone. If I were to withdraw My help, you would be a dismal failure. Instead, give thanks and praise to Me for all you have received. You cannot have two masters. It is better to have Me who can give you everything for body and soul than to believe you or your possessions are gods and more powerful than Me. Those who have given themselves to the world and are self-centered and not God-centered, are headed for a rude awakening both here and at judgement. So see My light, that you are My creatures and not gods. You were made to adore and serve Me and not the devils or the world. Listen to these words leading to eternal life, or you will fall with the others going to hell."*

Later, at church, I saw a light gradually turn into darkness as I looked into the sky at night. Then I saw a grotesque demon outstretched come down. Jesus said: ***"My people, you are in a time of evil, where it will be allowed a time to test man. In your affluence you have lost touch with Me since you have most of what you need physically, but spiritually you are poor and sinking more. It will only change if you are brought to your knees to see how much you depend on Me. I will pull back My love but an instant to let you see how little you can do by yourself. Once you become aware of how evil will drag you down, you can more fully understand My place in your life. You will see that My love is strength and you need to draw on it for your survival. Without My help you are nothing and once you understand this, you will see how you need to be one with Me forever. It is your eternal commitment to Me that will gain you eternal peace. This is what your soul seeks most, not fame or fortune or putting yourself on a pedestal. Pray for strength and endurance through this time. Being with Me will protect your soul. Keep hope in Me and you will see your salvation."***

Sunday, September 11, 1994:

After Communion, Our Lady in the sky, standing to the side. There was a bright band of light wrapped over her head. She was ushering the new little souls to earth. Mary said: ***"I am assisting all my little ones to come to their new mothers. I, as your spiritual Mother, am asking each parent and even grandparents to watch over these precious little ones. It is up to you to see that they receive a Christian upbringing so that they will be acquainted with my Son. In many cases you must direct them back to Church or pray for their conversions. These are your charges, your responsibilities since you helped to bring them into the world. You are called to be apostles, but your own relatives should receive your first attention. My Son loves the children and wants them brought up in a loving Christian environment which you can provide."***

Later, at church, I saw a fast train coming to a crossroads. Then I could see a large letter ***"T"*** for trial which was followed by seeing a crucifix. Jesus said: ***"Many of you will face trials worse than those you anticipate, but fear not, I will be with you. You will see many tortured for the faith, but these things will happen. Concentrate on the end of evil on earth, which will come soon. No matter what you face, with hope in Me you will succeed in winning your crown. Justice will be served when you receive your reward of being with Me forever. If you think about the beauty of eternal bliss with Me, you will see this trial as a woman's birth pangs before rejoicing over a new life. You too will have a new life in My oneness. It will be so wonderful to be fully wrapped in My love. You will not find words enough to express your joy or your thanks to Me. Believe Me, My children, a life of prayer is all you need to please Me. If you follow My commands, you will not be disappointed."***

Monday, September 12, 1994:

After Communion, I saw row on row of many earthen graves. Jesus said: ***"You are seeing the result of man's continuing foolishness. Wars will breed nothing but more graveyards. Why is your greed so consuming as to kill many people for ill gotten gains? It is too severe a price to pay for that which is never attainable. Men's hearts have grown so cold that killing lives does not even affect certain consciences. Therefore, you will see increasing wars and more severe ones. Many lives will be lost to***

satisfy a few in high places. Ultimately, it is the devil's agents leading you through this strife, but know that you have been forewarned. Continue to pray for peace in your world among those who want only war."

Later, at church, I saw a spiraling cloud with concentric circles. There was some darkness, yet there were rays of light on the fringe. Jesus said: ***"I come to you with a message of love. You have witnessed a birth of life and with it you can see the miracle I create with each new life. Each soul comes forth from My love endowed with all the special gifts I have given that individual. From the time of your Baptism I have been drawing you to Me so that you may seek greater perfection by following My will for you. You must strive for a higher spiritual plane by your prayers and actions. My love envelops you, so I ask only that you accept My invitation to join My heart. You will be seeing a great testing time of evil, but I will be with you through it all. After this trial you will witness a new life as at creation where harmony and My love will abound. You must live for this day of glory, since this was why I created you—to love, adore and praise Me. Have faith and trust in My word, My people, and you will receive peace and love beyond your heart's wildest dreams. I long to cherish each of you with Me in heaven. That is why you must help Me to bring as many souls as possible to see this light of faith. You have free will to choose, but what an opportunity you all have to enjoy My gifts while I am waiting for your acceptance. Do not treat this choice lightly, for you have a limited time to convert. Come forward to Me now or be lost to the demons."***

Tuesday, September 13, 1994:

After Communion, I saw our pastor at the altar. Jesus said: ***"I am devoting a special time to show you My love for My priest sons. Every priest is special to Me not just because I love each of My creatures. They are special since they have given up many earthly opportunities to want to be My ministers of My Sacraments. They are My instruments through which I come to My faithful. They preach My word and bring My teachings to the ears of those who need to hear of My love and care for them. These ministers are worthy of My praise and worthy of your prayers to help them be the best priests possible. My priests are called individually not only for their mission in My vineyard as***

harvest masters, but they too, must acknowledge Me as Lord and follow My will. The priests, more than anyone, need to be an example of My love since they represent Me on earth. I ask all of them to follow their office religiously to keep close to Me in daily prayer so that they will not lose that initial fervor they had as they were ordained. Be thankful to Me, My people, for each priestly vocation granted to you."

Later, at church, I saw a telescope focused up into space and a picture of the earth was being viewed. Jesus said: ***"My people, your scientists are delving into areas of life where they should not be manipulating. The area of new life is what I am referring to. Creating life in test tubes or the using of sperm banks is a serious abuse of the way I meant life to be reproduced. This is a serious sin as well as is the masturbation required for sperm banks. All forms of blocking life's transmission and abnormal means of fertilization should be stopped. My plan for procreation was to come within the environment of marriage out of love. All acts should be open to life and desired, with the intent not to thwart procreation or abuse the good I have put in place. I am the Creator and you are My instruments, but there is severe sin in abusing the pleasures under the marriage bond. See to it that you obey My commands and if you are weak, seek out Confession. These sins of the flesh and their abuses are very serious and you should know when you are doing wrong. Pray to Me for strength and guidance that you will have the knowledge and the courage to follow My will in these matters of life."***

Wednesday, September 14, 1994: (The Triumph of the Cross)

I looked down an aisle of a dark church and I saw a large bare cross standing there with an old man beside it. Jesus said: ***"Each person is appointed their own personal cross crafted by Me. You each will encounter certain trials throughout life, but do not despair. You have been given many graces to endure your trials since I do not test you beyond your endurance. Each trial is a test of your faith and your resolve to keep My commandments. You do not successfully meet every challenge. By those faults or failings, you should learn how to perfect yourself, so that you will be pleasing to Me in My sight. Little by little this earthly testing will bring you closer to Me as you see how you are humbled as a sinner.***

I have gone before you and have conquered sin on My cross. I place My life before you as a model. So, once your pilgrimage comes to an end at Calvary, you will be readied and prepared by Me to accept your triumph of your cross."

Later, at the prayer group, I saw the teeth of a shark. Jesus said: ***"My people, do not be ensnared by the mind control of those things in the programming of your TV. Many poor examples of living and exploitation of people's money result from this source. It would be better to pray in the quiet of your room than waste your time with such a disgrace."*** I then saw someone smoking drugs using a pot. Jesus said: ***"Pay attention that you do not become controlled by any substance abuse such as drugs and alcohol. They will gradually weaken your mind with addiction, such that you could lose your faith worshipping an earthly high rather than My heavenly joy. Pray much for those with this problem that they may return to society and get hold of their senses."*** I saw Jesus on the Via Dolorosa carrying His cross up the hill. Jesus said: ***"I am showing you the road to salvation by enduring the suffering you will receive from this earthly life. Your trials may appear to you as the stations of the cross. Each event has its place in molding you to the spiritual person I expect you to be. Live for the cross as your guide and you can fight even the demons."*** I was at the base of the cross at Holy Sepulcher Church in Jerusalem. Jesus said: ***"Many unbelievers see the cross as foolishness and personal humiliation, but My faithful understand the power of the cross against evil. It is very much used in exorcisms because My death conquered sin and put it under My power forever. If you ask anything in My name, it will be granted according to My will. Use this power of the cross in helping you through life each day."*** I then saw a Chinese man and I was led to believe we will need to understand them more. Jesus said: ***"The countries from the east will have an increasing influence on your way of life. It may even be threatened by war as evil builds up for the great battle of good and evil."*** I saw a champagne bottle stored away. Jesus said: ***"You should be in more preparation for My glorious return in My Second Coming. This joy will be so wonderful in your eyes that you should ask for it to come faster for you to enjoy. My friends, place more attention on My promises of heaven than on any fear of the evil one's threats. Do not credit the evil one with anything since he***

was given all he has and he will only be allowed a short time." I finally saw Mary at the foot of the cross. Mary said: ***"It was a time of great sorrow for me to see my Son crucified, but in my heart I know His sacrifice was for a greater good in the salvation of men. He gave me to be your Mother which is another triumph of His cross. He suffered for all the sins of men, because this was His best way to show His true love for mankind in gaining heaven for all who were previously lost."***

Thursday, September 15, 1994: (Mother of Sorrows)

After Communion, I saw Marie E. with her face down and then lifted up. She said: ***"Pray with me."*** I then saw Our Lady in darkness beneath the cross. She said: ***"My dear children, as I drank in My sorrow that infamous day of my Son's crucifixion, may you try to understand how much my Son suffered for each of you on the cross. You, too, should have sorrow for your sins since they collectively caused my Son to have to do this for you, but His heart goes out to all of you and me and He would do anything to bring you before Him. Since He has opened the gates of heaven, we both invite you to accept His will and be with Him in paradise. I did suffer on earth since I knew from Simeon His destiny from the day of the presentation in the temple. Now I ask all of you to seek forgiveness of your sins in Confession and accept my Son's knock on the door of your heart and soul. Receive Him in and you will taste and see the glory of the Lord."***

Friday, September 16, 1994:

After Communion, I saw a cave with water and then I came outside to experience a beautiful scene of islands. Jesus said: ***"My people, do not become so taken up with yourself or your material things that you lose sight of Me and your eternal destination. Even though you may be impressed with the new and latest fads of life, these things will pass and become outdated. Look to the things that are permanent and lasting in peace. Nothing or no one can be found on earth to give you eternal happiness. All things on earth are only temporary. Look to Me for your joy and excitement and you will be completely satisfied both physically and spiritually. See that real power is in Me and you have not always realized it. Once you are at peace in My love, you will see that a*** *life of prayer is much more rewarding than following all the latest earthly sensations. Pray to Me often to keep your life focused on the things which should mean most in your life."*

Later, at church, I saw some yellow flowers and then I saw some native Indians. Jesus said: ***"There are many peoples under My care in this world. I have suffered and died for each of you. You are all equal in My eyes, so do not lord it over others, or feel you are better in any way than they are. You must, instead, be more concerned with pleasing Me and following My commands. If you spent as much time praying as you do talking about others behind their backs, you would be farther ahead spiritually. Greed and desire of power over others can misdirect your life and keep you from Me. Be prayerful, therefore, and help your neighbor rather than run them down before others. Treat people as you would want them to treat you and you will have started on the road to perfection. Look at how I dealt with people when I walked the earth, and follow My example."***

Saturday, September 17, 1994:

After Communion, I saw outside in a field a stack of pallets and then I saw to the left of it a large hole which seemed to drop endlessly. Jesus said: ***"My people, you have heard the Gospel about the seed of God sown in the field. I tell you to be on guard and be ever faithful to your daily prayer since this is your life link with Me. You have seen how the world tugs at you, always seeking your attention with its duties and delights, but do not become so distracted from Me that you lose sight of your faith and fall into sin and leave Me. For if you risk falling away, there may not be someone to bring you back to Me by deed or prayer. Once you leave Me, you could be lost forever and become eternally lost in hell. If you value My love, or at least try to avoid hell, then be attentive to your spiritual life since it needs daily feeding."***

Later, at Nocturnal Hour, I saw the earth in space and it was bright blue. Then it grew cloudy around it and then it was cast into darkness. Jesus said: ***"I am showing you again My chastisement not to frighten you but to tell you it is close for the comet to come. You will be joyous once it arrives, as it will bring My Coming that much sooner. I have shown you the path of fire and the resulting fumes which choke some as the sun's light will cease for a time.***

Be in a spot protected from the air so you do not have to breathe these fumes. Much of the oxygen will be consumed and breathing will be difficult, but once this trial has passed, you will be resplendent in My glory, for no one can imagine how beautiful life will be for My faithful. On the other hand, those not loyal will meet a bitter fate."

Sunday, September 18, 1994:

After Communion, I saw a king in his robes with crown and scepter walking up the steps to His throne with the people crowding on either side cheering as he sat down. Jesus said: ***"My people, it will not be much longer when you will see Me majesticly coming on a cloud on the day of judgment. It will be a glorious triumphant entry when all the faithful will be honoring and adoring Me for they know I am the conqueror of sin in the world. For the worthy, they will celebrate with Me a peace on earth as it was originally meant to be. This will be a day of hope all good people long to see. They cannot conceive how glorious it will be but, trust Me, those who are faithful will no longer have to worry about receiving a just reward and then some. Give glory and praise to your God now and forever and I will take care of you as a most loving parent, spoiling you to death."***

Later, at church, with the image of Our Lady of Guadalupe I saw Our Lady come dressed in white as at Fatima. Mary said: ***"My dear young adults, I am coming today thinking of purity of heart and body. How sad it is for me to see so much abuse of chastity and purity. My life has been a model of what a woman should strive to imitate. Instead of being ruled by your passions and your selfish independence, it is your place to follow my Son's commandments and take care not to abuse your bodies. You must think of your bodies as temples of the Holy Spirit, which they are. It is not for you to violate your bodies simply for a short earthly pleasure. This union of man and woman was reserved for the sacred Sacrament of Matrimony. My children, you are foolish to think you know everything and can do as you please without any thought to the responsibility of your actions. As a Mother I must chastise you for some of your selfish behavior. You must ask my Son for the forgiveness of your sins. Strive through prayer to be more chaste in your lives and see how fol-***

lowing my Son's plan for you is much better for you in the end. It may take some patience to wait for the proper time for things, but you will be well rewarded for living a good Christian life."

Monday, September 19, 1994:

After Communion, I saw a doorway to heaven and the door swung open with a bright light behind it. Jesus said: ***"I stand here at the doorway of heaven beckoning you to come as you are with all of your imperfections. Do not worry whether you are worthy enough to come. If you are faithful to My commandments and willing to adore and serve Me, you will be welcomed with My loving arms waiting to receive you. Do not tarry, since there is not a long time for you to decide. A time will come soon when this opportunity will no longer be available. In other words, My judgment time is approaching and you will be forced to account for yourselves at that time. So be on guard lest you are found wanting in My eyes and not fit for the wedding feast."***

Later, at church, I saw a huge temple and there was a large altar of sacrifice displayed in front of the temple. I also saw a large number of locusts descend upon the people as some sort of punishment. Jesus said: ***"My people, during the tribulation you will see many give praise and honor to the Anti-Christ. They will treat him as a god because of his miraculous powers. They will make sacrifices to him even, possibly, human sacrifices as they do even now in hidden places. I will send a curse upon these demented souls for blaspheming against Me. There will be many pestilences and plagues of locusts and scorpions which will be sent to bite and sting those accursed for their evil deeds. They will know that I am the Lord and I shall not have any strange gods before Me. Prepare, My people, for this evil time. You must muster all your spiritual strength to endure it. I will shorten the time of this evil scourge lest even the elect would be lost. Believe in Me and I will save you through it all."*** (Rev.9:3)

Tuesday, September 20, 1994:

After Communion, I saw a woman I did not recognize wearing a white top. Jesus said: ***"You must be the servant of all if you are to be My disciple. I ask you to imitate My life and that of My Mother in all your affairs. Think of how we would have acted in*** *any given situation. In leading your lives as such, you also will be examples of Christian lives to those around you. Your actions, as well as what you say, must speak in unison and you can evangelize others to the faith. Pray especially for those close to you that you may influence as many souls as possible to come back to Me while they still have time. Keep in constant preparation by a prayerful life."*

Later, at church, I saw an altar and a cross was in the center on a stand. The scene moved around and I was looking at it from all directions. Jesus said: ***"You can see that life is a constant cross you must bear. You are buffeted with life's problems and concerns at all times with never any true peace. But do not despair about your cross for I am always at your call for help. I am asking you to be careful how you spend your time and set your priorities. Set aside some time for Me in prayer each day. If you say that you have no time for prayer, then maybe you are too busy with life's concerns and need to set new priorities. If you are to keep close to the One you love, it is important that you allow Me some of your precious time. When you do pray, concentrate with your whole heart and mind on what you are saying in prayer. Do not rush through your prayers, so you can rush to your agenda. If you are truly following My will, you will be only too ready to give Me as much free time to work with you as possible. In that way I will be running your life and not you or the world. If you keep things in proper perspective as to what is most important, you will see that your prayer life comes first before all other earthly distractions."***

Wednesday, September 21, 1994: (St. Matthew's feast day)

At church, I saw people crowded along the edges of the street and their shadows were on the road. It was as if Jesus was walking by. Jesus said: ***"I am here calling all My disciples. Each of you that has been called and given the gift of faith, is given many gifts through the Holy Spirit, as the apostles were on Pentecost. You each have been called forth to use your individual gifts to spread My word and evangelize as many souls as you can, both by deed and example. Those with gifts of teaching shall teach. Those with gifts of healing shall heal. Those with gifts of tongues shall interpret My instructions. Whichever gifts you have been***

given, you cannot hide them or not use them. They were given to spread the faith and using them will indeed build up your treasure in heaven. So go forward and do My will and you will see how rewarding your work will be."

Later, at the prayer group I first saw Pope John Paul II walking outside with other prelates. Jesus said: ***"Listen to My Pope, John Paul II. He is My vicar I have appointed to you at this time. I am guiding his every action and teaching so that you may be reaffirmed in all the teachings of My Church. He is standing the test of time in all the Church pronounces on modern day problems of abortion, war and the way priests and laity should live."*** I then saw an icon of Our Lady encased in glass. Mary said: ***"This day is very prophetic in honor of the evangelist Matthew. You are all called by your Baptism to go forward and teach all nations. By your word of encouragement, work everyday to help bring souls back to my Jesus. You, too, are to evangelize as the apostles gave you the example. By spreading my Son's word, you can see how faith will come alive in those you touch."*** I saw a picnic table and a green drilling machine about to dig a water well. (Note. Magdalena asked for donations for a well to be dug in a Phillipine town with no water.) Jesus said: ***"Trust in Me always for your sustenance when you are in need and I will provide food and drink for you. I bring you 'living water' which a man will drink and never thirst. For My heavenly gifts are much more enduring than earthly ones which only last a short while."*** I then saw an old victrola radio and then some modern appliances. Jesus said: ***"Do not treat science as a god to be worshipped. I have endowed inventors with their ability to help you live a little more easily, but do not abuse your inventions for evil purposes and do not think that science has all the answers of your life. On the contrary, when you gain full knowledge, you will see how little you know and understand. You have only scratched the surface of what can be known."*** I saw a skull in a burning flame. Jesus said: ***"I am warning you, My people, those who go to hell do not realize how final this decision will be. For those who are being led astray by the evil one, wake up before it is too late. You will be forever in torture and never at peace in hell. If you desire My peace or fear hell, come to Me at once and do not waste time to be reconciled of your sin lest you be lost in your procrastina-***

tion." I saw some modern day skyscrapers. Jesus said: ***"Man builds many tall structures which become monuments in his attempt to show off his skills. These remind Me of the Tower of Babel which was built long ago. My people, do not think you are so great and proud of all you have accomplished. For all that you do I have helped you and you could hardly take full credit, but be thankful for My help in your work and give proper credit to Me. If you do not and think yourselves like gods, you will soon come to a failure much as when I toppled their towers of old and confused their speech."*** I saw a small church. I opened the front door and saw a scene of green trees and a blue sky. Jesus said: ***"I want you to have a deeper understanding of My creation and how beautifully made it is. If you were to even look at a tree, try to think how you would make one yourself. Also, just think of the detail in how each cell has its genetic code structured to produce only one type of tree. Think even how it grows each year, fitting in as just one part of creation and how without that part, the world would suffer. Now praise Me for giving all of this world for your use."***

Thursday, September 22, 1994:

After Communion, I saw Marie E. receiving Communion and she said: ***"Receive your Lord."*** I then could see a very ominous light from above as Jesus parted the heavens to show Himself. There was a feeling of a direct supernatural intervention which willl come at the time of the warning. Jesus said: ***"Woe unto you, O people of the earth. I have said, 'When I return, shall I find any faith on the earth?' Your generation has been very much attacked by the devil. His deeds are everywhere to be seen in your many abominations. For this reason of your plight, I will offer you one last chance to choose Me on terms where you cannot refute My presence. Nor will you not know of My existence. With this warning, you will come face to face with your Lord to show you all your sins and how they offend Me. At that moment you all will have an opportunity to either choose Me or the world. Take time, though, to judge your actions for your decision now will be final with no grey areas and no excuses will be taken after this. For you will truly see Me as I am in glory. There will be no doubt about which you are choosing. 'Choose life,' therefore, that you may be with Me forever in My graces and splendor. Otherwise, a choice of the***

world will leave you empty with eternal chaos in hell and no hope of ever finding My peace. This will be the most important choice you will ever make in your lifetime, so choose wisely."

Friday, September 23, 1994:

After Communion, I saw a huge field and there was an irrigation ditch with water in it running down the middle of the field. Jesus said: ***"I am the living water come down from heaven which all men thirst after. Apart from Me you are nothing. Join in praising and adoring Me since I am the one you are seeking. Your souls clamor to be with Me since it is your spiritual nature which seeks My peace. In the world you will never find My peace. Much as you try to satisfy your earthly cravings, you can never reach pure satisfaction because you are incomplete without Me. It is with resting in My spirit of peace that you will see yourself satisfied. Once you understand My love and your craving for it, you will only then be fulfilled. For My peace and joy are your eternal heart's desire. Keep close to Me in prayer and your joy will be complete."***

Later, at church, I saw a great darkness and a few shadows passed in front of me which could be spirit souls. Jesus said: ***"I am the Light of truth which dispels the darkness. I have come into the world to light a path to Me through the darkness of sin on this earth. It is important to know that there will be no improvement in your world unless I am instrumental in it. If it be your wish through prayer that I help man in his troubles, it will happen only if you accept Me and believe I can change the world's direction. These later years of evil are only a glimpse in time. Do not think I have abandoned you. On the contrary, it is by seeing your helplessness without Me which will turn this world around. Once this world falls on its face worshipping other gods, it will one day wake up to the reality of your dependence on Me. Come to Me in Confession to forgive your sins and your lives will be turned around to accept My light and shun the darkness of the world."***

Saturday, September 24, 1994:

At church, I saw a wall with what looked like a safe at a bank. Then the door opened of itself and Jesus walked forward. Jesus said: ***"I am your deposit of faith stored in My tabernacles around*** *the world. I present you with this image since I am the most important being in your life. Money and the world are so inferior to My purpose; they are like the dust of the earth. All in the world I have created is good in and of itself, but your abuse of these things has polluted their appearance. My friends, the faith and My body that I deposit in you at Communion is like a bank deposit. As you grow in My love and your faith is perfected, you become the interest on that deposit. Once you have been instilled with Me, you all become new bankers as you and I now must spread My deposit of faith in the hearts of all the rest of humanity. By bringing souls to Me, My body in the Church will grow and flourish as I intended it to be in My image. See how My plan for you centers your life in Me. Put nothing before Me and always be ready to do My will each day. It should be a joy for you to walk with Me each day in fulfillment of all My commands with your faith perfected through Me. You will long to be in My Kingdom as soon as possible. Pray and abide in My love and your life's ambition of being with Me will come to fruition."*

At church, I saw a dark night and I saw tire tracks on the road as if someone sped away fast. Jesus said: ***"My people, I was with My apostles and left My mark of faith on them. They knew and experienced My teachings. I am calling on each of you to do the same with the people you come in contact with. Be willing to share your faith and life experiences with others. Then you, too, will leave your mark of faith as an impression on each person who took your word to heart and followed Me. You will not travel to many towns before the end times will be drawing nigh. Know that My children are crying out for My message of love. They want to know I am coming to help them and are rejoicing when My messengers give My word to the many. Know that I am with you to help spread My word as the Holy Spirit was with the apostles. It will be Me speaking through you. So do not worry what you will say—I will give it to you."***

Sunday, September 25, 1994:

After Communion, I saw a tall empty cross. Then I saw a man and a woman holding a Bible. Jesus said: ***"There are many ministries I call My faithful to carry out. There are, indeed, some messengers among you whom I have called to prophesy among My***

people. Especially in these times, My messages are being given to many to warn My people and reeducate them to the evil going on around them. Many have been lulled to sleep spiritually by the devil's cunning ways taking advantage of man's weaknesses. You yourself are an example of such a ministry. You should be faithful to helping Me spread My message. Do not fear reproach, but speak openly to those who will listen. I need many such instruments to prepare My people for the great trial about to come to the earth. Did you think I would forever tolerate this evil in your world? So pray much and work hard to get My message out to those that would listen and take it to heart."

At church, I saw closed blinds on a window. Someone pulled up the blinds to let the light in. Jesus said: ***"My people, I come to you many times struggling to get your attention. If you are to give Me a chance to win your heart and soul, you must be open enough to receive Me. If you do not open the door to your heart, how can My love try to soften it? You must desire My heart and My love in order to come to Me. If you do not take a chance on meeting Me halfway, you will never have a chance to improve. Come to Me, My children, and you will see the graces I wish to pour out on you. You will be rewarded for your effort with everlasting life as long as you hold on to My call. Once you have accepted Me, you must nourish your faith with prayer and suffering. If you do not take time to better your spiritual life, it will be much harder to make any spiritual gain. Be sincere in your love for Me and I will assist you to your heart's desire of heaven with Me."***

Monday, September 26, 1994:

After Communion, I saw a dark night and police were apprehending someone. Jesus said: ***"My people, do not deceive yourselves that you can keep your transgressions secret from Me, for I see what you do in secret, even understanding the intentions of your heart with every action. You may fool other men, but you will never keep secrets from Me. Be on guard lest the evil one coaxes you to sin in secret. I will see everything and expect recompense for everything you do. If you catch yourself in such sin, then come to Me in Confession and I will forgive you and free your guilt. It is better to have a free conscience knowing you are forgiven than to remain in sin with all its guilt feelings in your***

soul. I love you, My people, and I long to have you love Me all the time. But you must clean out the evil trash in your souls and hearts and set your track on good things through My help."

Later, at church, I saw several women in a beauty contest. Jesus said: ***"My people, do not be taken up with all your vanities, for your physical beauty is fleeting. The beauty you should concern yourself with most is your inner spiritual beauty before Me. Do not be so concerned with being better than someone else either in appearance or in your belongings. For even some of My apostles sought to be at My right hand. I tell you as I told My apostles. If you desire to be great in the Kingdom of God, you must be the servant of all. When you conform your life to My ways and you confess your sins in Confession, then your soul will be filled with My graces and be truly beautiful to Me. I tell you when that soul radiates love and peace, there is an inner glow to that person's outward appearances. When you seek My will, that is what you should be concerned with, not following your own designs. My love permeates the souls of My faithful so they think only of pleasing Me and not themselves or others around them. Lead your life in this way and your joy will know no bounds."***

Tuesday, September 27, 1994: (St. Vincent de Paul)

After Communion, I saw a priest serving Mass. Jesus said: ***"I direct your attention to My priest sons who indeed are serving the rest. Imagine if you did not have your priests, you could not receive Me even in Communion every day. My priests should be honored and praised for carrying out their priestly functions. They have many problems to deal with as the laity has. Pray for them just the same despite any of their failings. You need My priests now more than ever to fight this increasing battle of evil. My priests should be thankful for the opportunity to lead My children to Me. May they keep faithful to Me in their daily prayers and concentrated on their dedication to leading My people to My Kingdom in their service."***

Later, at church, I saw a long narrow line which looked like a narrow road. I then saw a very flashy car drive by on a big superhighway and on the guard rail was a man with green glowing eyes. Jesus said: ***"My people, follow Me on the narrow road to heaven. Do not be persuaded by the evil one to seek only the things of this*** *world. I have planned your life for you and if you follow My will, it will be enough for you both on the earth and in heaven. Do not be distracted by the evil enticements of possessions and a life following only your passions and appetites. Be satisfied with your lot in whatever life I have given you. It is not necessary to be rich and successful in the things of this world. It is sufficient to have a moderate living without any excesses. If you are to desire more let it be a desire for more of My graces and heavenly gifts. Your world is in a dark night of the soul and only asking for My help will save you. Continue to lead a life of prayer and follow My commandments to keep on your narrow road to Me. Do not wander off on your own or seek more than you need of this world's goods. If you should enter on the road to hell, you may have a hard time returning to My love, if indeed you ever return. I love you My people and I do not want to see you lose your souls for only temporary comforts. See clearly how you need to seek Me if you desire any worthwhile future."*

Wednesday, September 28, 1994:

After Communion, I saw the mitre of a bishop and then I saw Pope John Paul II sitting on a chair outside on a sunny day. Jesus said: ***"My children, I call your attention to My bishops. These are My priest sons and shepherds of the people but there are some with earthly failings like all of yours at times. Look to whether their teachings are in conformance with My representative on earth in My Pope John Paul II. I tell you it is a most serious sin for those bishops to be contrary to My teachings of faith and morals. They shall not dilute My word with their own interpretations of My law. They will be held responsible for any souls they may misdirect in their pronouncements. I tell you to look to the Scriptures to validate what they say. If such a bishop proclaims things not in the Church's traditional teachings, then you are not obliged to follow him. You must follow a higher law in conformance with My teachings and My will. If you follow Me in this way, it will save your soul from any of these wayward prelates."***

Later, at the prayer group I first saw a bright angel come down from heaven. It was revealed to be St. Gabriel, who said: ***"I am Gabriel who stands in the presence of God. Hear My message,***

dear people. Your Jesus is coming once again to receive His people. I have come to both warn you of His coming and ask you to prepare yourselves for His triumphant entry." Then I saw some angels in the sky that were the angels who heralded Jesus' first coming at Bethlehem. They were, as one, trumpeting the great Second Coming of the Lord. They are greeting us as the shepherds and asking us to go and see Jesus in His tabernacle and praise Him. I saw a mirror and it reflected an image of a person contemplating. Jesus said: ***"Look into your inner soul as you would see yourself in a mirror. Reflect on how your spiritual condition is right now and how you could improve it. If you find many ugly things displeasing to Me, then make haste to Confession to ask for My forgiveness. The peace of the priest representing Me in this sacrament is always awaiting you there."*** I then received a message from my guardian angel Mark: ***"Many ask how they are to know and follow God's will. My advice is to follow His commandments in all your actions. Also, imitate your Lord in the way He led His life here on earth. In other words, it is God's will for us to be perfected to the point where our every thought and deed are meant to please Him. Once you become one with His spirit, you will be doing His will."*** I then had a beautiful picture of what life will be like when there will be heaven on earth. A very exhilarating feeling came over me with peace and love at a high pitch. You could sense everything in creation was in harmony and each thing became so completely understood as if a surge of all-knowing pervaded everything. There is so much hope in this vision that all will strive to be in tune with Jesus so we can experience this wonder. I then saw Mary coming as she said: ***"I am happy to see Gabriel announcing to you how I felt when the Lord was coming the first time. I also am asking you many times to prepare for His coming. I heard and received your many Rosaries. Your prayer intentions I have set before my Son as your intercessor. Continue your prayer efforts and you will be very close to my Son's heart."*** I finally saw a circling of bright lights over us. These lights were heavenly beings of angels and saints who were watching each of us playing out our lives. I felt we were on a stage of life and it was up to us to perform as Our Lord wants us to, following His Will. We should be proud to display our faith and ask them for their help on earth.

Thursday, September 29, 1994: (Sts. Michael, Gabriel, Raphael)

After Communion, I could see a long tunnel with light at the end and gradually I could see three angels. St. Michael came forth in splendor with a spear, St. Gabriel was kneeling as he came to Mary and St. Raphael passed by. St. Michael the Archangel gave the message: ***"I stand before God the most powerful angel in heaven. The Lord has given me to guard over His people from Lucifer and his angels. I have heard your many prayers to me and I stand by watching over the Church and all who invoke me. I am ever at your service to provide for the Lord's faithful. Call on me often when you are threatened by evil or if evil angels are about. During the tribulation you will need me most when all the angels of hell will be allowed to roam the earth. If you humans only realized how powerful even one angel is in your earthly terms, if allowed by God, you would praise God more for these beings. Continue your many prayers as I will continue to guard over you all."***

Friday, September 30, 1994:

After Communion, I saw some people in a little room with a light on and they were looking for food but the pantry was bare. I then saw a yellow warning sign in a diamond shape but could not see any writing on it. Jesus said: ***"My people, you will see a famine come over your land as this will lead into the end times. Many will be looking for food, and chaos and riots will reign in the streets with people pillaging anything they can find. Those who do have extra food will be ransacked by the hungry crowds. But know that the monied people will have their food in safety since part of this famine will be contrived by the rich for control of the people. These people, though, will meet with My swift justice at the appointed time. You are now forewarned of these events and this is another reason to flee your cities, for men become mad in search of food. Pray now to be spiritually ready for the trials that will come."***

Later, at church, I was looking down from the top of a throne. But the one who sat on the throne was the Anti-Christ. I then saw a second throne for the evil successor pope who will be second in command over the evil days. I saw both together and there were colors of blue around Anti-Christ and some green around the black pope. Jesus said: ***"You are seeing a picture of the rulers of evil. Their reign will be very short, but they will cause much pain and hardship to the faithful. You will need an abundance of My help and you will need to call on your guardian angel to protect you from the powers of evil. Do not seek to follow them even out of curiosity, but avoid their influence at all costs. They will be much more powerful than humans. This is why you need to hide from their powers of suggestion and persuasion. Know, though, that I will stop their reign to usher in the new heaven on earth. I will not leave you alone to Satan's men, but I will protect you physically and spiritually. Have faith in Me and you will see My promises come true."***

Saturday, October 1, 1994: (St.Theresa of Lisieux-The Little Flower)

After Communion, I saw a nun standing with a bright light behind her. I could see her silhouette and then her face. She carried red roses. She said: ***"I am happy to be with you, my son, but it would be better for you to think of me more often. I have come to you several times to help your spiritual life. You have been called to spread God's word in a special ministry, not given to everyone, by your messages. You owe it to your Savior to be more close to Him. Keep in constant prayer or you will lose your gift. You must be most pleasing to Jesus in your actions to be His messenger. Guard your anger under trying situations and do not be distracted by the worldly events. Be as perfect as you can and do everything for Jesus, not yourself. You will be asked to help Jesus farther in the future, so keep close to His heart by following His will. As you become one with Him, your mission will take on more importance and your spirit will be fulfilled in His peace."***

Later, at church, I saw a tall dingy brown building and a door opened. As I drew closer the door opened into stark darkness. Jesus said: ***"My people, look to Me in faith that you will hold steadfast to your promises from Baptism, for Satan is calling the darkness upon you. He wants to snuff out life and especially he wants to put out the light of faith in your world. My faithful, you are on the side of good in this battle. You must hold up your flame of faith brightly with your prayers and fasting. By keeping strong in***

your faith, you will be a witness to those around you. You can be an inspiration for others to follow Me. You can instill in others an eternal flame of faith which no evil spirit can extinguish. So fight on in this battle of good and evil with My help as your Bulwark. Keep the light of faith burning brightly to dispel the darkness of the evil one. With such a light you will be preparing the way for My Second Coming. Have faith in Me and all else will be taken care of for you. Be at peace, My people, and you will see Me shortly in My reign."

Sunday, October 2, 1994: (Guardian Angel feast)

After Communion, I at first saw Our Lady in heaven with a halo of light around her head and rays flashing out around her. I asked permission from Jesus for Mark to speak: ***"Thank you for welcoming me on our feast day. Those things in the future of which you are concerned must be taken up with Jesus Himself. He will not tell you the day of the warning or the miracle until it is time. Do not be concerned over dates, especially if you are not meant to know them. Be more attentive to how you can perfect your spiritual life. The Lord has a higher calling for you to do everything for Him and in accordance with His will. If you find the purpose of some actions not directly helping spread the Kingdom, then it may be you are following your own will instead of His. Be careful to direct all the intentions of your actions toward what He wants you to do. You must discern in your conscience what you believe His will is for you, but know in the future you will need to call on me for your protection. I will help you and lead you, if you ask my direction."***

Later, at church, I saw a branch with some ice on it. Then I saw another scene with a baby's carriage and a blanket. Jesus said: ***"I am calling your attention to the survival of two institutions—My Church and the family. The evil one is making great attacks against each of these because he knows how important they are to maintain the fabric of a good society. In your churches if I am not at the center, how can it survive? You must know that many abuses are seen in My Church—the worst of which is the many sacrileges of those who do not worry about their sin. How can you receive Me in the Eucharist if you are not properly disposed in your soul? If you have sin, especially grievous sin on your***

soul, then go to Confession before you receive My body. Many hearts have grown cold in their love for Me and only go through the motions on Sunday. Renew your lives with a real fervor for My love since I am the source of grace to make you holy. Also, the family is not putting Me in My proper place in their homes. Without prayer in the family, there could be much strife and division, but if you do pray and keep My remembrance in your pictures, statues, and Rosaries, you will see My love bind that family and keep it together. Satan is trying to divide you and remove love. You must see his attacks for what they are and avoid his temptations. Keep close to Me in the Church and the family and you will have enduring peace without wars."

Monday, October 3, 1994:

After Communion, I saw some empty pews in a church with the doors wide open. Jesus said: ***"Everyday My Body and Blood are made available to you My faithful. In this I give you My graces and Myself for you to treasure as frequently as you wish, but alas, only a select few wish to participate in receiving My daily offering. Where are the rest who are weak and could profit from this strength for their souls? Most of My faithful are missing a golden opportunity which may not be available much longer. Those who come to receive Me on Sunday only out of duty fail to appreciate how much I love them and how I want to be a part of each day with them. If you can receive Me daily, I can be a daily bread which indeed can nourish your souls. Then you can realize the importance of My love. These faithful come knowing My love and will realize more of My graces out of love and not just duty."***

Later, at church, I could see some demon faces trying to break out of the ceiling of hell. There was a great fiery flame. Then I could see ugly slithering spirits or evil souls about me. Jesus said: ***"Wake up, My people, from your spiritual blindness. You are witnessing a ferocious battle of good and evil before your eyes. You see it at every turn in your life, be it at work, on the street, your TV and your society's morals. Pay attention to what is going on before you at all times. Even though evil and its effects are about you, have faith and call on Me and your guardian angel for help. Each and every day you awake, pray for My strength to endure*** *the day. Each day think of yourself as going to the battleline to fight for your Lord. You must struggle every moment of your lives to give witness to My light of truth. By your speech and good deeds you must show My example of love. You cannot fall lax at any time, but you must be ever vigilant. The devil is lurking and ready to attack when he thinks you are weak. So keep strong with your prayers and if you are under duress call on My help and I will come to your aid. In all of this, do not ever give up the fight even though you feel outnumbered, for I will give you what to say and how to deal with the evil around you. Have peace in My love and you will see My day. At the end I will say to you, 'Well done, My faithful servant, for you have fought the battle and completed the race in My glory.'"*

Tuesday, October 4, 1994: (St. Francis of Assisi)

After Communion, I saw some kneelers and people praying. In a final scene I saw a monk in his cell. Jesus said: ***"It is good to lead a contemplative life. It is in seclusion that you can recollect your soul and see how your spiritual condition is doing. There is much beauty in time of prayer to lift up your soul to Me in complete surrender of your will. This dying to self is a good practice which you can find in your reading of your*** **'Imitation of Christ'** ***book. You truly should seek humility in all you do. It is truly following My life in imitation that will show you the way to heaven. Be sincere and pray from the heart in your room away from the trials of the world. You will find My peace in the serenity of your prayer time. Combine both your strength from prayer and your good works into a life which is befitting a true Christian life."***

At church, I saw a lily and then I saw some man laid out at a funeral parlor. Jesus said: ***"This earthly life is not your final life but only a training ground for where you are to go. If you are greedy all the time and are constantly seeking things for your self, you will be training to see hell. In hell there is always chaos and torment. You will never be at peace there. You will always be striving for something, but you will never reach it. You will be suffering an eternal frustration because you never sought to do My will. On the other hand, you can train for heaven by trying to please Me right from your start here. Once you are accustomed to following My will, it will be easy to make a transition to My***

eternal peace in heaven. For you will possess what your soul desired on earth—to share in My love and My oneness in body. Once you realize how to live your choice on earth, you will be delighted at death to receive Me, but if you seek only yourself, you will meet with deep disappointment in your incompleteness. Follow Me or your end will be sad, indeed, without Me."

Wednesday, October 5, 1994:

After Communion, I saw a picture of a quarter indicating money and then I saw some camera lenses pointed from above followed by a person's face. Jesus said: ***"Beware My people of the coming times when your money will be controlled and you will be under constant surveillance. The evil one will control the people through electronic devices. He will control people's thoughts by his suggestions and they will follow him like blind cattle. I tell you beware of this time when evil will appear to reign everywhere. Go into the fields away from any of these devices to flee the evil control. Do not worry what you will eat or wear and where you will live for I will provide for you. Your main concern is to keep focused on prayer so you can thwart the evil one's attempt to control your soul. By keeping close to Me, you will save your soul and in a short time you will be rewarded by enjoying My new world to come both here and in heaven."***

Later, at the prayer group I first saw a picture of the Liberty Bell in Philadelphia. Jesus said: ***"In the future days your freedoms will be taken from you one by one. As the evil times draw near, you will see your president through his decrees and your congress usurp your rights with warped laws. As your country moves farther away from Me, what has made you great now will make you diminish in power."*** I then saw some stacks of books in a library. Jesus said: ***"Religious books will be banned from your libraries where federally funded. Gradually, other books will be censored as well, much like under Hitler's reign."*** I saw a monstrance with a white covering over it. Jesus said: ***"You must treasure the special time you have left where you can visit and adore Me in exposition and My tabernacles. I have told you before there will come a time when you will have a hard time finding My Eucharistic Presence. Preserve this tradition of My adoration however you can."*** I then saw a beautiful sword with jewels on it in a nice sheath. Jesus said: ***"Remember how I reprimanded Peter when he used his sword. Do not take up arms in these evil days. The devil wants you to fight each other over anything. Give up what you have rather than fight, for I will provide for your needs."*** I saw a very ornate Church with many gold objects. Jesus said: ***"What you are seeing is a representation of the Church's traditions carried down throughout the ages. Hold on to your roots dearly and do not listen to those theologians who would water them down or call them old-fashioned. You are in the world but not of the world. Preserve My teachings for your future generations."*** I felt the Real Presence of the inspiration of God in the Scriptures. Jesus said: ***"If you long to know the coming events, read Revelation, Exodus and the other prophetic books. Listen to the Church's interpretation of the Bible and discern the meaning of My word. Everything you need for salvation has been revealed to you there."*** I finally saw Mary coming, holding out her Rosary to Me. She said: ***"Here in my Rosary is your pathway to heaven. The more you pray it sincerely, the closer you will draw to me and my Son. I thank you for your Rosaries tonight and I encourage you to use your Rosary every day. Its graces are needed by many."***

Thursday, October 6, 1994:

After Communion, I saw Maria E. and she said: ***"Praise the Lord God in heaven."*** I then saw a circus coming to town and an old wagon like the tonic salesman used. Jesus said: ***"Do not be fooled by the many false prophets who will come in My name. Discern very carefully each person's message to determine if it is of God. For by their fruits you will know them. If they do not lead proper lives according to My law, this will cast doubt upon their ministry. If they teach things contrary to the Gospels, know again their false ways. You must be clever as foxes to know who is with Me and who is against Me. If such people are very proud and boasting of themselves or worldly, know also this is not in conformity with a man of God. Trust only those who are humble and trying to follow My will, for this is what I ask of all My disciples."***

Friday, October 7, 1994: (Feast of Our Lady of the Rosary)

After Communion, I had a beautiful sense of the presence of Mary and I saw her as a very young girl kneeling and then again standing with her Rosary. The vision ended with a flash of Jesus in the Garden and a silhouetted view of Calvary with the crosses. Mary said: ***"My son, you have been very faithful to my Rosary. Thank you for listening to my wish for prayers. You know how I am linked in union with my Son in one spirit. Even on earth we acted as one as I followed His wishes for everything in my earthly life. You, too, must walk in His footsteps on your road to your salvation. You must not take your Rosary lightly but think of your prayers as a heavenly communication which keeps you linked to both our hearts. Think of each prayer on each bead as a jewel of worship, a personal bouquet you are sending to us. By focusing your mind on the mysteries of the Rosary you relive both our lives every time you say the blessed Rosary. This is your weapon against Satan's attempts to divide my children and cause wars. By your many prayers offered in sincerity you can join my battle in helping save souls and join in helping my intentions. Thank you, my son, for answering my call to prayer and fasting."***

Later, at church, I could see a large map of Europe and Asia and it was all covered with red. Jesus said: ***"This part of the world is in constant turmoil and it will continue to be a place of constant wars. Different peoples have dominated given areas over the years. Each feels a right to certain territory because of their ancestry. That is why there will be constant fighting to control land since many feud over who has the right to the land. You are seeing red because of the sins in this area and the hatred between these people. It cannot be that way with you My faithful. You must love one another and do not be greedy or envious of the things of this world. It is your faith in Me that will give you peace. This is a much more desirable treasure than earthly things which will disappear or change hands. Pray for peace in the world or man will live to repeat the mistakes of the past. War is futile since there are never any real winners. Come to Me and be reconciled and that should be enough for you."***

Saturday, October 8, 1994:

After Communion, I saw a dark basement with a little window and some light coming in. Jesus said: ***"My people, many times the cares and troubles of the world occupy your minds even to the exclusion of thinking of Me. My friends, you must keep an open***

mind to your Lord. Leave a crack or small window open for Me to enter your hearts. If you do not allow Me entry, I cannot give you My graces of peace and consolation. With Me your troubles would be glossed over as you see the importance of your eternal life far surpasses any consequences of this life. If you do not make a forward motion to accept Me into your lives, you will stay in your darkness of sin and rejection. You will be as if in a cold, dingy, dark basement with no light the rest of your eternal life with torment besides."

Later, at church, I saw a long sagging telephone line down a road with thick woods on either side. Jesus said: ***"You will be seeking out to live in the fields and woods away from the evil authorities. It will seem like a long time to you to be in hiding but, not so, in reality. You may think it impossible to survive without help, but with Me all things are possible. You should seek out a more southern area to avoid the cold winters. Also, look for water and a hill to dig out a home in the ground. You must survive off the land but, if you cannot, I will provide for you. You may suffer for a short time, but once I take back control over evil, you will marvel in My plans of glory. All the evil spirits and men will be driven off the earth into the pit prepared for the bad angels. A period of peace on earth will reign and you will see Me, as Adam did, with all your concerns relieved in My peace. Your struggle against evil will earn a place for you in the new heaven and the new earth. Never fear for I am right beside you guiding your every step."***

Sunday, October 9, 1994: (Joselyn's Baptism)

I saw a lady holding a baby and the priest performing a Baptism. Jesus said: ***"My people, you must live your baptismal promises every day. You must realize you do not just renounce Satan and his pomps one day. Your recitation of the creed and giving Me adoration and praise is an ongoing devotion which is why you were created. Every day of your life is a witness of your Baptism. It is the living water that is used to bless you and make you one of My disciples. Remember, also, you are obliged as a disciple to spread My word in the world. You are given the light of faith represented in the candle and you must carry your light into the darkness of the world and witness Me publicly before men. You do not hide lights under a bushel basket, but you place*** *it in a wide open spot so the light can spread to the whole house. So, also, spread your faith to the world around you by example and good deeds. Show through your prayerful life how much I mean to you for all to see."*

Later, at church, I saw a beautiful blue sky with a sunset and several clouds. Jesus said: *"My people, I need you to be ever confident in My love, for you are full of hope for My Second Coming. At the same time you must guard yourself of any complacency so you do not despair waiting for Me. With trust in Me your faith will guide you through life in My peace, and you will have no fear of what is to come. You know that while you are faithful to Me, you can expect Me to watch over you in all you do. I will be testing you in many ways as I tested the saints to see how you endure suffering and hard times. Many of you have been spoiled with peaceful times and very little persecution. You, at times, have grown apathetic to My word because you have most of your worldly wants satisfied. Know there is more to life than just surviving. You are here to serve Me and fight in this battle against evil. Be ever prayerful and protect yourself against evil influences in asking My help. You will live to follow My will since you will learn it is in your best interest both spiritually and physically."*

Monday, October 10, 1994:

After Communion, I saw a volcano spitting out rock with white hot pieces in different directions. Jesus said: *"This evil age asks for a sign much as in the days of old, but I tell you that you are a rebellious people. My brothers, why do you seek more than what you need? Do I not grant you gifts so that you are provided for? But alas, you have designs of your own to take from your neighbor that which is not yours. When your greed consumes you, you will reap the whirlwind. For wars beget more wars and I declare you will never be satisfied with only stealing once. As soon as you lower your morals to stealing by force, you will see a pattern continue until your evil will bring you down to the pit. Do not continue your greed, but be satisfied with your lot or your last state will be worse than the first."*

Later, at church, I saw a man with a miner's hat on and then I saw a truck with troops on it. Jesus said: *"My people, beware of the UN police state. Much will be made of sanctions and punishments*

of nations who violate the wishes of the UN, but the UN leadership will soon go awry and many unusual demands will be made of people without their consent. There will be much anarchy since the people will not wish to follow the commands of their leaders. As a result power will go to a few elite and things will be ripe for the coming of Anti-Christ. All of these things have been planned before, as these monied elite will try to take the world by force. When the Anti-Christ does come, he will soon become a worse tyrant than those before him. You will see no justice until I return to claim the earth for My own. The evil men will be cast aside and will wait in judgment. When you see the signs in the sky, you know when these things will start and then finish with My reign over them. Pray for swift justice when I come again. You will be joyous to receive Me. Keep close to Me in prayer."

Tuesday, October 11, 1994:

After Communion, I saw a light shining down on me and it seemed like a Bible, representing the Word of God. It was coming down on me and then it stopped. Jesus said: ***"I have revealed My word to you but many have not taken it completely to heart and have not always lived it. You must go forward in public and be willing to share My word with others. Let your life be an example of My love by showing others how much you care for Me. You can also start by being humble in all you do. Do not be so quick in your speech to brag or show off your accomplishments. You must remember to credit Me if you must boast. By not being so prideful you will be more at peace, and people will not claim you are too self-centered. You must step back and see how you appear to others. If you are to live My message, you must be ready to witness to Me in public and not be ashamed of your faith in Me. Watch over your pride, so that you do not think all your success is due only to your talents. Remember, I have given you those talents and work with you every day."***

Later, at church, I could see a cross at a distance without a corpus and then I could see the cross vanish and an angel appear in its place. Jesus said: ***"My people, you will see many crosses come into your lives, but do not be alarmed, for I have suffered much, also, before you. You will see, these testings will strengthen your resolve to fight evil and they will bring you back to Me on your***

knees for help. I love you, My friends, and I will gladly answer your prayer for help in your need. You know I am at your service if you just call on Me in prayer. I am showing you how I protect you through your guardian angel. They help you in many ways you do not always realize. Call on your angel to help you perfect your resistance to evil temptations. While you are on earth, you will always suffer crosses of temptation. Learn to discern how and when they come, so you are prepared for these attacks. Cast them out of your mind with small prayers to Me. Be ever expectant. They will come since Satan will attack you frequently. You can use your angels to help you during those struggles and they will keep you from harm. Know you will have some failures, but be ever vigilant to confess your sins and keep Me close to your heart through all adversity."

Wednesday, October 12, 1994: (sprained ankle)

At the prayer group, I first saw a golden goddess as in Thailand and then I saw a picture of the golden calf. Jesus said: ***"You cannot have two masters. You cannot love money and Me at the same time. You must give up all other allegiances to other gods in this world. I am the only one to worship and you should have not other gods before Me."*** I then saw an altar set for Mass. Jesus said: ***"You must offer up your entire being to Me as your daily offering. Then I can mold you into the plan I have for each of you. If you frustrate My will and follow your own ways, you will never fully achieve all you could be. Without Me you will always be incomplete, so cling to Me as if I was part of your body."*** I saw a lot of chaotic activity and people were hyperactive and not sure of themselves. Jesus said: ***"Put your trust in Me to give you direction and settle down your restless spirit, with My peace. For when you partake of Me at Communion, you have all you need with My help. Do not be concerned so much with the needs of this world which are passing away, but concentrate your efforts on acquiring holy treasures which you can store up in heaven and which will not corrode."*** I saw a good size wooden cross and had a sense of the suffering Christ went through on Calvary. Jesus said: ***"Offer up to Me all your sufferings of the day since there are great merits in this sacrifice, if you offer it from your heart. Many sufferings go wasted when they could be offered to save souls***

both here and in purgatory." I then saw a burning flame come down as it illuminated a dove representing the Holy Spirit. He said: ***"I am the light of love and I come down to grant you My blessing of graces. My favors will enable you to see more clearly how to follow your Jesus in imitation of His life. With My gifts you will begin to feel complete in the love of the Trinity."*** I saw an icon of Our Lady and Jesus as an infant dressed as royalty with crowns. Mary said: ***"Honor my feast days and celebrate the 13th of the month, especially October. This is a commemoration of my visits at Fatima. My messages asking for prayer, fasting and repentance have been echoed at all my apparition sites. Live these messages and you will be led to my Son, Jesus."*** I then saw a golden triangle representing the Trinity. God the Father said: ***"As you have seen My works in the Exodus, you will also see my Son triumph over the darkness of sin by His suffering and death on the cross. Adam was the first man and brought the fall of all of mankind, but my Son is the new Adam who will restore everything to its original beauty I intended it to be at the time of creation. Look and prepare for my Son's Second Coming."***

Thursday, October 13, 1994:

After Communion, I saw Maria E. and she said: ***"Suffer with me."*** I then saw a bright white cross and it came down close to me so I could look up and see it clearly. Jesus said: ***"Your pain you are going through is but a slight touch to that which I suffered on the cross for all of you. Offer your pain up for the souls of poor sinners. It is through suffering that you feel a little of what others are going through on earth. Pain as I have experienced was a most acceptable reparation for sin. You must dispose yourself properly though and keep charity in your heart. Do not harbor ill thoughts over your temporary misfortune. Pray to Me for strength to endure your pain gracefully."***

Friday, October 14, 1994:

After Communion, I saw a triangle and then some light came on it from the opening of a cave. At the mouth of the cave I could look up and I saw an eclipse of the sun and felt this was a sign for the end times. This vision lasted for a minute. Jesus said: ***"I have told you before you will see many signs and wonders to announce both the***

beginning reign of Anti-Christ and My Second Coming shortly after. Know that the eclipse will usher in the evil age of darkness. At that time, you should be in hiding to avoid the powers of darkness. Many will be persecuted in various ways, even some will face martyrdom. Pray for the strength of My help and your guardian angel to get you through those days. Life will be hard for a while, but your experience in My reign of peace will more than make up for it. Have faith and hope that I will protect your soul."

Later, at church, I could see several tiers in a stadium and the people were making sport of persecuting the Christians. It was as in the days of the Romans. Jesus said: ***"Many will suffer for My name at the hands of the torturers. Those faithful who are caught and tortured will be suffering much more pain than yours. In your pain you can understand a little of what they will go through. Prepare, for some will suffer much even unto death. These are My victim souls who will offer their trials up to help free sinners of their bondage of sin. There will come a day not long hence when I shall comfort My people with My all-consuming love and peace, but those who reject Me will find eternal torture in hell in answer to their deeds of evil. Pray for the strength I will give you to endure the coming evil days and whatever lies ahead for each of you. Do not fear, My faithful, for I will see your souls are protected from the evil ones. With My protection they will not have power over you, no matter what they desire in their evil."***

Saturday, October 15, 1994: (Feast of St. Teresa of Avila)

After Communion, I saw a nun in her habit and she was kneeling down facing toward the tabernacle. She said: ***"You have been humbled in your pain. This can be a good experience for you so you will remember to stay humble before your Lord. Keep your eyes fixed on Him first and follow His will for you. To do His work you must be ever ready to do what He asks. Put aside your own intentions so you can do His bidding. It is hard to throw aside our human nature, but we must do it if we are to be one with Him. Treat your Jesus as the rock of your salvation and you will always be close to Him. Call on Him for help in prayer and He will see you through to your victory in heaven."***

Later, at Nocturnal Hour, I saw three candles burning in the darkness and I sensed this was during the three days of darkness.

Jesus said: ***"Fear not, My people, during this hour, for the time of the final chastisement will cleanse all evil from the earth. It will be much like when the angel of death came and the first-born of all the Egyptians were slain. When you are enclosed in your room with burning blessed candles and closed windows, you will be as the Hebrews were with death all around them. Pray to your heavenly Father that you will be saved from this evil age. For if you truly follow My commands and My will, you will know your salvation. Once the earth is cleansed of evil I will renew the earth as at the creation. Man will once again enjoy all that I had intended for Him before the fall. You will live for that glorious day when I invite you into the new heaven on earth."***

Sunday, October 16, 1994:

After Communion, I could see God the Father in the clouds in heaven and He was receiving us. Then there was a scene of a vast number of people in a huge temple. There was a prominent chair on the altar and the people were worshipping the Anti-Christ. Jesus said: ***"You will be entering a time of a faith decision. My faithful must be in prayer asking for My help to endure their trial. Men will be given a time to choose either Me or the Anti-Christ. For a while the evil side will look attractive to the earthly senses and his powers of suggestion will be at their worst, but know you will be either with Me or against Me. There will not be any middle ground. No longer can you put off to tomorrow your decision. Since once you take the mark of the beast, you will have fallen into his clutches never to be with Me again. Know the finality of your decision. What will appear the easy way out, will in the end lead you to eternal torture in hell. So do not be deceived by the wiles of the evil one, but remain faithful to Me no matter what you must suffer here on earth. If you are faithful to Me, you will see My eternal bliss of joy and happiness with your Lord beyond your dreams."***

Later, at church, I saw Jesus on the cross and it was turning in a circle so all the world could view His saving act for humanity. Jesus said: ***"My children, I am showing Myself in this way to remind you of the importance of My death on the cross for your salvation. In the days of Moses, he held up a stick with a bronze serpent that all who looked on it would be healed of the bites of the seraph serpents. Today, I hold up Myself to you to heal you*** *from the attack of another serpent, the devil, who has misled many people on the earth. See My love for you and come to Me all who are seeking My peace. For with My help and your trust in Me I will save you from the many temptations and sins of this world. Many are caught up with satisfying themselves in the pleasures of this world. But the things of this world were never meant to be an end in themselves. All here is good, but you must seek Me only, to be saved. Desire My love and return My love, and your heart will reach its destination. For if you depend only on yourselves and this world, you will be frustrated by their inability to satisfy your soul's peace. Pray and stay close to Me and My crucifixion will be most meaningful to you."*

Monday, October 17, 1994:

After Communion, I saw a huge rounding device that was digging out a good size cave, but this time I saw it working from inside out. It was yellow in color. Jesus said: ***"My people, many will be in need of shelter with little time to provide for one. I have told you not to worry about what you are to eat or where you are to stay; I will provide for you. You will see the miracles I will perform for you. I will make caves for you if you cannot make one or find one. The same with the food. I will provide manna when none is available. I will be guiding your way much like God the Father helped the Israelites in the Exodus. Be confident in Me and pray for My help and you will receive it."***

Later, at church, I saw a purple flower open wide and then hang limp as if ready to die. Jesus said: ***"I am seeing many of My faithful as sorrowing flowers not reaching out for all they can be. My people, do not be overcome by the trials of life. I look upon you many times and I am saddened by those who reject My help in their lives. Look upon My crucifix and remember how much I have loved all of you, such that I suffered and died on the cross. Each one of your sins is responsible for Me being there on the cross. I have suffered for each and every one of My human family. Whether you receive Me into your hearts or not, I am always here waiting for your return. So do not forget why I have saved you, My friends. I want you to live life to the fullest, but to do so, you must reach out to Me daily and accept Me into your life. Ask for My help and you will truly come to your destined reward as***

all of My faithful. I am here to suffer for you, to open Heaven's gates to you. All I ask is that you take My hand and give your love and your will over to Me. You will then be one with Me and have all your soul desires."

Tuesday, October 18, 1994: (Feast of St. Luke)

After Communion, I saw a man standing and he was preaching. Luke said: ***"Many people have been brought the faith, but few are willing to take responsibility to spread God's word as their***

own mission. It is true. God calls special people as the priests to preach His word and bring the sacraments, but I, myself, took Jesus' word to heart so that I had to tell all those I could of His saving act of salvation. Even though all are not called to be priests, you all are called by your Baptism to bring up your children and help your relatives in the faith. You, too, can help spread God's word to others, since there is only a short time left to evangelize many potentially lost souls. Your word of encouragement to follow Jesus may be the only warning these souls may receive, so do not hold back bringing anyone to the faith."

Later, at church, I saw a pyramid of good size and there was darkness all around it, but for a few lights that were directed upward to the top. I was looking down at it from some distance above it and I slowly drifted around it for several rotations. Jesus said: ***"You are seeing a representation of the power of the one world order, men who are currently manipulating the Middle East for their own power. These are the monied people who are controlling the world events. They are planning future wars to gain more access to people's money and to gain power by usurping other men's rights. They know only one thing and that is greed for more power and money at the bottom line. There is much wealth in the oil and the control of armies contributes to their means of controlling the people. This group is very devious in their plans but all will be exposed when I come once again to judge all mankind. Pray, My people, for you will suffer much before My coming. Know that I am testing your resolve until you are lowered to your knees to ask My help. You will need Me to get you through. Learn to come to Me beforehand, so you do not need to learn the hard way."***

Wednesday, October 19, 1994: (St. Isaac Jogues & Companions)

After Communion, I had a vision of a cross and a flashback to the Auriesville grounds where these saints died in the ravine. St. Isaac Jogues said: ***"You have many physical things which distract your prayer efforts. This is even still a potential missionland since many people do not practice a good Christian life. My friends, stay close to Jesus in the Blessed Sacrament and He will direct what you are to do and how you are to live. You will soon be coming to a time of history when religious persecution will be***

rampant. You will know, again, how we faced death to teach the Gospel. Yet with Christ, there is a peace which will get you through without any fear of death. If you should have to suffer as we did, keep faithful to God through it all."

Later, at the prayer group, I first saw a truck which was carrying prisoners to a detention center. Then there appeared a huge green serpent on the front of the truck. Jesus said: ***"You will soon be entering the tribulation time where many Christians will be persecuted for believing in My name. Have faith, My people, for you will endure many difficulties for a time. But if you ask My help, I will protect your soul from the evil one."*** I then saw St. Isaac Jogues come forth and he gave a blessing over the people here tonight. He said: ***"Pray to endure your trial."*** I saw a large floor with ornate markings and then some long halls with big arches. Jesus said: ***"My people have grown weak in the faith and they have desecrated parts of My churches. During the coming tribulation your churches will be taken from you and they will no longer be houses of prayer to God. Have faith in Me and I will bring you rest in My peace. You will suffer a while, but My saving power always waits for you. Pray much."*** I saw the flooding rivers. Jesus said: ***"You are being tested with the elements of water and fire and still you fail to see the connection with your sins of abortion. Your testing will continue on into the winter months. You will not listen until you are brought to your knees. Why do you refuse My answer for your life? Give yourself over to My care and your needs will be cared for."*** I saw pictures of Hitler and Hussein. Jesus said: ***"You will see many tyrants cause wars in your time. Be at rest, for you will see wars and hear rumors of wars, but the end is yet to come."*** I then saw a large microscope focused on the family. Jesus said: ***"My people, your society is slowly accepting Satan's demise of the family. Through an abuse of sex, homosexuality and your lack of family prayer, the family unit is breaking down. Please pray and struggle to preserve the family or you will see chaos undreamed of as a result. By your acceptance of one parent families as "OK" you are encouraging more breakdown in morals and less respect for a true Christian marriage."*** I finally saw Our Lady coming in darkness to grant us her blessings for the trials to come. I saw a bright light in the heavens as angels of judgment were descending. Mary said: ***"My children, I come to comfort you with my Son's***

graces to quiet your fears even while adversity will come around you. My Son's coming will purify the earth for My triumph. But you must pray often for the strength you will need to ward off the increasing evil trials. By keeping faithful to my Son, you will have all your heart desires."

Thursday, October 20, 1994:

After Communion, I saw Maria E. with her eyes lifted to heaven as she said: ***"I love my Lord."*** I then saw myself driving in a van or truck out on some hilly country roads. Jesus said: ***"My people, much suffering lies ahead through this tribulation. I have warned you often of what is to come, but still it will seem as a shock to you that it could happen. You will see many events quicken. Pray, My children, for I want to protect all of you from this evil age. Many men have chosen the way of the world to Me, which makes Me sad. They are giving Me up for temporary comfort. Inform My people that the road to heaven will not be so easy. My life was an example of your suffering to come."***

Friday, October 21, 1994:

After Communion, I saw the mouth of a cave from inside and then there was a very bright light at the entrance. Jesus said: ***"Fear not, My people, for I am always with you. You may sometimes see Me as a vision of light to guide you in the coming trial. I tell you that you will not travel more than a few towns and then you will see Me coming to judge those evil men who lord it over you. My glory is waiting patiently to receive My faithful. Those who remain faithful to Me will receive a just measure of My glory and peace. You will be completely satisfied in Me and justified in your reward. Live on in My love and you will enjoy My eternal bliss."***

Later, at church, I saw a beach and on the sand I saw a baseball. Jesus said: ***"Life can be considered a game of sort. It is not only if you win or lose in the eyes of the world, but how you played the game. Do not go through life as a braggart trying to make yourself successful for just the sake of money or fame. If so, you will be putting yourself first and have no time for Me. On the other hand, do not go through life in despair where you let discomforts and misfortunes rule your life. But have faith and give your life over to My will. Let Me lead you on your path to heaven. Let your*** *control over your life fall to Me as I ask so often. In that way, you will find peace, since you will not have to meet your hidden agenda for success and comfort. If you let Me lead you, all will fall into place. You may have to suffer some, but I will get you through. If you seek Me first, all will be given you besides what you desired. If you follow Me, you will win the most important battle—saving your soul in heaven. This will be the best success you could hope for in life, to live with Me forever in My love."*

Saturday, October 22, 1994:

After Communion, I saw a door open with a light on the inside and then I could see to go into a house. Jesus said: ***"My people, I am always knocking on the door of your soul. I am standing here as your Savior. I, who died for you to give you the opportunity of entering heaven, am waiting for your response. You come to My Church expecting things to come to you, but I tell you that if you do not bring yourself to offer everything you have over to Me, you will receive nothing. Do not be disrespectful and turn your face from Me, but please open your soul and heart to Me so I can come in and dwell with you. If you let Me lead your life, you will see the door open to you for all My graces and gifts to give new meaning to your life. I am your life if you really want to recognize Me. Without Me you are nothing and will accomplish nothing of lasting importance. Pray, My children, that you accept and share My infinite love with you."***

Later, at church, after Communion, I could see people in a temple and I felt very fearful omens in that place. They were worshipping Satan through his high priest. This will be one of the future uses of our Churches. Jesus said: ***"During the evil days many will worship the Anti-Christ with the help of the high priests of Satan. Those who do not worship him will be sought out as for the mark of the beast. Those who will not adore Satan will be tortured and some martyred even if they will not worship Me. So there will be no middle ground for anyone to hide. You are either with Me or against Me, but if you are persecuted for My sake, I will take care of you spiritually and soon even physically. Satan's reign will be shortened for the sake of the elect. I will not let him prey on My faithful's souls. Pray to Me for help and your trust in Me will win you your salvation."***

Sunday, October 23, 1994: (Fr. Gobbi in Auriesville)

At the church in Fonda after Communion (Mass at 3:30p.m.), I saw a crucifix posted on a tree in the woods. Jesus said: ***"My people, I am trying to keep you focused on prayer since your life through the coming trial will be troubled indeed. You should build up your good spiritual habits now, since you will be in deep need of My help then. I am telling you during those times you must not leave your eyes off of Me for one moment. The evil in these coming days will be so intense that you will wonder how you can make it. Remember, with My help everything is possible, but at that time if you leave for a while, you may not find your way back to Me. You will have to follow Me at all times, if you are to save your souls. Rely only on Me and not your own abilities. Put your trust in Me solely and I will lead you through this time. Be constant in your vigil of prayer to save sinners as well as yourselves."***

At Auriesville after Communion, I at first saw a door closed and then I saw Our Lady inside at the top of a church. All the people in the pews were all resting in the Spirit and fell backwards. Mary said: ***"You must pray sincerely from the heart, my children. There will first be a difficult time of evil which all must endure with my help and that of my Son. After a short time though, you will see my triumph in all its glory provided by my Son. All my children will then be blessed to be a part of the elect who were chosen to be saved from the evil days. You will be so enraptured with the joy of this experience that you will forget even all the trials you had to endure. At that time, you will see me and my Son with a permanent vision so that we will be with you until the final judgment."***

Monday, October 24, 1994:

After Communion, I saw the priest holding up the Host and a bright light shone out on all the faithful. Jesus said: ***"My dear children, look to Me in the Eucharist as your focus of life. Look on Me as being as necessary in your life as the sun is to your seeing things. If you could only understand how without Me, you are walking blind spiritually. With accepting Me in your life, My grace guides you closer to your goal in heaven. Give thanks to God for this opportunity to receive the bread of angels. This is the heavenly manna I have left you so your faith in Me can survive. Stay***

close to My Blessed Sacrament as often as you can for you may not have this occasion as such much longer."

At church, I saw a large white cross hanging in the sky. Then there was a beautiful sunny scene of green trees and gardens. Jesus said: ***"Dear children, I am drawing you especially close to My heart this evening. I want to draw you into My one burning love that loves your utmost attention to Me. My love for you is so great. It is hard to convey it to you in earthly words. I want you to be in tune with Me in your every thought and action. I want to be so much a part of your life that your following Me is like a second nature. Keep close to Me in My Blessed Sacrament for My rays of love and My graces are showered on you so beautifully tonight. In the quiet of your soul let Me enter to strengthen you for every day's toils. You are so precious to Me, My faithful, that you must rest assured how I will take care of you. Those that return their love to Me have a treasured place in My heart. You all are so magnificent to see your trusting faith. I reach out for you to hold Me close in all you do. Walk with Me every day as I cannot wait for you to see Me face to face and enjoy My glory."***

Tuesday, October 25, 1994:

After Communion, I saw Jesus standing among the trees. Jesus said: ***"The foxes have lairs but the Son of Man has nowhere to rest His head. Just as I gave up everything and roamed from place to place, you also will be nomads and have little possessions. In order to be free, you will have to keep moving away from your persecutors. I will strip you of your possessions so you will have to place your trust in Me wholly for your survival, but you will see living your life to follow Me, even though you want stability, will be much less tedious. By giving your trust in faith to Me I can feed you better both physically and spiritually. Follow Me wherever I take you."***

Later, at church, I saw a stage for actors and later I saw a puppet with strings working the motions. Jesus said: ***"You are actors on the stage of life. Many times in life I am trying to direct your life to Me. If you go through life and do not listen for My word, you will be taking paths I have not planned for you. I will be always playing on your strings to bring you back to My plan. If you continue to follow your own will, I will withdraw My help***

and let you fall on your face. If even after many attempts to wake you up, you still refuse Me, you may close your cold heart to Me forever. Many souls are going to hell since they are not conscious that they are sinners. Without acknowledging Me and My love for you, how can I accept you into heaven? So pray to Me for discernment on what you are to do and how you are to live. If you work in harmony with My will for you, life will go better for you and you will be able to offer sufferings up for yourself and others. Only once you control your life through My help will you be able to evangelize other sinners. Pray and be a good example for those you see in your daily works."

Wednesday, October 26, 1994:

After Communion, I saw a bright light and then a fence of barbed wire. Again, I saw a rose with thorns. Jesus said: ***"You are seeing detention centers where political and religious prisoners will be kept. America in its decadence will be sliding into oblivion much like the Roman Empire. It will go from persecuting the unborn and the aged on to those who are openly religious and those who do not believe in the workings of the government. As the citizens are selected and tortured, all will be suspect eventually, thus degrading your democracy into a blatant tyranny of dictators. This chaos will cause revolutions and the last state of your nation will be worse than the first. As you take Me out of your life as a partner in forming your government, you are inviting the control of the Anti-Christ and disaster. Pray, My people, to endure this trial."***

Later, during the prayer meeting, I was continually harassed in that I was losing the thoughts of the messages and I needed prayers to bring them back. The first message was a picture of our prayer group angel Meridia who appeared holding a sword. He said: ***"I come from Jesus to bless you with His graces to strengthen you in your trials. I bring my sword to fend off all evil influences which try to distract you from your prayer meditation. I also will convey your prayer intentions to Jesus as your messenger. Pray and continue to hold Jesus close to your heart."*** I then saw a vision of a man and woman kissing. Jesus said: ***"To you husbands, I say, love your wives. And to you wives, love your husbands. Keep your bond of love intertwined with My love which binds your union***

and makes it holy. Pray as a family, often, to keep My peace in your midst to fight the division thrust on you from the evil one. Also, pray for your children that they may remain faithful to Me." I saw a man with a black mask and sensed this was the anti-pope. Jesus said: ***"The imposter pope is lying in wait for the opportunity to seize control of the Vatican. He and his cohorts are trying to either kill or exile My Pope John Paul II. Be wary of him and do not follow him since he will decree all sorts of abominations which will spread confusion throughout the Church. Keep your traditional faith preserved as I will be with the faithful remnant."*** I saw a picture of some bread and grapes. Jesus said: ***"I give you My Eucharist so you can treasure My presence and receive the many graces I pour forth from this sacrament. When you receive Me, it is like the joy of your Baptism revisited each time as you receive strength to carry on."*** I then saw some computers and Jesus said: ***"Avoid the use of the Internet and all other forms of the future information highway. These will be the tools of the Anti-Christ and his agents to control your money and information on everyone. What sounds good will in the future be abused by evil."*** I then saw Our Lady appear with a great glow of light around her. Mary said: ***"My children, I come often to nurture you in following the will of my Son. Jesus wants to make saints out of all of you if you would accept His help. All the saints also are there to encourage you to follow in their footsteps to renounce the world and accept my Son to lead you. You can become saints if you follow My requests for prayer, fasting and the sacraments."*** I saw a man with a colonial hat on and I saw him as one of the framers of the Constitution. Jesus said: ***"Your forefathers are shuddering in disgust at how the people allow those in power to usurp the rights of each citizen. Still worse is your steady erosion of My presence in your halls and proceedings. The Ten Commandments have been stripped, Nativity scenes are banned, prayer in the schools are silenced and abortion is made lawful. When religion is replaced with atheism, your future will be less without My blessings on your nation."***

Thursday, October 27, 1994:

After Communion, I saw Maria E. and she said: ***"Put on the armor of Christ."*** I then saw some pictures of stained-glass windows in a church. Jesus said: ***"I call on My people to stand up to change for change's sake and hold fast to the traditional teachings of the faith. Do not let theologians or modernists change My views on the commandments, Church laws, or the rightful respect for My Blessed Sacrament. Those that claim the faith needs to always change are listening to the sirens of the devil and have itching ears as in the Scriptures. The faith and belief in Me should be like the rock on which I built My Church. Following My ways have been changeless throughout the ages. Be forewarned about those meaning to change My laws and continually reinterpret the Scriptures to follow their agenda of breaking down the Church."***

Later, at church, I saw a stand with an open Bible on it. Jesus said: ***"My people, I give you My word in revelation in the Holy Scriptures. All that is given you will show you how to live as a good Christian. You have everything in My holy book. Praise God for revealing to you all that is necessary to reach heaven. My word is a light in the darkness as proclaimed by St. John. My children, you have all the teachings of My word in the Gospels. My very own instruction is there for you to meditate on. You should make it a practice to read from the Scriptures every day and meditate on the readings at Mass. My word is forever yours to enjoy and appreciate. I love you so much that I died for your salvation."***

Friday, October 28, 1994:

After Communion, I found myself flying in outer space and there was a wooden cross leading myself and others. We kept flying until we came to alight on the earth with lush vegetation. There was a bright glow around the earth as it was renewed. Everything looked beautiful and there was the Lord's peace and harmony in all the plants and animals. Jesus said: ***"You are seeing the renewal of the earth as I have shown you once before. This is a message of hope to all My faithful. This is how I originally intended man should live before the fall of Adam. I ask you to pray and keep focused on this moment since this will be the beginning of your reward for remaining faithful to Me. All who are written in the Book of Life and who lived at the time of the tribulation will be allowed into My wedding feast. You will enjoy My true peace and see Me face to face often as I visited Adam and Eve in the garden. All will enjoy My presence and give glory and praise to Me***

for conquering evil and giving of Myself. My love will envelop you so much, that you will seem like you are floating about in ecstasy. Pray again that you will be saved and that you will be able to save sinners around you."

Later, at church, I saw a little window on the side of a building on the first floor. Jesus said: ***"Enter by the narrow gate to find heaven in your life. I freely offer myself to everyone, but it is their free will to accept Me or not. My graces are being offered, if you would only come forward and accept them as your own. I love you My children and I continue to wait to receive you. Please pray to find the grace of conversion for yourself and others. I bring many souls the opportunity to reach out to Me. You must choose to follow Me on your own with your own free will. I will come to you only if you invite Me. Be calm and discerning and I will reveal My understanding to you. Pray often to understand My calling to each of My children."***

Saturday, October 29, 1994:

After Communion, I could look out across a field and I saw a casket ready for burial. Jesus said: ***"My people, I am asking you to be ready for death every day. You may worry about dying but if you are faithful to Me, you have nothing to fear. If you should find yourself with serious sin, go to the priest quickly and confess to make your peace with Me through the priest. In Reconciliation your sorrow for your sin and your seeking My forgiveness will set you free from Satan's hold. Not only should you be in sanctifying grace before death, but this is the state of your soul which most pleases Me at anytime. Strive to be free of sin at all times so when I gaze on your soul each day, you will be radiating the reflection of My glory. You will see also the world, and all that you experience in life will be more peaceful and loving while you are in My grace than when you are with sin on your soul. So frequent Confession always and you can be close to Me as I desire you to be."***

Later, at church, I saw a very ornate pyramid. It was lit with lights of different colors and there were spotlights shining on it from several directions. Then gradually the lights went out and the pyramid was in total darkness. Jesus said: ***"I tell you, many of the one world order people are basking in the sun of importance and are lauding their power and authority over others. As the Anti-***

Christ comes though, there will be division in the ranks of the rich since he will want to control the whole world by himself. That is why the pyramid will be cast into darkness. Satan will exploit the positions of these people but they themselves will no longer have any glory. When people listen to the lies of Satan, they are always disappointed when he does not fulfill all that he told them. They will suffer in the end as a punishment for going against Me. Even Satan and his minions will have sport in tormenting these duped One-Worlders. They fell for his lies and now they will reap the harvest of their mistakes. When I judge them unworthy, they will even suffer more in hell forever. The lesson is to not be misled by Satan's lies of this life. Follow Me and you will not be disappointed for I will feed My lambs with the real truth of life in heaven."

Sunday, October 30, 1994:

After Communion, I saw someone up in some dark clouds and it was a man as he descended down. He was blinded with a white bandanna around his eyes and he was carrying a scale of justice. Jesus said: ***"I tell you your justice system is an abomination. Your lawyers are the same blind guides I condemned in My own time on earth. They still are placing burdens on men and do nothing to lift them. The root of their evil is the power given as law keepers and the money they extort from the people. Today, your law is governed by money and not justice. The laws which are kept, like that of abortion, usurp the intent of My divine laws. Instead of protecting the people and their rights, they exploit their position for ill gotten gains. At the judgment these money and power worshippers will line the lower recesses of hell since their hearts are the farthest from Me. If you want to gain heaven, you must give up your selfish ways and follow My will and My commandments. Only then will you be worthy and ready to enter with washed robes of forgiveness."***

Later, at church, (to celebrate Christ the King) after Communion, I saw Christ coming on a cloud and then a second scene of Mary on a cloud. Jesus said: ***"My people, for those who doubt My kingship, I tell you that you will see Me coming in glory on a cloud to judge all of humanity. I have told you many times how I am in control of things at all times. I have created you in My***

image to have free will to choose to follow Me or not. I tell you all those who praise Me and give Me glory will enter into My banquet feast in heaven. I am all loving to each of My creatures and by My death on the cross I have opened up the opportunity for everyone to gain heaven. Seek My Kingdom first and all else will be granted to you."

Monday, October 31, 1994: (Halloween)

After Communion, I could see darkness and I saw one eye of a wolf which seemed very sinister. I looked away and the same vision kept returning. Jesus said: ***"In your vision you are seeing the evil of Satan as he increases his grip on parts of humanity. His power will reign for a while rising to the power of Anti-Christ who will be coming soon. Pray, My people, for strength from Me during these evil days. Your days of struggle will worsen for a while. You will need great faith to overcome the increasing temptations of the evil one. I have allowed this dark night of the soul to test My people to see who really believes in Me and acts on it. When My Mother crushes the head of Satan, then you will see our triumph in glory and evil will be no more."***

Later, at church, I saw some horsemen and some dogs and I had the sense of hunting. Jesus said: ***"Many times I have been called the Hound of Heaven. I love My children so much that I reach for every opportunity to bring you to My bosom. I come to you in many ways to try to make you more perfect in your faith. Some have many prayers from others which allows Me to pursue them. In other cases I have chosen to shower some with extra graces which have yielded still more good works as a result. Still others are not always attentive to My word. To these I sometimes allow them to have their possessions fall away from them. Indeed, by bringing some to their knees, they eventually see the futility of doing everything on their own and return to My altar. A good portion, though, still do not listen to Me, but I do not give up on them right up to their judgment. Remember, even up to the eleventh hour you can be saved. Pray, My people, to protect your faith and through your intercession you, too, can help save sinners. Then, on that glorious day of My triumph, all My saints can join Me in My heavenly splendor."***

Tuesday, November 1, 1994: (All Saints Day)

At church, (Eric's Mass) after Communion, I saw a long winding line of people and it stretched up into the sky. They were walking from earth up to heaven's gates. Jesus said: ***"I am calling all My faithful and all My future saints to place their faith and trust in Me that I will one day lead them home. I love you so much. If you could only bring Me more into focus as the center of your life, I could wrap My arms around you with a joy of conquest over your selfishness. For once you give up your control, to follow My will, you will see the angels rejoice as sinners are brought to conversion. You see the saints and angels are here for you, anxiously waiting to help and console you, if you would ask their help as intercessors. Do not forget My many holy saints for I wish you to follow their lives so you can imitate them. They all struggled through life to please Me in every little thing they did. You, too, can become saints by praying and offering up all your daily sufferings and disappointments without any complaints."***

Later, at church, I saw what looked like huge blotches of pink lightning across the sky. Jesus said: ***"When you see this phenomenon of pink lightning, know that it is the time of the Anti-Christ. He will call this form of lightning to the ground as if bringing fire out of the sky. This will so mesmerize some with his power that he will convert many nonbelievers to his side. His wonders and powers will be a new reign of principalities and powers which will overcome those souls who are weak and not full of My grace. He will lead them as a Pied Piper to a deception of his lies such that they will do everything he says. They will even seek out Christians for him to persecute. They will be acting as robots under his complete control. This is why I tell you, My people, to build up your spiritual strength now since the evil one will test even My elect to the breaking point. But reach out to Me, My children, and I will protect you. Have faith in Me always no matter what the odds, and you will have a peace which no other creature can give you."***

Wednesday, November 2, 1994: (All Souls Day)

After Communion, I saw what looked like a dark black pool and it enlarged as I came closer. I could see some icicles on the edges and a deep sense of loneliness and a damp dark place as I was immersed lower. This is indeed a place of torment. Jesus said:

"I tell you many souls have come to this place you call purgatory. Let Me assure you, it does exist and indeed it is a part of My justice. It is a place where souls who had died and had not yet reached a state of spiritual perfection worthy of heaven. It is rare that souls avoid this without some major suffering or great spiritual awakening. You should pray to help these souls, especially your own friends and relatives, but also there are souls which no one remembers that need your prayers as well. Many do pray for these poor souls, but remember once they are freed from this bondage, they will be as your guardians praying for you on earth. Continue your prayers, for your reward will help you during your hour of trial."

Later, at the prayer group, I first saw a dark night and there was a car stopped with a helicopter overhead shining lights down on the car. The car was being scanned for people with the mark of the beast and the engine had been stopped by some radiation. Jesus said: ***"I have mentioned before how the Anti-Christ and his agents will use many electrical devices to seek out My faithful. Beware of their devious methods and hide from them as much as possible."*** I then saw the faces of many friends and relatives whom I recognized and they were in purgatory asking for my prayers. Jesus said: ***"Continue to pray for your friends and relatives since you do not know when they go to heaven. For those who already have reached heaven, those prayers will go to other friends. Do not forget these deceased you know since there may be very few others praying for them."*** I saw St. Francis of Assisi come and I had a flashback to when we visited his tomb. He said: ***"I come to you on these beautiful feasts to ask all of you to strive for sainthood in all you do to please God. Do not be concerned over those things you cannot change, but move forward to continue your battle against evil."*** I then saw a picture of a holy book in the dark. Jesus said: ***"You should make a point of doing some spiritual reading every day. It is this quiet time of contemplation which each soul should be open to in growing in your faith."*** I saw a crowd of people who were faithful to the Lord and they were all encouraging each other to help those around them come back to Jesus. Jesus said: ***"Be beacons of hope in faith to your friends. By your good example you can bring great encouragement to one another. Those who are good role models can help lead many souls to Me. Keep up your***

efforts to your dying day since there are many souls yet to save." I saw Mary come in blue and she stretched out her arms and she asked us to send her our Rosaries so she could grant them to the souls in purgatory. This I requested of our group. Mary said: ***"Thank you for responding to my call for prayers for the poor souls in purgatory. On my feast days I visit these souls to console them. On All Souls Day and Christmas I apply your prayers and many souls are released to heaven on those days."*** I could then hear a drove of voices and it seemed like those souls in purgatory were voicing their thanks to all those praying for them. This was a confirmation that our prayers for them do make a difference.

Thursday, November 3, 1994:

After Communion, I saw a raging furnace of fire underground through a grating. Then later I could see raging fires like firestorms on the surface of the earth. Jesus said: ***"You will see even more signs of My chastisements in the future. Your country will continue to experience attacks from the elements and some fires in other cases. You have seen imagery in the vision how the demons will be unleashed from hell to raise havoc all over the earth. My faithful I will protect from evil, but those who choose the world before Me will be tormented by the demons. All will at one time meet with your just reward. For those who reject Me, they will find unrest and torment in the flames of hell. But for those who believe, My peace and comfort await them in heaven."***

Friday, November 4, 1994:

After Communion, I saw a doorway and it opened and many people went through and up a stairway into a bright new world away from hiding. Jesus said: ***"My people, you will go through a trial time, but fear not, for it will not last long. I love you all so much and when you are able to come out of hiding at the appointed time, you will be protected. Then I will renew the earth and all will be made over beautiful as before. You must have hope and trust in My word, for My graces will carry you through to My triumph."***

Later, at church, I saw someone holding a baby. Jesus said: ***"My little children, call to Me often. These young innocent souls I treasure the most over all the earth. Why is it your society at-***

tacks these defenseless little ones? Has your society gone mad that it kills its babies and future progeny? Convenience and a lost sense of the value of life have clouded your thinking. You must wake up, America, before it is too late. Do you think I will allow this killing to go on without any recompense? I tell you, your country will pay dearly even materially for your spiritual ineptitude. For all the reasons you use to have more pleasure and the ungratefulness for My gifts of life, I will repay you. I will thwart those who seek any gain for killing My innocents. Their lives will be reprobate and distasteful no matter what they do. Pray for these confused souls to see their errors and ask for My forgiveness. If they do not repent, they will pay dearly both here and in the next life."

Saturday, November 5, 1994:

After Communion, I saw Yassar Arafat at first and then later on a stage I saw a man with a blue and white turban. Jesus said: ***"My people, I am warning you again that certain Arab elements will play a role in helping the Anti-Christ come to power. They will also be involved in the Battle of Armageddon. Know that the rulers of the world will be forced to go along with the Anti-Christ in order to keep their power. This greed for power will so drive these men that the evil one will exploit this to his advantage. Pray to Me for strength to endure this evil time which will have tyrants constantly attacking My faithful."***

Later, at church, I saw someone laid out in a casket. It was a view from the foot end. I then saw a huge cross over that person. Jesus said: ***"This is the time of year when you see the leaves fall and another season of nature comes to an end. So it is with your life. You should always be prepared when your life will come to an end. The world and life I give you is beautiful, yet it is not without testing. You must see that your time on earth is very short by all comparison to history. So I say to you, use your time wisely for the best advancement of your spiritual life. Make it a point each day to have time for Me in prayer. This is honoring Me, your creator. Make time, also, to help your neighbor with corporal works of mercy. In doing so, you store up treasures in heaven which will never rust or corrode as the passing riches of this earth. Be thankful then for every moment of life you have been en-***

trusted. For each day is an opportunity for conversion and a chance to win your soul's salvation. For My faithful, it is also an opportunity to send your prayers to Me for sinners on earth to come back to Me and, also, for those souls in purgatory who long for heaven. Once you understand My ways, you will see how glorious life can be. Most of all when you can reach heaven, you will enjoy My peace and glory as your eternal reward."

Sunday, November 6, 1994:

After Communion, I could see the faces of some recent relatives who died, that were mentioned at the Mass for those who died during the year. Then I saw a dark sea where people were trying to keep their heads above water. This appeared to be the upper part of purgatory closest to release. Jesus said: ***"It is good to remember those souls who have gone before you to their judgment. There are many friends and relatives who are soon forgotten once they have departed. Remember to continue praying for them. If they are in purgatory, your prayers can help alleviate their time of suffering. You will not be sorry that you prayed for them when it comes your turn, should you go to purgatory. Then the friends you made by your prayers will return the favor by praying for you. You can each help each other. I have allowed this for My communion of saints that you help one another. So do not forget these souls or your duty to pray for them."***

Later, at church, I was looking up a dark corridor on a ramp. Then there was a bright light and I saw a radiant angel come forward and show me the way with his light. Jesus said: ***"My children, when the time of your trial arrives, put all your faith and trust in Me. Call on Me to help you and lead you and I will send My angel to show you the way to safety. While you are in hiding, My angel will advise you where to go to be free from your persecutors. In the Exodus My angel led the people in the desert. Even now, this protection will soon be available to you when you need it most, so do not fear as I have told you, but have faith that I will take care of you. Pray often for your future strength to remain faithful to Me even when things look helpless in your eyes. Many miracles await you in answer to your prayers, if you would just ask at that time."***

Monday, November 7, 1994:

After Communion, I saw a road with many holes and in need of repair. As I continued down the road the ride was very bumpy. Jesus said: ***"As you go through life your road to Me will not be very smooth. Instead, the road to heaven is narrow and full of many pitfalls. In bodily terms you will encounter many sufferings, but offer all your problems up to Me and I will bless them as daily prayers. Have faith in Me no matter what in life you are asked to face. Know that I have suffered before you and also faced persecution. The follower of the Master should be ready to follow in My footsteps, but I will be beside you to pick you up from every fall. All I ask is that you remain confident in Me that I will bring you home to Me through all your difficulties. Stay close to Me in prayer and you will have nothing to fear."***

Later, at church, I saw through the Eucharist a doorway which was bright and it represented a gate to heaven. I then saw life as we know it in a room, but the colors of everything were very sharp and pure. Jesus said: ***"This is, indeed, a time of preparation at this time of year. It is a time to take inventory of your life and where you stand before God. I am telling you this for the day when you will be called to stand before the gates of heaven. All throughout your life you should be focused on this end, for this is the eternal destination of your soul that you are considering; therefore, take time now to look at your life and all its spiritual defects. Ask for My grace of understanding to know how to approach each problem for a future attack from the evil one on this subject. As you anticipate how to handle each problem in life as I would, you can bring yourself closer to Me and you will need less purification at the end. If you come to My gates too soiled with the earth and do not love Me, I will say I do not know you. If you come with marginal goodness, you will need much purification in purgatory. On the other hand, if you have trained yourself in My ways and have asked My graces to purify you along life's road, I will gladly welcome you to all your heart's desires in My perfect love in heaven. So choose now how you will approach My gates and you will receive My happiness with the measure you have prepared."***

Tuesday, November 8, 1994: (Election Day)

After Communion, I saw an eye at the top of a pyramid which became like a green playing field. Jesus said: ***"My people, beware of your leaders especially those you elect this day. For there is a pervading effect from the monied people who in essence control these elections. Even though there are multiple choices, many are made from the same mold. Such are those controlled that no matter who wins, the same people work behind the scenes to do the work of Satan's agents. It is still money and greed for power which still influences your politics, and as long as your leaders are more intent on themselves and not Me, your country will continue to be misled and will suffer the moral consequences of the actions of your leaders. I tell you there will be continued unrest and many natural disturbances."***

Later, at church, I could see someone's kitchen window and a table. Jesus said: ***"I am here for you always so that you can come to Me in your need and I will help you. You should treat your neighbor and your friends and relatives the same way. Be always willing to help someone when you are given the opportunity. If you have plenty of this world's gifts, you should be free to help those in need. When I see you not selfish but willing to share your goods, I will store those treasured acts for you in heaven. Remember when you help others you are really doing it for Me. Being outgoing in every way for others is the way I want you to be generous as I have been generous to you with good fortune. If you do these things in little matters, I will put you in charge of greater things in the hereafter. Pray, My people, and reach out to help as if it was second nature and you will be doing it out of love for Me as well."***

Wednesday, November 9, 1994: (St. John Lateran Dedication)

After Communion, I saw some people and received the word ***"Church"***. Jesus said: ***"My people, I want you to know the real meaning of Church as should be taught. First and foremost is that My presence is required in anything holy. It is My body joined with My people which is Church as you know it. Without the 'living stones' there would be no soul to My Church. That is why you as faithful are so important to Me. The house that you attend, again, would not be holy unless My presence in your taber-***

nacle was there. This is why I expect your reverence for My most Blessed Sacrament. If My tabernacle is the reason for the house of God, then do not hide Me away out of sight. I must be available so the people can worship Me and not man. Keep your priorities of what is important foremost in your thinking of Me."

Later, at the prayer group, I first saw Our Lord wearing a crown of thorns and He was silhouetted against a bright light. I then had a flash of the negative image on the Holy Shroud. Jesus said: ***"My dying on the cross was My greatest love message to all of you. That the Son of Man would suffer greatly for all mankind's sins shows you that I have not abandoned you, but I want to unite your suffering with mine. The negative image shows how I used My ignominious death to make a positive of bringing you salvation."*** I then saw a wooden cross which represented Christ's Church. Jesus said: ***"The gates of hell will not prevail over My Church for I will watch over it till the end of time. You must not lose hope, My faithful, even though Satan seems to be tearing the Church apart from the inside. You will see, the evil doers who threaten the unity of My Church will one day lose any control they seem to possess."*** I saw a picture of Clinton as a king on a card face. Jesus said: ***"I have smitten the power of your president because of his decrees on abortion and his leading of your country close to the One World Order of Anti-Christ. His reign will be fraught with chaos and disarray as His goals will be thwarted. Others, though, will continue his direction, but in more devious ways."*** I then saw a beautiful sunny fall day as I looked down a road with trees. Jesus said: ***"My people are here as a testing ground, but it can be a very beautiful experience even in these times. If you have faith in Me and follow My ways, you can go through life always cheerful without letting the difficulties disturb you. When you live your life for Me, each day takes on a glow of its own which is uplifting to the soul. Even amidst pain, if you stride over these problems, you will be at peace in contemplating My beauty."*** I saw Mary coming and she said: ***"I want you to pay special attention to following the practice of the prayer of my consecration. Take time out for this preparation for my feast, December 8th, and make your consecration a true devotion to Jesus through me as the mediatrix of all graces. Jesus has allowed me this means to bring you closer to Him. Take advantage of my request and it will bring you closer to heaven."*** I saw many intense flames burning. Jesus said: ***"You will see many fires and testing by the elements. These flames will be as a purification of your country's sins which are many. You who live in America must stop the trend of your moral decadence or your hearts will grow cold to Me. You must keep My flame of love flickering in your hearts or you will lose your way towards heaven."*** Finally, I saw some ornate statues and vessels in the Holy Sepulcher Church in Jerusalem. Jesus said: ***"The Anti-Christ will try to remove all remembrances of Me in the Holy Lands. He will attempt to destroy all the holy places. This will be the reason why the Battle of Armageddon will be so significant."***

Thursday, November 10, 1994:

After Communion, I saw Maria E. and she said: ***"May the Lord be with you."*** I then saw a picture of a sword. Jesus said: ***"In your own day you will see religious persecution. All eras have been tested to see the roots of their faith under duress. If you choose to follow Me without being tested, that is one state. But if you still follow Me under pain of suffering, then I see you really are sincere under any condition. Be thankful to Me for My help both in good times and in more difficult testing. It is only when you are really tested that your true colors appear as to whom you will go to."***

Friday, November 11, 1994:

After Communion, I at first saw some concrete blocks and gradually I could see it was a pathway disappearing at the horizon. I was given later that it was a pathway to heaven. Jesus said: ***"Many people go through life without thinking that their life here on earth is a pathway to heaven. Your life is short and it is a testing ground to see if you are worthy of heaven. Some may want to go to heaven because of how good it sounds for people to be there, but they do not want to go through the suffering and purification which is demanded. If you are My disciple, do not expect any less persecution than I received. It is not easy to achieve heaven, but it can be done only with My help and grace. Do not expect a spiritual life to be easy, but it comes only with work to root out your earthly desires to follow My ways. Do not put off to tomorrow trying to find your path to heaven, but start every day with your intention to strive for heaven through prayer."***

Later, at church, I saw a picture of a bike's wheels and I knew we would be traveling. This was again a message on hiding. Jesus said: ***"Your time of persecution draws near. I have given you many messages that you are to go into hiding from the Anti-Christ and his agents. At the same time, I am telling you not to fear what will happen for I will be leading you. Do not fear either for others, for I will direct them as well. You may have to split into smaller groups to avoid detection. Where you go you will not be able to take your cars very far, since they are traceable to your whereabouts. Take some basic necessities, but do not worry. I will provide for what you need. The main concern is your care to remain faithful to Me to save your soul. In the end this is all that matters. To survive this time or not is not important, for I will bring all My faithful back to My renewed earth. This is your hope I give you, that I promise to save you if you keep allegiance to Me and not Satan and the world. It is the hard way of the cross that will set you free. Do not be clinging to the burdens and cares of the things of the world. These things will pass away, but your soul will live on and your choice for Me is all that will save you from hell. Pray much and keep strong in My graces."***

Saturday, November 12, 1994:

At Christ the King (Fr. Rookey - Healing Mass) I saw rays of light as they came down from heaven. At a distance, it was a dove as the Holy Spirit came closer. He said: ***"I am the Spirit of Love and I am spreading My graces over all of you. You have been faithful to Me and you believe in My healing graces. Many are touched by Me in special ways. You, My people, must glow with My love as I infuse you with joy and peace of mind and soul. It is My spirit in you which keeps your flame of faith going. Each of you are made to God's image and are special gifts of life to this world. Each of you are holy since you are a creation of God. Give reverence to all life and have no fear of what is to come. I will protect you and give you what you are to say and do at the time of the trial. My faithful I will always cherish."***

Later, at Nocturnal Hour, I saw a big black pit and demons were coming out onto the earth's surface. Jesus said; ***"My people, prepare for the evil days of the end times. There will be many demons loosed from hell to claim their own—the ones who have***

rejected Me by worshipping the Anti-Christ and the worldly things. This will be a troubled time where you will need My help for your soul to reach heaven despite the attempts by the demons. You must make yourself ready to put on your armor to fight the evil ones with your Rosaries, holy water, crucifixes and blessed candles. After your brief testing time, you will revel in My glorious triumph over Satan who will be chained for a thousand years. My faithful will come forward then to give witness to My word which is true and will be accomplished soon. Trust in Me, My people, and My peace will make you fearless of any evil which may want to attack you."

Sunday, November 13, 1994:

After Communion, I saw circles of light in the sky which were like angels. Then I saw festivities on earth in a huge celebration. Jesus said: ***"I want you to see and appreciate My triumph when it comes. You will see a beauty on earth that will astound all those worthy to see My day. Know that in those days you will all be of age in your twenties with glorified bodies. This will be a taste of heaven on earth. You will see sun by day and My light by My heavenly luminaries, the angels, by night. For a thousand years there will be no death, no illness, and no necessity to eat or work. You will see Me face to face periodically. Life will be so joyful that you will be ever praising Me and thanking Me for all I have lavished on you. Your eternal life with Me will be My most precious gift to those who accepted Me and followed My ways. Keep this hope on My day uppermost in your mind and your goal of this life will stay in focus with prayer."***

Later, at church, I saw some football players playing a game and then I saw a red spotlight flash for a few seconds. This seemed to indicate some kind of warning would occur during the football season. Jesus said: ***"My people, I have warned you many times to be prepared for My Second Coming. As I look out over My people, most of you have not taken Me very seriously on My request. If you do not ready yourself with spiritual armor for the test, Satan will sift you like wheat when the Anti-Christ comes. You are in the midst of a battle of good and evil whether you want to believe it or not. Read My signs and that of the world and you will see evil is having its day. But pray and fast now at this acceptable*** *time to be saved. For if you approach the end times with a lackadaisical spirit, you will not be ready to fight your evil adversary. It will only be through My help and grace that you will save your soul. So stay close to Me for your spiritual survival."*

Monday, November 14, 1994:

At church, I saw some old women dressed in black praying outside before a shrine. Jesus said: ***"My people, I have been instructing you often about death at this time of year. Lend your ear and listen to My words. As you have seen by the vision, it is not only the old that I call back to Me but the young as well. So do not put your preparation for death off until a future day. If you are younger, do not feel you have plenty of time to make preparation, since tonight your very life may be required of you. Instead, My people, be in constant preparation to receive your Savior, for you know not the hour I will call on you. You will see, also, by being in preparation as if you will die tomorrow that the things of this world will no longer be so alluring. Since, if you will not be here long, what good is it to pile up so much wealth that will go to others anyway? Be focused on Me, always,so when I do come to take you to heaven, I will say to you: 'Well done good and faithful servant. Because you have made yourself ready for My wedding feast, come and join in your master's celebration.'"***

Tuesday, November 15, 1994:

After Communion, I could see stadium lights at night but it was a place of persecution and not just a sporting event. Jesus said: ***"My people, you will soon witness a time of persecution your country has yet to face. As evil will abound for a time, you will see My faithful exposed to more harassment and even torture for believing in My name. Christians, indeed, will be fighting for their lives to avoid their persecutors. Men's rights will no longer be equal. You see this even today with the rights of the unborn so violated. I tell you ever more perverse morality will be occurring. This is why you must pray and endure this trial in hiding. For they will drag you through the streets to shame you, and they will ridicule your belief in God even to the point of killing as sport in your arenas. Be watchful, My friends, for your lives will be in jeopardy, but through your faithful service, you will win your salvation."***

Later, at church, I initially was on the ground in a woods when gradually I was rising alongside a tree. I saw myself getting higher from the ground as my speed upward seemed to increase. I could then see that I was above the earth in orbit, but I was in a safe place not worrying about eating or breathing. Then I could see a miraculous transformation of the earth. I could see the finger of God as a light and the earth was being renewed. Jesus said: ***"You are seeing how I will protect My people as I renew the earth at My triumph. I will restore it to its once pristine state of complete harmony between nature and man. This new age of peace is synonymous with My Mother's triumph and will be for all My faithful to enjoy as was intended for Adam and Eve before the fall. You will then see an age where giving Me praise and thanks will overwhelm your spirit. You will be drawn to Me in so much love that it will be hard for you to understand now. You will live for this day of mine without evil and you will wonder how you could have any of the earthly thoughts you once had. Following My will, will seem so natural that you could not focus on anyone else but Me. Pray, My people, to remain faithful and hope for this day to come as soon as possible."***

Wednesday, November 16, 1994:

After Communion, I saw bright lights coming down from heaven to the earth. As they grew closer the lights appeared as angels riding horses with swords. Jesus said: ***"These are My angels who do My bidding. You are seeing a preview of the great harvest of souls at the judgment. I will call My angels to bring all those souls before Me. You will see the harvest at My thrashing floor. Here those souls judged unworthy will be condemned to hell. Those judged worthy will be brought safely into My barn where the wheat has produced thirty, sixty and one-hundred fold from My faithful servants. The message to you is store up in heaven your treasures of good deeds, for your love and actions will be your own testimony. I wait to give you your heavenly reward for the just but those who refuse Me will be thrown outside to wail and gnash their teeth."***

Later, at the prayer group, I first saw a very elegant looking crown of gold with jewels on it. I gradually backed away and I saw it rested on Jesus as Christ the King. He was sitting on His throne in the glory of heaven with angels all around giving Him praise. Jesus said: ***"My people, I am showing you a glimpse of My glory and how all of My creatures are giving Me praise and thanksgiving to be with Me and for their very existence to enjoy My love. Many times I have told you how each of you are so precious to Me that I would not want to lose any of you, but I have given you free will to accept Me or not. Loving must truly come from the heart. This is why if you love Me, it is a freely given act which I treasure very much since it was not forced on you."*** I then saw several people in graduation caps and gowns. Jesus said: ***"When you are ready to come to Me in death, I am ready to receive you with your washed robes at your final graduation. This life is truly a testing trial to see how true your love is for Me. For those who pass the test of time and this trial, you will come to the end of your life as a culmination of all that you are in life."*** I then saw a rather large golden calf image. Jesus said: ***"There are many people on earth who want their life to continue as it is and never change. They have grown so accustomed to its pleasures of the flesh and the things which please the body that this has become their god. I tell you, My people, all creation is good but your end is to eventually be drawn to be one with Me. If you have more love of this world than for Me, you will not witness to My love in heaven. Again I have told you to live more on a spiritual plain above the body's carnal desires."*** I saw a young woman dead in a large glass casket. Jesus said: ***"As I have talked to you much about facing death, I want to stress to you that living in serious sin is living a spiritual death. This is important that you keep alive in My grace of Confession. I have given you My Sacrament of Penance to be reborn through My forgiveness. Throughout your physical life be ever attentive to stay close to Me in prayer and away from serious sin. If you are faithful to Me, you will always be alive through Me in My mystical body."*** I then saw someone sitting in a chair with a small light reading a spiritual book. Jesus said: ***"I have encouraged you often to take time each day to recollect your thoughts so as to guard yourself from life's many temptations. Always contemplate how you can improve your spiritual life and check yourself each day to see your progress. By following instruction from a good book, you can apply that counsel for your improvement."*** I saw Mary asleep in the Dormition Abbey scene and then I could see her Assumption into heaven in glory. Mary said: ***"God has granted me His favor of being sinless in life and He again has shown His graciousness by my Assumption into heaven. I am showing you this because your resurrection to my Son should be your life's hope and eternal destination. If you believe my Son is the resurrection and the life, you will come to Him in all you do to please Him. I am praying for all of you to see the light to follow Him as I lead you to Him."*** I again saw an image of Mary as the mediatrix of all graces and I saw a picture of her crushing Satan's head at her triumph. She said: ***"I bring my blessing on you all tonight and thank you for your many Rosaries. I have heard your prayers and have directed them to my Son. You will see my triumph in due time and it will represent a conquering of evil. You will then enjoy my Son's deepest love and peace in a beautiful age. Live for this moment to treasure being with my Son forever."***

Thursday, November 17, 1994:

After Communion, I saw Maria E. and she said: ***"Love your God with all your heart and soul."*** I then had a vision of Pope John Paul II. Jesus said: ***"Listen to My beloved John Paul II. He is My representative on earth, who leads you in faith and morals. Abide by his decisions since the Holy Spirit is working in him. He will lead you well, since I have brought him up especially for your time before the trial. He it is whom I have appointed to prepare you for the tribulation to come. Give thanks for the gift I bring you in His life."***

Later, at church, I saw a plain bench and then later a jug of water was on the bench. Jesus said: ***"It is not much that I ask from you in life – that you be faithful in your true love of God. I give you many blessings throughout life to make your life even less burdensome. Recognize that all you have has come through Me, so do not be proud of all that you have done. Remain humble and you will always treasure an inner peace no one can take from you. When you are at peace with God, you have all you need in life. My cleansing waters of Confession are always at your call to keep you in My grace. Do not let things disturb you when My love protects you. Many of you worry too much over things you cannot control. Pray to Me for understanding to do your best and leave all else up to God. This life can be so much a pleasure if***

you just give everything over to Me and let Me lead you. Have faith in Me and I will never leave your side."

Friday, November 18, 1994:

After Communion, I saw a person bowed and praying to God and the words ***"Penitent Sinner"*** came to me. Jesus said: ***"Many times this month I have been preaching to you during this time to take stock of your spiritual disposition. In this time, My friends, you should be discerning how you are to improve and be adamant in your resolutions. I am pleased for those first who are able to admit they are sinners. This is the first step on your pilgrimage of purification. All souls must walk this path of forgiveness if they expect to enter heaven. In addition to making reparation at this time I would request that you be open to this contrition throughout the year as well. As you have thoughts of settling your spiritual accounts at death, you begin to realize how important the disposition of your soul is in the hereafter. Your spiritual life and love of God should be on your mind constantly, for this is why you were brought into the world—to know, love and serve your God."***

Later, at church, I saw a field and some tall grass and a few inches of snow on the ground. The words ***"Winter wasteland"*** came to me. Jesus said: ***"You must know that many souls are experiencing a spiritual wasteland. Keep focused on Me at all times, so you know from whence you came and where you are to go. Have peace among you, My friends, for I bestow My peace on all My faithful. Do not be concerned if I wish to test your country with the elements for its many crimes. Beware, though, about abusing the power of prophecy. What I give you is freely given for all, but not to be sought after for its own sake. Do not seek foreign sources to know the future, for this enables the evil one an entrance. Be content with your lot and listen to those words and signs I give. My Word is real truth and it is not to be abused for anyone's gain. Be faithful in prayer, My little ones, and My favor will continue to rest on you. Avoid the temptations of the evil one in all his enticements for fame and fortune."***

Saturday, November 19, 1994: (Christ the King)

After Communion, I saw some people in a misty place with light all around. Then gradually I could see angels come forth with trumpets. Finally, I could see Jesus seated upon His throne in glory. Jesus said: ***"My people, you will one day witness My glory in heaven, for this is the true Kingdom all aspire to achieve. You will see also a taste of My peace and kingship in your soul after Communion, for where My presence is, there also is the Kingdom. I am King of the Universe and when you love Me, you give witness to that Kingship. Be focused on Me always and you will enjoy My Kingdom wherever you are."***

Later, at church, I saw two tablets with the Ten Commandments written on them. Jesus said: ***"My people, I give you My covenant from years long ago to Moses. These are My commands that you may have a model society. You can consider My will for you lies with the basics in My commandments. I realize in your weakened state that you will undergo trials to keep holy, but for those people who do not believe they are sinning against My commandments, they must not have a right conscience. Those who do not admit they are sinners cannot be My disciples or humble before Me. Without asking for forgiveness, how can you come to Me, or what reason do you need a Savior? I have died on the cross to forgive your sins but it is your decision with your free will to accept Me and appreciate My gift of love to you. When you feel hurt out of love that you caused My passion then you will begin wanting to be one in My love. It is this divine calling of My love that you seek that will give you spiritual freedom. I love you, My people, with My infinite way in all I do. Be most appreciative of My help to you when I reach out. Accept My gift and you will be rich in My blessings."***

Sunday, November 20, 1994: (Christ the King)

After Communion, I saw a gleaming bright pyramid and it was blasted to pieces as a piece of glass shatters. I then saw a half-moon representing evil forces and fortune tellers who were destroyed. Finally, I saw a beautiful glow as Jesus came on a cloud to proclaim His new Kingdom. Also, I saw bodies rising from the dead. Jesus said: ***"I will break the fetters of those who oppose Me. I will dash their hopes of success with evil forever. They will know that My power reigns supreme and that I allow only a time of evil as a test. My glorious Kingdom will begin with a reign of peace at My triumph, on earth as it is in heaven. You will see glorious***

miracles at My first resurrection of those who witnessed to Me during the tribulation time. I will uplift all My faithful at that time as their eternal reward unfolds before them. You will be fulfilled in My everlasting love and peace. At that time, My reign will know no bounds. You will experience a joy of all knowledge which will consume you and give reason to praise Me and thank Me for all My gifts. Live in hope for this moment and your joy in Me will be one and complete."

Later, at church, I saw a car with its lights on during daylight. Then I saw a hearse carrying a black casket. I was led to believe that this was meant to be America dying. Jesus said: ***"My people of America, how long will it take to see your errors in casting Me aside? How do you expect to live in peace and prosperity without My help? Initially your country's religious freedom put you on the right path to Me, but somewhere on the way wealth has made you arrogant and selfish—thinking you could do everything on your own. Your country is slowly sinking into an abyss of sin from which you may not recover. Because of your path without Me, I am withdrawing My blessings and help. It is only by letting you fall on your face that you may get on your knees and ask My help and My forgiveness of your sins. Your sins as a nation are so scarlet that only dire disasters are in your future. Do not expect to stay in good living if you turn your back on Me. You have made money your god and have forgotten Me. You will find hard times as a result, so prepare for the consequences. Pray that you save your souls, My faithful, despite the curses around you."***

Monday, November 21, 1994:

After Communion, I saw a white house fall down a slope into the sea. Jesus said: ***"America, America, why do you not listen to Me? You are now as the unwise builder who built his house on sand with no firm foundation. Instead of relying on Me for help, your country is crimson red with sin on your hands. How can your kingdom stand without Me? If you trust only in men, expect your house to come tumbling down in short order. At your beginning, your founders established your country on God and His commandments, but know you have cast this trust to the winds and will be subject to the buffeting winds of My fury. Do you think I will wait long to test you? Expect My wrath to satisfy My*** *justice for those who do not believe in Me and utter every abomination. My faithful pray much to be spared from those evil ones around you."*

Later, at church, I could see Our Lady coming with a crown and I could even sense her presence. It was a beautiful uplifting feeling. Mary said: ***"My children, it is good to be with you this evening on another of my feast days (Presentation of Mary). I am this night presenting you also to my Son in heaven where we are one. If you would please my Son, think of Him as often as you can during the day. When I was on earth, I was joined to His every wish at every moment of every day. You too can come closer to my Son, if you could just close out the things of this world from your mind. Go to your room in private and pray such that your spiritual ears may be opened so you can listen for His word to you. As you grow in perfection, reach out to my Son and follow His every wish for you. By doing His will, you too can come into His oneness. Let Him lead you through life and every moment of your day can be a living prayer to Him. This is where your perfection begins, with your eyes and ears fixed on Jesus. You will then receive His abundant blessings and be allowed to carry on in helping His faithful. Look to both of us for help in all you do and then one day you will witness our triumph."***

Tuesday, November 22, 1994:

After Communion, I at first saw an altar at Mass and then I saw an open gravesite. Jesus said: ***"Remember, My people, thou art dust and unto dust thou shalt return. No matter what status you may arrive at, you still are no more than a mere human being subject to death and all your other frailties. Do not be overtaken with visions of grandeur in this life. Your life here is one of suffering, unrest and the trial. This life is your opportunity to find Me in prayer and learn how to prepare for the life to come, for you are living for the life of tomorrow where My faithful will enjoy full freedom of your spirit to worship Me in heaven. So do not be overly concerned with the cares of this world, but ready yourself to receive Me when your hour of death will arrive."***

Later, at the prayer group, I first saw a table of pictures of relatives, saints, Mary and Jesus. This was a sense of family coming together for Thanksgiving. Jesus said: ***"As you meet with your*** *family on Thanksgiving, remember your greater spiritual family as well. All the saints in heaven and Myself are offering you our encouragement in your life's trials. Draw comfort from each other both on earth and with those who have gone before you. Give thanks at your meal for the many blessings of friends and relatives. Each person affects your life as much as you affect other people's lives."* I then saw an ornate steel grating and it appeared as cemetery doors opening with a large colored building of the world in the background. Jesus said: ***"Remember your destination is at the end of your life. Everything you do is directed toward that end. If you are faithful to Me, your fruits of good deeds will go before you, as you prepare a spiritual treasure in heaven. If you are not with Me, your evil deeds will abound out of your heart of evil. Prepare, My friends, for you choose your end by how you live your life."*** I saw some water fonts and a river. Jesus said: ***"Water is a very strong symbol both in your earthly and spiritual life. On earth it keeps life refreshed and is central to survival. In the spirit world I bring you living water in Baptism to sustain My grace in you to lead Christian lives witnessing My word through evangelization. Be thankful for these gifts, for a font of grace is always here for those who ask."*** I saw a picture of St. John Lateran Church with some balconies. Jesus said: ***"This will be a serious time for My Pope John Paul II. He will be deeply tested by those who want to remove him from office. Know that these things will happen, but in good time you shall not worry, for I will at once triumph over evil."*** I then looked through some silver saloon doors which opened to a train leaving from the station. Jesus said: ***"Many people are found wanting when their time has come to die. Their spirits are restless and do not want to leave the earth. Many also are not very well-prepared for this journey, but still they must go with no choice. Those who have tried to love Me, but only with a short time, may require a long purification to be worthy. As I have mentioned, train yourself to be close to Me in prayer and you will be well-prepared at this junction of life and death."*** I then saw a man with a black mask on. Jesus said: ***"As you come on the end times, be watchful My children and do not be misled by the false witnesses you will see come to you. Many will say they come in My name, but their deeds are far from Me. Know I have forewarned you and ask for My grace of discernment to follow***

only Me." Finally, I saw four objects of light flying in the sky. It then became apparent that they were angels who took their positions at the four corners of the world. Jesus said: ***"The time of harvest is ripe. I will soon be calling My angels to gather in the people for the judgment. All will know by the signs in the heavens when this time will come. At that time, all will be judged by their own deeds as to whether you are with Me or against Me. In the end there are only two options—glory with Me in heaven or a horrific condemnation to hell with Satan."***

Wednesday, November 23, 1994:

After Communion, I saw people coming together for a feast. Jesus said: ***"My people it is good that you take time to give thanks for all your blessings, but besides the festivities, it is also good to remember that you should be thanking Me most for all your gifts in America. Many enjoy the feast but do not always understand their heritage from days gone by. Your nation, at that time was more God-centered than today. It would be good to dwell on some of those thoughts of how you enjoy peace and prosperity in your country. Again, let your celebration be a foretaste of the great celebration you will have once you reach heaven. For here in My presence you will be giving thanks to Me for the most generous banquet of all. Keep focused on Me in your prayers and dedication and you too will share of My meal which I have prepared for you."***

Later, at church, I saw a picture of a cross laying on the ground and when I looked at it, I saw a picture of Christ's face with a crown of thorns. Jesus said: ***"My people, look for Me in all your daily crosses. When you are experiencing pain, see My suffering face in it. When you are enduring any trial, see Me in that also. I ask you to offer up your physical pain in reparation for your sins, the sins of others or for those in purgatory. Do not waste your pain which you can magnify into a prayer for good. Know that any pain you suffer, I have suffered in a similar way. I know you need My grace to comfort you and get you through any feeling of loneliness or despair. You can offer up all your spiritual trials as well. Your whole life can be offered each day as a prayer. I am asking you, My friends, to suffer for a while as I did but then you will shortly receive your resurrection. Live for that day***

of spiritual metamorphosis, for you will then share the glory in My splendor of heaven."

Thursday, November 24, 1994: (Thanksgiving)

After Communion, I saw a deep dirt pit dug out of the ground leading to some underground tunnels. Jesus said: ***"My people, I will always be watching over you even during the tribulation. Once the warning comes, be forewarned to make ready your preparations for hiding from the Anti-Christ and his agents. One of your necessities will be a shovel for areas where you can dig out a house or tunnel. You must be below ground to avoid detection from helicopters and satellites who will be looking for My faithful. This also will serve as good protection from bombs or other chastisements. Be hopeful My people. You may suffer a short time, but your quest of heaven will be your reward. Pray much for My graces to help you through this time."***

At church, I saw several small airplanes flying into the sky. Jesus said: ***"My people, I love you so much that I care for you. I want you to learn all there is for you to know of My ways and how to lead a good spiritual life. With Me at the center of your life, you must earn your spiritual wings. Through a pruning process of cutting out this world's goods, you will see that heavenly things are much more desirable and longer lasting. I need you to come to the full realization that doing My will for you is My plan for you. Keeping obedience to My commandments gets you started on your road to heaven. Again, all must be as humble as innocent children trusting in Me as children trust their parents to provide for them. Come to see Me often in My Blessed Sacrament and learn to adopt a life of constant prayer. The more you dedicate your lives to Me, the richer life will seem to you. Come and get refreshed with Holy Communion and keep your soul cleansed with Confession. In this way, life will be a joy for you no matter what trials you may face."***

Friday, November 25, 1994:

After Communion, I could see Maria E. briefly and then some very grotesque demons were coming toward me. She said: ***"Pray to Jesus to fight the demons."*** I continued to see more demons after I looked away. Finally, I could see white globules of light like angels coming from heaven to put down the devils. Then all was calm again. Jesus said: ***"Woe to you all of earth's inhabitants for an evil time is approaching when there will be previously unheard of displays of evil power. This is the same time I have told you, if the time were not shortened, even My elect would be at risk. You will be fighting principalities and powers in angelic powers from below. You must pray to Me for strength to repel these attacks and have plenty of holy water and your guardian angels to ward off these demons. They are seeking only souls to destroy. They will use all manner of deception to achieve this end. Be prepared with your holy weapons of the Rosary and My holy objects as blessed palms or scapulars. This truly will be an open battle of good and evil all will recognize. You have been warned many times in Scripture about this time."***

Saturday, November 26, 1994:

After Communion, I at first saw a picture of Christ's face with a crown of thorns. Then it was as if He drew His hand up to heaven and the world turned into total darkness. Not long after I could see Him returning on a cloud in glory and celebration. Jesus said: ***"Prepare, ye My people, for My Second Coming. I tell you prepare because it is not long off. Remember, no one will know the day of My return—only My Father in heaven. So be on the watch and make your souls ready to receive Me. If you keep your souls cleansed through My forgiving waters of Confession, you can be the faithful ready with their washed robes. Know that these are indeed the end times and the events foretold in Revelation are taking place. Remain trusting in My word through all the tribulation, for your reward will be great to remain in My service and stay obedient in defending My name."***

Later, at church, after seeing a shooting star and watching *Star Trek* I had a vision again of the renewal of the earth. I could see flames go ahead to purify the earth and a great light caused a renewal of vegetation. All again was beautiful and people were enjoying a joy that cannot be expressed. Jesus said: ***"I am showing you a taste of what heaven on earth will be like. Your joy of My presence will be so overwhelming that nothing else will matter. For when your soul experiences what it craves for, there can be no other option. To know Me totally as you will at that time will***

be so fulfilling, you will never cease praising Me and thanking Me. You will have so much a sense of My love that My glow of love will be a light before you. You cannot imagine how this life will so draw you to Me as a piece of iron to a magnet. Now, My people, you must direct your lives to Me in anticipation of this eternal joy. With such a glory awaiting you, how can you let earthly longings hold you back from Me? I offer you so much for eternity. All I ask is your allegiance and faith in Me. Direct your lives to Me by following My ways and you can partake of My glory. Tell your people with such a gift waiting for them, how can you choose to follow Satan's lies? He offers you a death in self-love, while I offer you an eternal life of joy with Me. See the importance therefore of passing your earthly test of loving Me over all obstacles before you. When you can see a glimpse of your future with Me, how could you desire anything else?"

Sunday, November 27, 1994: (First Sunday of Advent)

After Communion, I saw Jesus under a dark cloud and barely visible. Then He rose above the clouds and He became radiant as the sun. Jesus said: ***"Come to Me, My people, you who are heavily burdened, and I will refresh you. I am here waiting to give you comfort with My graces. You are seeing My light as it tries to find its way to your heart. When I come for each of you, will you be spiritually ready? Take care, My people, and live in the present how you will receive Me when I come. Then, when you live a holy life, you will have no fear of My visitation. You are beginning the commemoration of My first coming, but be always ready for My Second Coming which is soon. This Second Coming will come to fruition in My appointed time, because all of the Scriptures will be fulfilled."***

Later, at church, I saw several tanks moving and then a great white light blotted them out. Jesus said: ***"My people, why must you continue to cause wars and make more arms? I tell you My Mother's prophecy will come true, if the latest war in Europe becomes larger. A greater conflict would lose even more lives. You must pray that this conflict does not widen. It will be to no one's advantage. The innocent lives lost in warfare are so heartrending to Me, when it is only greed at the bottom of men's hearts. Come and ask for My peace or you will see only destruction. There***

will come a day soon when I shall blot out all evil from the earth. I will carry off all potential arms and there will no longer be any more conflicts, for I will provide everything. My people, come to Me in prayer and I will satisfy your every need. If you would give Me a chance to console you even now, you would see how futile earthly desires are. Seek those things of heaven and you will have all you need."

Monday, November 28, 1994:

After Communion, I saw a cave or barnlike structure as the place where Our Savior would be born. Jesus said: ***"I am showing you My place of birth on earth in a stable. You yourselves may one day have a humble dwelling place. I go before you in many of life's experiences. Even in suffering and persecution, I go before you. As you prepare in Advent for My coming, keep your spirit humble and not dependent on this world's goods, for when you are stripped of the things of this world, you will indeed be dependent on Me for your very survival. It is better training for you to follow Me than to depend on your own or man's means. Look to Me for leading you in life no matter what your status is in life."***

Later, at church, I saw a picture of a big eye and I was looking into a blue pupil through to the soul behind. Jesus said: ***"Look with your eyes as windows into your soul and prepare yourself to meet Me at My coming at Christmas. Look to see how you can improve your prayer life and place more fervor in it so you can be drawn to Me and distance yourself from worldly concerns. Again, look to how you can be more gracious in receiving and helping your neighbor. In all you do in life, do it for Me, where pleasing Me and following My plan for you should be your only concern. When you give everything over to Me, now you will be ready to bring your gift of love to Me at the crib. Do not come to Me until you have made your preparation and are sincere in improving your spiritual life. When you are part of My oneness in doing My will, you will truly enjoy the peace I bring to you on earth. When you care only for Me first, then all else will be easy for you with My grace."***

Tuesday, November 29, 1994:

After Communion, I could see people at Mass and then in the background a shadow figure of what looked like royalty. This figure was Christ as King. Jesus said: ***"I am in your midst always waiting for you to listen to Me. I am always here to lead you through life. Those who follow Me and let Me lead them, will be the first fruits of the lamb. The reading today shows you a description of My new world for you. You will see at that time a harmony in the natural order both in the animals and plants. Those faithful, chosen worthy, will experience My banquet table where no longer evil will have its influence. At that time your free will, will be absorbed into My oneness and you will experience a glorified life in full knowledge with no death or pain. Have faith in My word that this will be your reward for believing in Me at your time of trial."***

Later, at church, I first saw a golden calf and then I saw a sky full of red to the horizon. This signified a time of flames and a time of evil. Jesus said: ***"This is an evil age much like at Mount Sinai when Moses condemned the revelry and idol worship. It is a time again as during Lot's day in Sodom where all manner of sexual misconduct took place. Your age is no better and soon it will grow so intense with evil that it will call for My justice of purification. The tribulation you are entering will seem as a godless society, for in fact they will be worshipping the Anti-Christ instead of Me. I warn you, My friends, to go into hiding to avoid these evil forces which will try to force their way on My people. These evil agents will have a strong power of suggestion and persuasion which will require My graces to repel them. Lean on Me for help at that time and be not prideful and think you can withstand them. I tell you, come to Me for strength and use your spiritual weapons of holy water and your Rosary. You will need to muster all your spiritual friends to fight this last battle of evil. At Armageddon, I will defeat them and evil and death will lose their sting in My triumph."***

Wednesday, November 30, 1994: (St. Andrew)

After Communion, I saw a speaker behind a podium. Jesus said: ***"To all those I call to follow Me, I ask them to give up the world to preach My message of love and My message of salva-***

tion. To all who commit themselves to be My messengers, I ask them to count the costs, but also to know that My strength will go before them in helping them proclaim My word. To My prophets I promise you a just reward and many persecutions besides. To preach My name will be increasingly difficult, but necessary for the many souls to be saved. For if on hearing My word, those refuse it, they will answer to Me and face the fires of Gehenna in their disbelief. For those who believe, I welcome them into My house and ask them to give thanks to the messengers who bring My word to them."

Later, at the prayer group I first saw a large scroll opened to announce both the Lord's First and Second Coming. Jesus said: ***"The scroll you see represents the prophetic words of Me in the Scriptures. Read and listen to the words of the Old Testament describe how beautifully I was to embrace My people at My First Coming. Again you can read descriptions in both the old and new testaments concerning My Second Coming as well. One thread of truth is evident that all these prophecies have come about and will continue to be fulfilled."*** I then had a picture of walking down some city streets at night and I could see murdered people with black shadows of their killers running off. Jesus said: ***"Many of you have noticed how the number of killings have increased in your streets. As you see an ongoing number of abortions continue, your society is witnessing less regard for the value of human life. This is how evil suggestions allow people to justify killing in their warped minds where nothing is sacred. During this Advent season make an effort to witness how beautiful life is and how precious a gift it is to be safeguarded."*** I had a picture of Mary as a reflection off of an ornate clock. Mary said: ***"Your time is limited and you will see a quick progression of important events occur. This will lead up to the tribulation but it will also hasten the time of my triumph. Prepare yourself this Advent as well as make ready to receive me near the end of this trial."*** I then saw an ornate picture of the Star of David. Jesus said: ***"Many of you know of My lineage which dated back to David in the line of kings, of which I am one. It is important to recognize your heritage, for it shows how each of you fits into My plan for all of mankind. You should also be thankful to your parents for bringing the faith to you. As Mary and Joseph watched over My preparation, you as***

parents should also carry on your responsibility to teach the faith to your children." I saw some glitzy decorations and gifts in some store windows. Jesus said: ***"Your society has secularized My feast day of Christmas as the most profitable shopping season of the year. In your quest for buying gifts for each other do not lose the true Christian spirit of Christmas. There should be joy and peace at this time and not fighting or bad feelings for each other. Try to cure old rifts and heal old friendships racked by many misunderstandings. Forgive one another and make this more of a season of love and family."*** I then saw a picture of a spinning saucer in a clear blue sky during the daytime representing the Warning. Jesus said: ***"Do not be concerned when My warning will come, for it will come at a time you least suspect it. Many are awaiting this time since they know it will be one step closer to My triumph over evil. It will be a time when all will know it to be supernatural in origin and you will be made well aware of your choice for either Me or the Anti-Christ. My mercy is present in this gift. Appreciate this opportunity for the time to be saved by choosing My ways and not that of the world."*** Finally, I saw a nun kneeling and I recognized her as St. Theresa of Lisieux. She said: ***"I come on this day to encourage all those blessed by God to be messengers and those committed to spreading God's word. You yourself have been chosen by your gift to bring an understanding of Christ's love to the people. All prophets who are called to follow Christ must also make an extra effort to be holy and a good example to others. Be thankful for your gift but live to preserve it with a good prayer life. It is only by being united with Jesus more intimately that He will shower His graces of inspiration on you."***

Thursday, December 1, 1994:

After Communion, I saw a swollen stream with a torrent of water running through it. Jesus said: ***"My people, I ask you to be in preparation not only for Advent but also for the coming tribulation. Be ready with My grace of strength to endure the trials that lie ahead. Keep a firm trust and faith in My word that you will be able to withstand the evil days which lie ahead. As the onrushing waters of this trial come, stand firm to withstand all those who will try to steal your soul from Me. Keep your resolve against all the powers of the Anti-Christ and hold fast to Me in***

prayer and humbleness. If you keep by My side, I will protect you and not subject you to being taken over. The demons will have no power over those faithful during this time. Then after I will quiet the storm of evil, you can once again join Me in celebration of My victory over evil."

Friday, December 2, 1994:

After Communion, I saw a road and I was traveling along it in motion. I then came to overlook a huge hill with a very dark valley. The road went down the hill and there was very abundant forests. I heard the words: ***"Though I enter the valley of darkness..."*** This seemed to announce a time of evil was upon us. Jesus said: ***"You will see shortly an increase in the power of evil as I have said. There will be such an appointed time to test all of humanity. You will see a day when My faithful will be under dramatic repression and vigorous persecution. Your society will become even more godless as the time of Anti-Christ draws on. Pray to Me for protection for I will be your only hope. This will be the dark night of the earth when I will truly know those who are faithful to Me. For when those reject Me in the green, who will be with Me in the dry?"***

Later, at church, I walked through some entrance rooms like in the tombs of Israel and in the inner room I saw a body laid out for burial. Jesus said: ***"My people, during the time of Anti-Christ and the tribulation many people will die. You will see many of My faithful who are captured by the Anti-Christ's agents and put to death for My name, but I tell you now to have no fear and pray for My peace of spirit to lead you. If you are chosen as a martyr, think of when I will come in a short while. I will raise up all those faithful killed in the tribulation to join Me in My triumph. You will enjoy heaven on earth with Me whether you survive or not. All you need do is ask My help to protect your soul from Satanic suggestions. I tell all of you now, do not take the mark of the beast on your hand or your forehead and do not worship anyone but Me. For your best defense go into hiding to avoid the evil influence. I will go with you and the Holy Spirit to lead you to safe places or havens. I will provide food and water for you if needed. So enter this evil time with hope and pray to remain faith-***

ful, for your hope will see you to your salvation. After the test, you will rejoice in My new heaven on earth and you will praise Me and thank Me for all the gifts I will shower on you then."

Saturday, December 3, 1994:

After Communion, I could see a strange eclipse of the sun by the moon. As the moon was in front of the sun, I could see huge fingers of flames come around the edges. Jesus said: ***"My people, this eclipse will be one of the signs in the heavens that will be your warning that the tribulation will start soon. This will also be the time of My warning as seen by the image of a life review. This will come first to allow you to decide between Me or the Anti-Christ. He will demonstrate great power but do not believe or worship him. They will try to mark you with the sign of the beast but refuse this even under pain of death. The mark may be in various forms or electronic devices, so avoid this in any form even if it may threaten your livelihood. Continue to ask for My strength in these trials so you can endure the test and trust I will help you."***

Later, at church, I saw a wall with book shelves up five racks with a tabernacle of the Lord in the middle of it. Jesus said: ***"My people, look to Me to lead you through all your life's endeavors. You spend many years training yourself in school to prepare yourself for life's work. I ask you, My friends, to make as much effort to train yourselves in My ways as well. For all that you learn, do not be arrogant or think yourself so smart that you can do everything on your own. No matter how much education you acquire, you will only be scratching the surface of all knowledge that is to be known. Therefore, I tell you do not be proud, but come to Me as a humble penitent and ask My help in your work. By using your knowledge with My grace, you can provide many beautiful good works, but remember to boast in Me and not your own accomplishments. Without My help you would be left to flounder in your human frailties of mistakes. So praise Me and follow My plan for you and you will receive great joy that your wishes of Me will be fulfilled. For if your life's work earns your salvation, it will be most worthy indeed."***

Sunday, December 4, 1994:

After Communion, I saw an Arabic looking young man who could have been in his thirties. He wore a turban and had a striped beard around the edge of his face. It was revealed that this was the Anti-Christ. Jesus said: ***"My children, you must recognize My sacramental presence in My Eucharist. When the priest consecrates the Host, this is My present reality in both My Body and Blood. Never doubt for a moment that I am with you, but give praise and glory to God that I have fulfilled My promise to remain with you as I instituted My Eucharistic gift at the Last Supper. You commemorate My first coming at Christmas and you look for Me face to face as I will come in glory at the first judgment. Never forget My gifts of My presence in your life—it is not even anything to speculate about. Now I am warning you of another coming of Anti-Christ who will be most devious. He will come as a man of peace with miraculous powers. He will come as Satan in an angel of light, but do not be deceived by his cunning and remember only God is worthy of being worshipped—never anyone else. Be watchful and pray for the grace to discern these coming events."***

Later, at church, I again saw a carved out tunnel for hiding. There was a pool of blue water in it. Afterward, I saw a ship representing our country sink into the ocean. Jesus said: ***"My people, your time of trial draws near. Many will be misplaced from their homes to avoid the evil ones, but do not worry about the uncertainty of what will further happen. Of more significance is the bad direction your country has taken. In all phases of life your morals are rapidly deteriorating. Unless prayer and good works turn around, you are bound for the same end as the Titanic. Without love for God in your hearts, you will fail to reach the perfection I desire from you. Please, My people, listen to My pleas to return to prayer and a good Christian life or you all will be doomed to repeat your past. You do not have much time to correct your wrongs, so prepare for your judgment."***

Monday, December 5, 1994:

After Communion, I was looking up at a concrete tower from underneath it. Then gradually I rose up outside to be even with the top of the tower and I could see a blue figure which looked like

Our Lady. Mary said: ***"My children, continue to be faithful in your prayers and devotions, for many are being called on to stem the outrage of sin in your country. Were it not for these few good souls, my Son's judgment would have fallen harder on you. Thank you, for responding to my call for your consecration prayers, but be more adamant in completing them. Some do not realize their importance at this crucial time. You are witnessing signs and descriptions of my coming triumph but first you must endure the trial. My day is not far off my little ones, so hold strong to your faith and you will enjoy much the glory of my Son."***

At church, I saw an older lady praying in a chapel and I could see the door was open and it was a beautiful sunny day outside. Jesus said: ***"My loving children, come to visit Me often in My tabernacle or in exposition. Take some time out of your busy and restless lives to come into My chapel away from the cares of the world. You need to make time for Me so I can refresh you at My oasis of graces. I pour My living water out over you so you can see how beautiful and generous I am to My people. I am always here, My friends, waiting as a prisoner in the Host to share My love with you through your prayers. If you could only appreciate how I am the very basis of your life, you would wonder why you would not want to be there all the time on earth. My love for you is overflowing and willing to be shared with all who come forward to accept Me in faith. It is this grace to know Me more intimately that I wish to give everyone. Once you become a part of Me, you will never want to leave Me. Ask Me constantly to share your life every day."***

Tuesday, December 6, 1994: (St. Nicholas)

After Communion, I could see a long narrow high corridor leading into a beautiful church. I received the words: ***"Enter through the narrow gate."*** Jesus said: ***"This is indeed a good day to think about giving and receiving gifts. I have gone before you to offer all sinners the greatest gift of all—My death on the cross for your salvation. I also offer My faithful the gift of faith in knowledge of My revelation. You have been offered many opportunities to save your soul. It is up to you now with your free will to accept or reject Me. If you do choose to be with Me for eternity, you can offer Me your gift of yourself at the crib. By giving over your worldly ambi-***

tions to follow My ways, this gift of your soul to Me will enrich your life as well. All those who do give of themselves to Me will receive My promise of their sharing heaven with Me."

Later, at church, I was on an airplane, but we were flying in space with the stars all around us. Then I could see people on the plane in their seats. It was as if everyone was tied down to the space in the plane. Their life was limited while they were on board. Jesus said: ***"You all on earth are on a big spaceship traveling around space. Your time and space is limited also. You must understand you were not created just to be on earth, but you were created for your eternal life after death when your immortal soul will continue on without earth's limits. Once you are outside of time, you will truly appreciate the life I intend for you in heaven. By your being faithful during this training time on earth, you will see and understand My beauty and endless love. Learn, My people, from your experiences here on earth. By letting Me guide you by the hand through life, you will be in much better shape spiritually, by putting your allegiance and trust in Me. Use your time wisely to please Me by your prayers and keep in daily communication with Me. In that way, you will see in only a short time how you will be with Me to enjoy your heart's strongest desire—full contemplation of My glorious presence in the beatific vision."***

Wednesday, December 7, 1994:

After Communion, I was looking into a big horn and then I could see angels making an announcement on their horns. Jesus said: ***"My people, as you commemorate My First Coming, My angels as you see are announcing My Second Coming as well. You will soon see the tribulation start which will eventually lead to the earth's purification and My coming at the first judgment. First My announcement of the end times will begin with My spiritual and physical warning. This will indeed lay down the battle lines between good and bad. This will culminate in the Battle of Armageddon, where the evil ones will be conquered and banished from the earth. Woe to those who oppose Me and welcome to those who receive Me with open arms to embrace Me. This will indeed be a time of trial, but My faithful must endure to win their salvation."***

Later, at the prayer group, I first saw a picture of a blue globe representing the earth. I then saw it become darkened as with the three days of darkness and it moved away from me as if it was going out of orbit. Jesus said: ***"You are seeing a picture of the final chastisement when a cataclysm will strike your planet. In the process the earth will be veiled in darkness and a collision will cause it to go out of its normal orbit for a time. You will see a great coldness come over the earth, so prepare with warm clothes and blankets. Fear not, My children, the earth must be purified before I renew it. Pray and I will watch over you."*** I then saw some toys for the children at Christmas. Jesus said: ***"Oh, you, My people, if you can give good gifts to your loved ones, how much more will your heavenly Father shower you with His gifts. You will need much help along the path of your faith journey. Reach out to Me and I will help you through your difficulties."*** I saw a detective with sunglasses that had a look of silver mirrors. He was riding in an old vintage car. I was given that Clinton's old deeds will come down on him. Jesus said: ***"Your president will soon be chastised for his many offenses against My laws. Anyone who mocks My laws and plays as innocent will be found out in the end. His last state will be worse than his first."*** I saw a picture of fall with many leaves abound on a sunny day. At the same time, I saw an auger digging a hole in the ground. Jesus said: ***"Be watchful in the fall for My signs of the end times. You may see warning signs at this time to prepare you. It will be as a sign to you like winter will be approaching."*** I then saw a bright chandelier in the middle of a dining room. Jesus said: ***"Look to Me as the centerpiece of your life. Focus all your attention on Me so I may lead you to a life of prayer and deep communication with Me. I will also be your light of faith—a beacon for you to come to Me. I will protect you from the worries of life's problems by giving you My peace, so you will see I am much more important than anything else in your life."*** I saw a large rectangular table with the heads of nations stationed all around it. Jesus said: ***"You will see a time when all nations shall come under one ruler who claims to be the prince of this world in the Anti-Christ. By proclaiming his message of a false peace, he will entice all nations to listen and follow him. He will spread his control over all the earth but his reign***

shall come dashing down as I triumph over him in battle. Then all will be loving and with the real peace of God." I saw Our Lady coming with a crown of jewels and a bright blue mantle. Light was radiating out from her. Mary said: ***"I come once again to prepare you to receive my feast day of the Immaculate Conception. I was blessed by Jesus to prepare a spotless place for His entry into my body at the angel's announcement. This is His coming at Christmas, but I have warned you many times, my Son is coming again soon. We will combine our triumph over evil and a new life will be born again on the earth. This will be such a joyful gift, you could not find words to express your thanks to my Son. Thank you for your Rosaries my children and be ever vigilant as the five wise virgins."***

Thursday, December 8, 1994: (Immaculate Conception)

After Communion, I saw Our Lady come in such brightness, I could hardly make out her appearance. Mary said: ***"My children, thank you for sharing in my feast day which your country has made your patronage. I have been indeed graced with my Son's gift of being sinless. It was His preparation to come into this world and become our Savior. It is by His grace also, that He prepares everyone of you for your life as well. Be sure to give Him praise in your humbleness and thank Him for His gift of salvation. He is the one to seek in this life. I will help you as a mediatrix to spread His graces and draw you to Him. Your soul seeks my Son, by the very nature that you are made to His likeness. Pray, my children, and give witness to my Son especially in this Advent season."***

Friday, December 9, 1994:

After Communion, I had a few whiffs of roses and I had a brief picture of Maria E. and she said: ***"Lift high the Lord."*** I then saw a heavy battle gun as an artillery piece and Jesus said: ***"My people why do you have an obsession with taking up arms against each other? Even in trying to help, men are always trying to force their will on others even when they are not welcome. There is an evil hand in this but it is part of your trial. I intend to bring you My peace at this Advent time, but beware of the evil one's intentions to disrupt harmony and bring discord. Do not listen to those temp-***

tations of jealousy and greed, but have sincere intentions of love for your neighbor. If you show only love to everyone, you will heap red hot coals on those only intent on evil and frustrate them."

Later, at church, I saw a ship at sea with an oil slick around it. Jesus said: ***"Your ship of state is in disarray with those who claim their rights to govern it. Many trials will toss you around, but I am the only one who can calm the waters. My children, prepare yourself for some dark days as you continue to be led into blindness by those who are not fit to lead. You must bring your country back to worshipping Me and not the world. Put your ship back on the right course to Me or you will see yourselves tossed about in the waves of unrest in your streets and the weather. Pray much, My friends, you have a great need to counter so much sin in your world."***

Saturday, December 10, 1994:

After Communion, I saw a little pool of water with people on the sides in the water. Jesus said: ***"A prophet is without honor from his home place. Many persecuted Me because they thought they knew My origins. This is because they cannot believe one among them could be so gifted. Even My messenger, John the Baptist, was persecuted for preaching repentance to the king. All authority feels threatened when preachers try to influence their subjects. For those I have asked to spread My word, it will be the same. Some will repent and praise God, while others will want to silence My messengers. History has been repeated because man wants to control his destiny instead of giving his life over to Me. This age old problem of pride still lurks in the hearts of some today. Pray, My children, to humble yourselves and see the beauty in obeying My commands. By following obedience to Me, you will be ordering your lives to My plan for you. This will bring you close to Me and give you My peace."***

Later, at church, I saw a cross in the distance and then it was replaced with a Christmas tree. I sensed Our Lord wants us to put Christ back into Christmas. Jesus said: ***"My people, Advent time should be more of a spiritual preparation than a commercial one. If you truly are thinking about Me, you would be concentrating more on prayer, fasting and Confession. If you would prepare to receive your King, these are the gifts that would please Me. As***

Christmas approaches, will I find room at the inn of your soul? Open your heart to Me and tidy up your soul so it will be worthy of My presence. If you do these things, truly you will experience My peace and joy more abundantly. At the same time, be very conscious of helping others in this season, for I am always asking you to love Me and your neighbor. It is a beautiful family for those who are united in faith. Those who see My star as one of hope, can conquer their problems in this life with My help. Pray to Me much and you will see an improvement in the attitude of your life. With hope in Me, you will be ready to receive Me even when I call on you at death."

Sunday, December 11, 1994:

After Communion, I was looking up from the floor and watching a column of people walk by in white robes. As I came up higher, I could see a very long line indeed. Jesus said: ***"As you prepare this advent season, focus on the purpose of My coming. I have come as an innocent lamb willing to give My life for you. The blood I have shed is meant to wash your robes clean of the sin of original sin and also for the forgiveness of your own personal sins. I give each of you a clean robe fitting to go before the Father in heaven. It is up to you, My friends, through frequent Confession to keep your robes of your soul unblemished by sin. Pray to Me, My loving children, that you will come to Me and live in My will for you. Express your love to Me in your daily prayers and actions. Through your fervor to join with Me, I will grant you your heart's desire especially room for you in heaven."***

Later, at church, I saw a forest of evergreen trees and there were people in among the trees. Jesus said: ***"My people, you may be forced into hiding in the woods to avoid the mark of the beast. It will be a desperate time for you. You will have to depend on Me for your sole survival. I have warned you, a day will be coming when you will be stripped of all your material things. You will see great famines and chaos in your streets. The godless men will hold reign over you for a time. Living in desperate conditions will be common place just to survive, but know that when you have Me with you, you will enjoy the time for prayer and sacrifice. I will test you with hard times but keep faith in Me and you will see your salvation. The battle with evil is your main concern.***

If you stay loyal to My words and commands, that will be enough to get you through this trial. After a short testing, I will welcome My faithful to a purified earth free from evil. At that time, all you endured will be worth being with Me. Pray to Me always for your spiritual endurance."

Monday, December 12, 1994: (Our Lady of Guadalupe)

I saw a picture of Our Lady dressed in blue and then I saw the inside of a simple old kitchen. Mary said: ***"I have come from simple means when I was on the earth. It is true that I have appeared to many of simple means as well, but most of all, I look into the hearts of those I ask to be my messengers. It is not how well off people are in this world that matters. It is how rich they are in spiritual treasures. I come to my children to instruct you how to receive my Son. I also come many times with warnings to amend your lives, for the sins of nations. If nations do not repent, often times wars and pestilence result at their own hands. I have brought faith and hope to many of my children that seeing my miracles, they will be encouraged to endure this life till they can come to my Son. After all, it is getting your soul right with God that is your life's goal."***

Later, at church, I saw a table with a white cloth. On it was a little Christmas tree. Then I saw a shadow come over it and a fist smashed it to pieces. I then saw in a mirror a figure of the Anti-Christ with a small beard. I sensed this was a reenactment of the Scripture where the devil laid in wait to strike the one who would be born of the Virgin. (Rev 12:4) Jesus said: ***"Hark, My people, with My coming there will always be the tempter. You will see the Anti-Christ come shortly and he will rule with a hard hand over his human subjects whom he detests. His reign will last only a short time, since I will bring it to an end. You will see a mighty Battle at Armageddon where Michael will lead the good over evil. At that moment of conquest, you will see My Mother crush his head and the devil and his cohorts will be cast into hell. This will be the moment of triumph all creation is awaiting. You will rejoice at My victory for it is then I will reward all My faithful. Pray and ask My help and that of My Mother to lead you on My righteous path to your glorious destination with Me."***

Tuesday, December 13, 1994:

After Communion, I saw a vase of tulips and some were drooping down. It came to Me that these were to represent burial flowers. Jesus said: ***"I have asked you many times during this time of year to always be prepared for the day you might die. As you draw to the darkest night, you may focus your attention on the subject of your eternal destination. It is good that you always pay attention to your spiritual lives. You should be in My grace and if I ask your life the next day, how would you respond? A person who is always ready will say, 'I continue to do the Lord's will every day the same.' This is how I ask you to stay prepared. So when I do come in glory, you will not be found wanting. You will see a dazzling light at the dawn of My new earth. Have faith through the trial and your true love will be happy to receive you into My banquet."***

Later, at church, I saw a Christmas tree in a living room and there was a white cloudiness all over it. There was a feeling of cold hearts toward Christmas. Jesus said: ***"Many of My people are taken up with gift giving during the Christmas season. It is good to have a feeling of charity toward each other at My coming. It is also one of your Advent resolutions to keep Me foremost in your thoughts. I am the eternal lover who never ceases holding My arms out to receive you. You for your part should also take time to greet Me as well. Even amidst the joy of this season there are still many cold hearts who do not warm up to My love. It is your responsibility to reach out and soften these hearts for Me. If you can prepare them to meet Me by your personal attention, then more can share in My love when I come. Live each day, My friends, as if Christmas was celebrated every day. For I am here in your midst ready to share My love with anyone willing to accept Me."***

Wednesday, December 14, 1994:

After Communion, I saw an angel standing alone with a great light over him. I then saw many angels come forth from heaven blowing their horns. Jesus said: ***"My angels are announcing to you My coming at Christmas. Greet them with the joy they are celebrating and understand how they go before Me to prepare the way. They are saying 'come to My wedding feast and share at My banquet' the graces of My first coming. This also is an an-***

nouncement of My coming as the beginning of man's salvation with the entrance of your Savior, but in order to be saved, My people, you must take Me into your hearts and embrace Me with acceptance as a good host. Then you will truly be saved as I write you into My Book of Life. For these are the ones who will stand at My gates of heaven waiting to be let in at the appropriate time. Rejoice, O mankind, for the time of your visitation is near."

Later, at the prayer group, I first saw a sick young girl in bed. Jesus said: ***"Many times in the Gospel I was moved with compassion to heal many sicknesses and infirmities. You in your world have many sick people as well. You know, yourself, how helpless you feel during a sickness. It is good that you visit the sick to lift up their spirits and pray for them to be cured. For those of you who have healing gifts, go out to all those who request your services."*** I saw a man go down into the basement to bring up a box of necessities in preparation to go into hiding. Jesus said: ***"Many times I have warned My faithful to make themselves ready both spiritually and physically for the evil tribulation about to befall you. Evil will have its time, but it will not be able to attack your soul while you are in union with Me through prayer. Have your blessed objects and necessities ready to flee at any moment."*** I then felt the presence of a saintly man praying before the cross of Jesus. St. John of the Cross said: ***"You must be always willing to follow God's will in making any sacrifices He requests of you. Even though it be against your will, you must remain in obedience to the divine wishes. It is by joining Jesus in our walk of life that He prevails over our thoughts."*** I saw what looked like an Oriental dragon going through the streets. Jesus said: ***"You must be aware and ready to do battle with the dragon of this world. His forces are the same that encouraged your first parents to believe they would be like gods. He preys on your pride to deceive you. Know this trick and be prepared for his attacks by keeping your thoughts on Me."*** I then saw a beautiful bouquet of yellow flowers. Jesus said: ***"My children, I have prepared many bouquets of graces for My faithful when I come at Christmas. By being open to Me I will shower these graces on you for your faithfulness. Pray and bring your many spiritual gifts to My crib."*** I saw a picture of Our Lady pregnant as she appears at Guadalupe. Mary said: ***"I gave my yes to my Son to conceive and bring Him forth. Many of my children***

have listened to Satan's voice of convenience to not give birth to their own children. Please pray for all pregnant mothers, especially those leaning towards abortion. My Son has stated any sin which takes a life—abortion, murder, or suicide—are the most grievous sins against His will. He is the one who will call you to Himself at the proper time for that soul. When you take a life, you thwart God's plans for that individual and you will pay accordingly. My Son will forgive you if you ask, but woe to those who do not." I finally saw a field and they were playing football. Jesus said: ***"All of you are appointed a length of time on the field of life. This is a great opportunity for all those granted the gift of life. It is up to you to make the most of your little time on earth and choose in your actions who you are going to follow—Me or Satan. If you choose to follow Me, live every day as your last and work to please Me in all your prayers and activities."***

Thursday, December 15, 1994:

After Communion, I was given physically three triangular pieces of the Host. I had another vision of a triangle representing the three persons in one God as in the Trinity. God the Father said: ***"You are seeing in the readings how I have kept My promises through the covenants over the ages. I have told you I will never abandon you. You may be tested at times, but I will always be available to help you. I have made My best fulfillment in making salvation available through the coming of my Son. After Adam's sin, I have promised you a redeemer through My prophets. At Christmas you will see fulfilled in all the Scriptures how my Son is the glory of My promise brought to light. Listen to Him and be glad that the grace of salvation is yours for the asking. You have all been afforded the opportunity to heaven which was closed before my Son's coming to earth."***

Friday, December 16, 1994:

After Communion, I saw some lilies or trumpet like flowers and I sensed all creation, even in nature, was getting ready to receive Jesus' coming. Jesus said: ***"My people, you are making great preparation to receive Me at Christmas. I tell you all of creation awaits My coming, even the plants and animals. They all are in eager anticipation of My peace which permeates everything. Do*** *you remember when I said in Scripture 'if man will not acknowledge Me, I will make the stones even rejoice at My coming and give glory and praise to Me?' I tell you even more will nature await My Second Coming. For at that time, everything will be in full harmony as it was in the garden of Eden before Adam's fall. Then will the words of the prophets be fulfilled when there will be no more violence between animals for survival. All, even you My people, will have new and glorified bodies. All will bow down and give Me praise, for I am truly worth your homage for your salvation and your existence."*

Later, at church, I saw a dark living room with just a little light shining away from me as I was behind the light. Jesus said: ***"I have come to you to dispel the darkness, especially the darkness of sin. My light is all powerful, eternal and never diminishes. You see now the time of Christmas has long nights, but I give you hope, much as you know the days will soon start to grow longer. So it is with faith also. I bring My light to curse the abomination of your sins. With My gift of faith, you can see the inner beauty of My love for all of you. With the light of My faith, you can see your purpose on earth is to please Me by your obedience and also how loving and helpful your God can be. If your light should go out with mortal sin, you have My gift of Confession to come and have your sins forgiven. Then it will be as you change a burned out bulb with a new one. Your faith will then be renewed and your soul will be radiant as ever to Me and those around you. So listen to My words of wisdom and follow My light wherever it leads you, for this is how I show you the way to your salvation."***

Saturday, December 17, 1994:

After Communion, I saw a priest distributing Communion and Jesus said: ***"My dear children, when you receive Me in the Eucharist, I come to you in a special way. As I draw near to you and you to Me, it is like being personally next to Me at My crib in Bethlehem. As you read of My human origins, know that I know of all your origins, as well, since I am, I was and I will to be. I ask that you would reverence My Blessed Sacrament with the same fervor as if I was before you in human form. Many of My people do not fully understand the mystery of My presence in the Host, but I am still there nonetheless. Pray for spiritual***

guidance in this life and visit Me as often as you can in the Mass and at My tabernacle."

Later, at church, I saw Jesus standing in His tunic with an outstretched arm to us. Jesus said: ***"I reach out to My people every day to come and visit Me. I am here in the tabernacle waiting to give you My graces for giving Me praise and adoration. My coming at Christmas is to remind you how I came to offer My life as a gift for you. This is your most precious Christmas gift that you will ever receive. I have loved man so much that I died for you on the cross. It is this commemoration of My coming that brought you the beginning of the salvation of all mankind. You can thank Me for this wonderful gift by giving your will over to Me and accepting Me into your heart each time you visit Me. At the Mass, pay attention to the offering of My Body and Blood, for this is the most important moment of the Mass. When I come down into the bread and wine to give you My real presence, that becomes your chance to reverence Me and thank Me for My gift of living faith for you. Be ever faithful to My laws and My will, and you will see Me in heaven in a short time."***

Sunday, December 18, 1994:

After Communion, I could see a picture of Our Lady in blue and white. I then saw a single camel tethered outside a dwelling. This seemed to symbolize the kingship of Our Lord at His coming much like the Three Kings came on camels. Mary said: ***"My dear children, prepare to greet your King and your Redeemer as He comes at Christmas. Shout with joy and enjoy the festivities in celebrating the coming of my Son, the Messiah. Here is your King. Here is your Creator. Here is your God-man to whom all His creatures should kneel to give Him homage. Think for a moment of His power and might. Think also of the generosity of His love that He would lower Himself to take the form of a man. He had a world to redeem of all its sin and He saw fit to suffer for all humanity. Give praise, honor and thanks to your Lord who brings you His love and your salvation."***

Later, at church, I saw an altar with a bright light behind it out in the open. I then was traveling in air moving over many waterways, factories and mountains. Jesus said: ***"I am showing you all the things of this earth to put in perspective the importance of***

your soul. Many people strive for the things in this world as an end in itself, but I tell you this world, all its money, treasures, and desires will all be of no account one day. So do not place your trust in things or men of this life, for these things are fleeting. Instead, put your trust in Me that I will lead you to your eternal home in heaven which will be much more lasting and of much more insurmountable value. You will see being with Me will put you in a far more beautiful being of existence. The spiritual world holds much more beauty and deeper meaning especially outside of time. My light will be your life. My love will be so complete that you will wonder how you could ever desire anything earthly. So, My friends, pray and live to enjoy the tomorrow in heaven which will be a life beyond your wildest dreams. Once you realize your choice of earth and Satan vs. Me, you will see living with Me is the most obvious. At the same time, you will be honoring your creator and lover who strives to save all of My beautiful children. Turn your heart to Me before it is too late."

Monday, December 19, 1994:

After Communion, I saw a microphone being held before me. It was time to announce Christ's coming, not only at Christmas, but also at His Second Coming. Jesus said: ***"In days of old I sent My prophets before Me to announce My coming as a man on earth. You are visiting these readings as proof of My plan. Even now, I continue to make announcements through My Mother, the new Eve. She is the new herald to make way for My Second Coming in judgment. At this time, also, I am sending this news through many visionaries and locutionists. Do not be surprised that this can happen even in your day, for nothing is impossible with God. I tell you, prepare your soul, for My day of coming to judge My people is quickly descending upon you."***

Later, at church, I saw a plant on a porch. The view overlooked some very poor houses. Jesus said: ***"My people, I come to you in poverty and I lived a very austere life. This was an example to you that you do not need much of this world's riches to survive. I have said before that you will not be judged on how successful you were in the world's eyes. Instead, it will be how rich you are in your spirit of generosity and love that will matter. If you have more than enough to survive, you should share your excess with***

those less fortunate than yourselves. It is good to help the poor. Then you will be enriching your spiritual lives as well. You will see many in life who seek after riches, but once they attain them, then they want to seek more. Still others are even more desirous of power, as well, in their position in society. It cannot be this way for My faithful. Be content with your lot and seek to serve Me only, not just your earthly desires. Then you will see in the end that everlasting spiritual treasures are more worthy to seek."

Tuesday, December 20, 1994:

After Communion, I saw Our Lady with a crown and she looked like the Fatima statue in white. Mary said: ***"When the Lord asks for your moment of truth in how you should serve Him, come forward in full trust and accept His will for you with no holding back. Take a lesson from Zechariah and have no doubt or disbelief in what the Lord can do with your life. Also, as Ahaz, do not make excuses or try to put off the Lord for your own designs. Have a blind trust in your God and He will see your sincerity and bless you with His gifts. If you should decide to do your own will, you will see how a dismal failure lies in wait for you. You cannot achieve His will for you without your acceptance. You must pray for discernment, how to follow what He wills for you. You will never be disappointed if you let Him lead you. You will see, your yes will be your most thankful decision."***

Later, at church, I at first saw a monkey with some bananas and then behind him I saw some huge skyscrapers. Jesus said: ***"My people, take heed of what I am telling you. Many of you are content to lead your complex lives in knowing all the things of your day. You are so intent on learning worldly things that you go to great lengths to understand their every little detail. Sometimes, you are so taken up with life's distractions that you leave very little or no time for Me. I tell you, do not waste your precious time trying to understand earthly things that will last only a short time. Instead, concentrate your learning on My word in Scripture and other spiritual devotions which are much more pleasing to Me and will lead you more to heaven. The more you seek Me and want to serve Me, your time will be well-spent for you will lift your soul to contemplating on a higher plane of life's meaning. It is the spiritual nature of your being which is most important,***

since this is to be your eternal existence. By drawing yourself to Me, you will be preparing yourself for your most worthy of goals in heaven. The more you can learn and understand Me, the more you will come to know complete knowledge."

Wednesday, December 21, 1994:

After Communion, I saw someone carrying a book which looked like a Bible. Jesus said: ***"My people, I prepare you for all My events with prophecy. As you read of the prophets concerning My coming at Christmas, you can understand more My grand plan for mankind. Since Adam's fall, I have promised a redeemer would come to free you of the shackles of your sins. Also, there again are many prophecies of My coming, again, to judge the earth. You have seen how I fulfill My prophecies. Know that not one jot of My promises in My word will ever be forgotten or go unanswered. I am coming again to fulfill My plan for man. It will be at this conquest of evil that you will see My joy for those faithful, that I will offer a measure of My heaven on earth. Have trust in Me that what you have seen in prophecy truly will come to fruition, and most likely in your lifetime."***

Later, at the prayer group, I first saw some oil derricks and I was given that there would soon be war again in the Mid-East among the oil countries. Jesus said: ***"Many times you have heard the signing of many peace treaties in the Mid-East, but I tell you there are still many hostilities in this area which will continue as some seek more land and oil riches. The rest of the world will be at risk because of the dependence on energy in the oil."*** I then saw several bottles of wine and alcohol as people were celebrating the holidays. Jesus said: ***"My friends, it is a good time of cheer and friends coming together, but I beg you do not disgrace My memorials by becoming gluttons or drunkards during these feast days. It is good to have friendship and charity, but keep your behavior as if I was present in your midst."*** I saw a barren tree in a field of sparse growth. Jesus said: ***"I grace each of you with many talents and I set before you My many plans if you would follow My will. Dear children, be sincere in what you do in life and do not squander your gifts or bury yourself in useless pursuits that do not bear much fruit. I ask you to go forward and do your best to bring My Kingdom to others by your good use of your talents. By following this path***

you gain great merits in heaven, but woe to those who are lazy and do not bear fruit, for what little you have will be taken away." I saw water covering much of the land. There will be places that will be inundated with water that are dry land today. Jesus said: ***"You will see many signs and wonders in nature. In some instances, chastisements will be sent as a punishment for sin and where there is much disrespect of God. Pray, My people, that My wrath will be lessened by your contrite hearts."*** I then saw a great darkness of night with stars and, then, there were angels coming in the sky dressed in white and shining forth light. Jesus said: ***"Just as you have seen My angels come to the shepherds to announce My coming at Bethlehem, you will see in the future how they will come again to announce My Second Coming. These will be the signs in the sky to you of My impending visitation."*** I then saw a gunboat in the ocean and behind it on the horizon were great black clouds which represented war clouds. Jesus said: ***"Beware, My people, you will see wars and rumors of wars before I come. Satan will stir up the people and their greed for power will consume them. For I have told you, those who take up the sword, will die by the sword. This vision is another war scene which lies on the horizon of your time."*** Finally, I saw a dove, representing the Holy Spirit, come down from heaven in glory. The Holy Spirit said: ***"I come as the Spirit of Love and I come in answer to your prayers. Continue to pray and communicate with your God and you will be protected. I shower My graces of My gifts upon you. This is your Christmas gift I bequeath on you this day for all here present. Continue in your love of God and neighbor."***

Thursday, December 22, 1994:

After Communion, I had a picture of Maria E. as she said: ***"Behold your Lord."*** I then had a glimpse of Our Lady and she said: ***"Everything the Lord has given is not your own but, only, given for you to care for, for all belongs to the Lord. So when my Son asks you to follow His will, He is directing you to give back to Him only what is His proper right. We are made to His image and, as creatures, all praise and glory should be given to our Lord, so that all that you have, has been given from above and holy is His name. Give forth, therefore, your prayers and***

thanksgiving to the Lord for all He has done for you. Greet Him in love at the crib."

Friday, December 23, 1994:

After Communion, I saw a bright light against some mahogany doors. As they opened, I saw Our Lady greeting me as a herald to her Son's coming. Mary said: ***"My dear children, the day of my great glory granted me by God is arriving in my birth to my Son. This was the fulfillment of His promise to me, that a Son would be born of the Holy Spirit. Jesus has spared nothing in His care for me. He also cares for all of you in a similar way. So I ask you to prepare to meet your Lord at Christmas. He comes to celebrate His redemption of all of mankind. This truly is a celebration of peace on earth, since He brings the opportunity of heaven to everyone. As His herald, I announce to you, again, to prepare for His Second Coming. He will come in glory and triumph on that day to judge all mankind. His plan is beautiful and wonderful to behold. Give praise and glory to your Jesus."***

Later, at church, I could see out of a circular hole I was in. There were steep sides and I could see some people on the edge. There was darkness as I looked out. It came to me that I would suffer some possible persecution and maybe even some kind of jail. Jesus said: ***"My poor little ones, many of you will suffer in the coming tribulation, but take heart because My peace and grace will go with you. You will never be left alone. I ask you many times to make your spiritual preparation to endure that day. Many do not know what lies in store for them, but I assure you with Me at your side, all will go well. You may have to suffer in My name for a while since much reparation will be needed to make up for the sins of the world. Your suffering will help some who are struggling to know Me but need other's prayers and sacrifices to go the last mile. Have faith, My children, that good will come out of this test, for man's complacency calls upon My justice. Give thanks that your prayers will not be in vain. They will be effective in helping bring My Kingdom to the earth. Be patient and accept My timing of events, for all that occurs will follow My plan. Have hope, My people, for a short time. Then you will share in My glorious love."***

Saturday, December 24, 1994:

After Communion, I saw a glimpse of a Santa Claus outfit on someone. Jesus said: ***"Many of you are sharing gifts at this time and giving money. While these things are thoughtful and require time for shopping, there is another dimension of giving I ask of you. It is one thing to give gifts once a year, but I am asking you to give a gift of yourself to people freely and without holding back for any selfish reason. Then you will truly be sincere and people will know you really mean what you say by your deeds. At the same time, I ask you to come to My crib to love and adore Me, but not just this one day, but every day of the year. Let Me into your lives so I can share in your joys and help you in your troubles. Do not leave Me out in the cold, but accept Me into the inn of your souls."***

Later, after Communion, (midnight Mass), I could see a great darkness with just a few little beams of light on high from the angels. Jesus said: ***"The joy of Christmas is being showered over all of you. Some take it to heart and are uplifted in faith, while others treat it as just another day. For those who realize the significance of this feast, they will receive My grace and peace. Those who are cold to Me will go about their dismal lives without any hope. Pray for all sinners, but especially those who are so lost in themselves. The friendship of this time should radiate to all men and My love and joy should be shared by all."***

Sunday, December 25, 1994: (Christmas)

After Communion, I saw a star and myriads of angels were descending down in a line of light out of the star. Jesus said: ***"My little ones, I reach out to you this morning from the arms of an infant. I am asking each of you to come to Me as innocent as little children. Have the faith of an innocent child who believes in full trust of your God without any care for the world. If you have such a blind trust, this is how Heaven's doors will open to you. When you can give Me your full attention every day, you will see what beautiful things are in store for you in heaven. Keep faithful to your prayers and continue to follow My will all the days of the year. Then peace will indeed come to the earth, one that is more lasting than a passing sunset."***

Monday, December 26, 1994: (St. Stephen)

After Communion, I saw a tunnel with a hole showing the outside greenery and sun. I saw a picture of something with teeth after us which looked like a shark. Jesus said: ***"My people, I am with you always. Many will die in My name before the tribulation is over, but know that I suffered before you. You will be tried by many who will stand by the evil one. I tell you, look for the signs of the evil one to come. Remember, his reign will last but a short time. So do not worry what you are to say, for I will take care of all My faithful. Those dedicated to Me can rest assured I will protect your souls from evil, but those who do not follow My word, these will be tortured the most in the end. Your suffering now will be but a test of your faith. So pray and hold fast to Me and you will not be disturbed. My peace will come and you will have a good measure of it."***

Tuesday, December 27, 1994: (St. John the Evangelist)

At St. Michael's (Easton, Pa.) after Communion, I saw a man I believe was St. John the Apostle. He showed Me a desk for writing and later I saw Our Lord in His crown of thorns bleeding for us. St. John said: ***"I am the beloved Apostle of Jesus. He is the holy one of Israel. He comes to you at this time to encourage all of you with His peace. It was the people He came to save by His death on the cross. You are seeing a portion of His suffering, but this is why He came into the world—to free man from His sin and to allow Heaven's doors to be opened to Him. You, my son, have been blessed to spread Jesus' word by your messages. There is a deep responsibility to be faithful to your Lord and to be an example for others to follow. Guard your spiritual life ever so closely and do everything for Jesus. Do not be selfish with your time, but use all you are given for His purpose only. It is by focusing on perfection that you can come closer to your Lord and He will direct you what to say and do for His Kingdom. Pray and stay close to your Beloved as I was. All writers of His word must pay special attention to how to spread His word."***

Wednesday, December 28, 1994: (Holy Innocents)

At St. Michael's (Easton, Pa.) after Communion, I saw a flower and an enclosure with a small coffin. I then walked through an area which looked like the catacombs. There was a train with many cars and it seemed to travel up to heaven. Jesus said: ***"Your killing of innocent unborn children continues to this day unabated. The original feast of such killing was a one time event, but you are continuing this offensive behavior even now. Do you not realize that each of their angels witnesses to Me in this slaughter? Do you think the injustice of this killing will go unanswered? I tell you all nations who participate in abortion will live to regret their actions. Those who would harm innocent children, would be better that a millstone be cast around their neck and then they should be thrown into the ocean. For their punishment lies in wait for them. Even if forgiven, they must suffer some retribution for their offense to My plans. My people, your continuing chastisements are in answer to the wanton sin which your nation continues to wallow in. Pray to make reparation for these many sins. You will soon see I will end all this evil which is detestable in My sight."***

Later, at Holy Name (Holy Innocents Right-to-Life Mass) after Communion, I saw a white robe and the priest offering Mass. I then saw some young children and later some mothers holding their infants. Jesus said: ***"Life is your most precious gift. Treat it with respect in all forms. Life is very precious to Me, also, and I nurture it in every way I can without violating man's free will. Each life, no matter what the world thinks, is important and meaningful to Me. It is up to you to respect each life as equal before Me and deserving of honor and recognition. Even though certain individuals may have less or more value to your world, they continue to be equal in My eyes. Each person is given an immortal soul and the talents I have bestowed on them. Each is made to My image, so do not run down anyone's worth because of what you think. Think only that any value you have has been given from above and is no more or less than that soul has received. My children, be kind and help each other. Then My love will permeate all of you and your world will be ready to receive My peace."***

Thursday, December 29, 1994: (Gospel on Presentation)

After Communion, I saw a strong ray of light shine down through the dust. In the background I could sense I was in Egypt since there was in the shadows a sphinx like stone statue. Jesus said: ***"My parents had taken Me into Egypt to avoid Herod's at-***

tempt to kill the newborn King which he felt threatened his earthly kingdom. I was presented in the temple to honor God's gift and already My persecution started. Man thinks more of himself than God, and any threat to his power is quickly thwarted, even if it is heavenly in origin. His sins he wants kept secret, but man enjoys all manner of human pleasure. You must not let the flesh and power so possess you as a drunkard yearns for drink. See that this life is only a training ground to graduate to heaven. I warn you, My people, soon you will also see the Anti-Christ presented in the temple of evil as he will rise out of Egypt, also. His power will rise from the evil influences that reigned there in days gone by."

Later, at church, I saw some blue and green objects. I saw at first a pyramid sign and then signs of big bomb clouds. Jesus said: ***"My people, I try to bring My peace among you, but you are still too intent on striving for material things and power. You do not seem to be satisfied with your lot and love Me as your only goal. As long as you put your own priorities first, you will never see peace on your earth. Many of the one worlders continue to plot for control of the whole world. They do not realize that they can never control all of the people all of the time. Their greed will drive them to their own destruction. You will see, men will attempt to seize power by force in the Mid-East. A war will come where there will be no winners, but the evil one will succeed in killing many in a large war that may encompass nuclear weapons. If men do not control their greed, you will continue to see unrest for years to come. It will only be when I defeat the enemy, that you will see My triumph conquer sin and restore heavenly peace and justice for all. Only then will things flow perfectly according to God's plan and not man's. It will take a supernatural intervention to achieve a lasting peace with no fighting."***

Friday, December 30, 1994: (Holy Family)

After Communion, my eyes were drawn heavenward toward a bright light which shone down on the earth. Then I could see a mother and her child and the light came down upon them. Jesus said: ***"My beautiful parents, this is the place in the family where I consecrate new life. It is in the framework of marriage that children should be brought forth. This is a holy responsibility, that you are obligated to bring your children up in the faith. It is up to***

you to plant the seeds of faith and nourish My word in their hearts. The family is precious to Me since this is the model I gave you for the fabric of your society. When the family is attacked and weakened, it is an attack on the stability of your society. As you see more one parent families from divorce and children out of wedlock, you will see more division in your society. You cannot stand unless you listen to My laws. Without these laws as your basis of life, your moral decay will bring your nation down to ruin from within. You must pray more to uphold the true family togetherness to protect your society from Satan's wish to destroy you."

At church, all I could see was the letter A for atomic. All the thoughts were focused on man's responsibility of an atomic war. Jesus said: ***"I love you so much, My people, and I have given you the power of your destiny in your own hands. I, for one, am standing here with My peace, encouraging you to follow My way. Satan, on the other hand, is encouraging man to bring Mass destruction on himself. Satan hates you so much, he wants man's demise in every way. He is trying to destroy all the good I have created. You, man, must stop and look what life is about. It is not to possess everything at other's expense. If you gain the whole world and lose your soul, what good is that when your wealth passes away at your death? So give up your greed and satisfy yourself with My love as the victory over Satan. It is love for God and neighbor that will frustrate the evil one. Live for Me, and not yourself and you will gain eternal joy with Me in heaven. If man continues on his current path, he will destroy himself in the process of his hatred. Pray much, My people, to sway those in power to seek peace over war. If you do not, there will be great loss of life."***

Saturday, December 31, 1994:

After Communion, I saw an empty floor where I understood other families would have placed a Nativity scene. Jesus said: ***"In the midst of all your holiday activities make room for Me both in your acknowledging My presence in your home and in your hearts. For I am true love and the light which shines over the whole world. I am always knocking on the door of your souls to let Me in and be a part of your everyday life. Your society is becoming more godless and I see many cold and angry hearts as the new year approaches. Pray, My people, and evangelize My***

word that all will be acquainted with My love. It is up to you to spread My love by your example. If enough do not pray and bring souls back to Me, many souls will be lost to curse the darkness in their despair."

Later, at church, I was in a small boat on the water when suddenly it became swamped with a wave. Jesus said: ***"My people of America, how blind you have been to My many warnings. You still go about life as you please, not caring whether your actions offend Me or not. I say to you, you will see many chastisements come to you through the elements. Further flooding is in your future, if you continue on your path to sin. You must pay close attention to your sins of the flesh and make reparation for them. Again, you must stop the many abortions and killings in your country. Pray much for these offenses and attempt to avert My wrath for your godless actions. If you do not come to Me for forgiveness, you will see much destruction and what little you have will be taken from you. Prepare to meet My justice, for your sins have raised a great cry to heaven. Make the most of what little time you have by keeping close to Me in My Eucharist. For those who take heed of My words, I will protect you from this evil time."***

Sunday, January 1, 1995: (Solemnity of Mary)

After Communion, I saw an ethereal angel with wings lead me up into the sky to see Our Lady with many angels around her. Mary said: ***"You, my son, have been led to my Jesus through me. Treasure in your heart the many gifts you have been given. My Jesus blesses those He favors with such a richness of love. You, for your part, must give back to Him all that He desires of you. You have been given many graces and insights. You must work more at striving for perfection as Jesus wants you to. The necessities of life are requiring your time, but give to the Lord His due in prayer, fasting and visits to His Blessed Sacrament. You can always work harder to please my Son and follow His will. Continue in your efforts and make more time for my Son Jesus. He is the one worthy of your praise. Use your gift to inspire others with my Jesus' word. It is spreading His word to sinners that will bring true peace to your world. Pray, my son, and keep close to your Jesus in all you do."***

Later, at church, I saw some beaches get washed away with some kind of tidal wave. Jesus said: ***"My people, you are facing a new year in which to make some spiritual resolutions to wake up to the battle of good and evil about you. I have given you and others many messages about returning to Me. You do not want to test My justice, for already the cup is overflowing with your sins. I ask you, My people, to look at the current condition of your life. Are you self-centered or God-centered? To be truly God-centered, you would give up your worldly inclinations and seek more to praise, love and serve Me. I did not create each of you to just do things to please yourself. Instead, you are a part of the plan I have for man to live peacefully with one another in love and harmony. When greed gets control of you through the evil one's suggestion, all harmony is lost. Pay attention, therefore, to the purpose of your actions. Direct them to help in the battle against evil, or you may be visited with the justice I will be forced to mete out. I love you and I do not threaten you, but if the world does not repent and ask forgiveness, I will be obliged to purify the earth in My own way."***

Monday, January 2, 1995:

After Communion, I first saw a priest giving out Communion and then I saw a large Host emanating a bright light from it. Jesus said: ***"I love you, My people, with an overwhelming abundance that I wish to share with you. I have left you with an example of that love in giving you My real presence in Communion. Some believers may not understand this mystery, or think it is impossible, but I am truly there, none the less. If you had the spiritual eyes of an angel, you could visualize how My power radiates out from the Host. You have felt My warming presence at exposition. I am eternally present to you in all My creation as well, therefore, ask anything of Me in prayer and I will answer it if it be My will for you. I am always in the tabernacle, ready to uplift you in any of your problems. I am your source of spiritual strength to get you through each day. Never rely just on your own devices, but take Me with you through each day, and you will see what a joy even living on this earth can be."***

Tuesday, January 3, 1995: (Baptism Reading)

After Communion, I was looking down into a pit. The next scene I was looking upward to some big thrones which represented judgment by God. The Holy Spirit said: ***"I am the Spirit of Love and I bring you great joy at the coming of your Savior. At the Baptism of Jesus, the Three Persons of the Blessed Trinity were presented to all. This was to announce the beginning of the mission of Jesus. He was the first to forgive the sins of His people, because He was the lamb who would suffer to free all mankind from original sin. Look to the Son of Man, for He reaches out to forgive you even now. His mercy and love is upon all His faithful as He beckons all to come and receive Him. Your Lord awaits you to come to Him and share His peace and His glory. Do not be fearful, but go to Him in faith and He will receive you. Pray, My sons and daughters, that your souls will be saved and you will witness His splendor."***

Later, at church, I saw some high mountains with snow on them. The next vision I saw was several people going down a long elevator. Jesus said: ***"My friends, you must be prepared to go into hiding. Do not be offended where I will lead you, for it will be for your own safety. Wherever I take you may seem impossible, but believe in My word. The coming trial will try men's souls to the breaking point. You must persevere for only a short time. Do not be disappointed if you must leave everything behind to follow Me, since I asked the apostles in the same way. The more you put your blind trust in Me, the more I will believe your heart is sincere in loving Me. It is this focus on Me that will gain you heaven, no matter how hard the crosses. Continue to pray and believe in Me and you will see Me shortly in a glorified state."***

Wednesday, January 4, 1995: (St. Elizabeth Ann Seton)

After Communion, I saw a woman in an old-fashioned habit of her order. St. Elizabeth Seton said: ***"My son, you have been faithful in coming to my memorial. In doing so, you received the graces of your visitation. My children, remember to take care of each other in the true sense of charity, as in the readings on love and family. Also, continue your faithfulness to Jesus in the Blessed Sacrament which is so dear to me, also. When you see your Lord,***

you will recognize His warmth and loving affection as seen by your gift. Pray to help others see the value of His word and follow His will."

Later, at the prayer group, I first saw a bare foot and a hand. Jesus said: ***"I have created all of you equal with but one purpose — to love and serve your God. Use all of your God-given abilities to spread My Kingdom on this earth to all those eager to hear My word and keep it close to their heart."*** I then saw a woman in black weeping over the loss of her child. The Scripture came to me, "Rachel was found weeping because her children were no more." Jesus said: ***"There are many of My young children being abused or killed in the womb. While some desire to have children and cannot, others are aborting their children. Pray for all parents and would-be parents that they see the evil in their actions against their children. If they could only understand the true value of life, they would not even think of harming these little ones."*** I saw a living room with old furniture and no TV. Jesus said: ***"My people, I desire that you lead more of a simple life without all your material distractions of the latest devices. Live to give Me praise and glory and direct your lives to doing My will in all your actions."*** I then saw a person sewing a black and red designed flag. Jesus said: ***"I am showing you how the Anti-Christ will be praised by the people and they will parade his flag giving him honor. My children, be prepared for this short reign of evil which will be given as a test to prove your faith and hope in Me."*** I saw some men in crowns sitting at a table to give homage to their new king in the Anti-Christ. Jesus said: ***"Shortly, you will be celebrating the Magi coming to give Me gifts of gold, frankincense and myrrh. I was given honor by the poor shepherds and the rich kings, but you will see, man will easily be persuaded to follow this evil king. Beware, My friends, that you worship God alone and give no heed to those on earth who claim fame."*** I then saw a picture of some sick in wheelchairs and then I saw Our Lady behind them. Mary said: ***"I ask you, my children, to pray for your sick so their spirits will be uplifted. Pray that they see to offer up their pain as an offering for sin in the world. I have heard your petitions and have placed them before my Jesus. Pray, also, for the poor souls in purgatory, especially those who have no one to pray for them."*** I finally saw Our Lord on the cross wearing a crown of thorns and suffering deeply. The next scene was that of winter and people were suffering from war. Jesus said: ***"Many of your fellowmen are suffering from the ravages of war because one faction wants to lord its authority over the weak. This injustice cannot go on much longer. Pray, My people, for peace in your world or these warlords will bring death and destruction to everyone, if they are not stopped. With prayer, all is possible with Me, but you must have faith that I will answer your prayer."***

Thursday, January 5, 1995:

After Communion, I saw a vision of Maria E. and she said: ***"Look to His star."*** I then saw a vision of a bright star, one that was connected to Bethlehem. Jesus said: ***"I have told you previously that a sign in the heavens, like a star, will announce the coming of the Anti-Christ much as I was announced at Bethlehem. But know that it will not be through any power of the evil one that this will happen. I will do this through My power as a sign to you. His moment of time will soon be upon you. Pray for spiritual strength, My people, to endure this trial. You must rely on My help or you will surely be lost. After this test, you again will be visited with My glory as My triumph will usher in a new era of peace on earth."***

At church, I saw a thin black cross very clearly hanging on a wall in a house. Then I saw a priest about to say Mass in the home. Jesus said: ***"At the time of tribulation you will be most fortunate to find a Mass in the home. Satan's agents will purge the churches and the religious from active worship. Instead, they will try to force the people to worship the Anti-Christ through suggestion and physical coercion. Avoid these people and do not give them any heed. If you should be faced with persecution, tell them you will worship only the one true God. This will heap hot coals on their ears and they will vent their anger on you. If you could hide at that time, it would be courageous and the smart way to avoid the evil one's attempts at winning your soul. Pray and trust in Me to help you get through this time."***

Friday, January 6, 1995:

After Communion, I saw a priest sitting in the first row with his parishioners. There was a light near the priest, but it was dark throughout the rest of the Church. Jesus said: ***"I have told you*** *many times that I am a light in the darkness who comes to free you from your sins. The darkness is the indifference of the world to the word of God. You, My friends, need My help and the grace I give you to carry on with your life. What better way to renew yourself than to receive Me sacramentally into your hearts. Then I can dispel the darkness and put My light of faith in your soul. Seek Me out and I will take refuge in My faithful. The light you see is from those who represent Me in the priests. It is through My priest sons that I am consecrated in the Host and distributed to all who are willing to come to Me. See that your strength comes from the Eucharist and receive Me as often as you can."*

Later, after Communion, I could see Our Lady dressed in blue radiate a light from her and it was black all around her. Mary said: *"Some of you may be anxious while others are excited about your pilgrimage. My children, be careful to go as a true pilgrim to my shrine. Do not expect so many physical or earthly experiences to please you. Instead anticipate the graces and spiritual blessings I will pour out on you. In the end, these are more lasting gifts. Enjoy visiting these people who do not have much in worldly terms, but have much faith and deep devotion to me. It does not matter how rich you are, but it does matter that you come to my Son in humility and let Him guide your lives. You will see, as at many of my shrines, your interior improvement will make you grow closer to my Son. Have faith, my children, and bear with one another, and your experience will be memorable."*

Saturday, January 7, 1995:

After Communion, I saw a stand of pines and there was snow on the ground. I saw another scene of a waterfall with a cave behind it. Jesus said: *"My people, you will come upon a testing time called the tribulation which will test your allegiance to Me. At that time, you may be stripped of all your comforts and material possessions. You will truly be offered a choice to suffer and be with Me or remain with the momentary comforts of the world. Know that when you choose Me, you will choose eternal life. Those who choose the world and the Anti-Christ, will choose eventual damnation in hell. So choose wisely, My friends, for I am a jealous God. All those in My Kingdom give glory and praise to Me or they are cast out to grind their teeth. Know that it can be no dif-*

ferent for men on earth. If you truly love Me as I love you, you will come to Me out of love and not just fear."

Later, I saw a cross come up out of the earth as Our Lord claimed a victory over evil. There was singing and celebration in heaven. At that time, the earth took on a special glow and all those whose robes were washed white circled down to the earth. It was a manifestation of heaven on earth. Jesus said: ***"Let true peace reign over the earth. Today, My people are still in agony as true peace has not as yet come to the earth. I have given you a taste of***

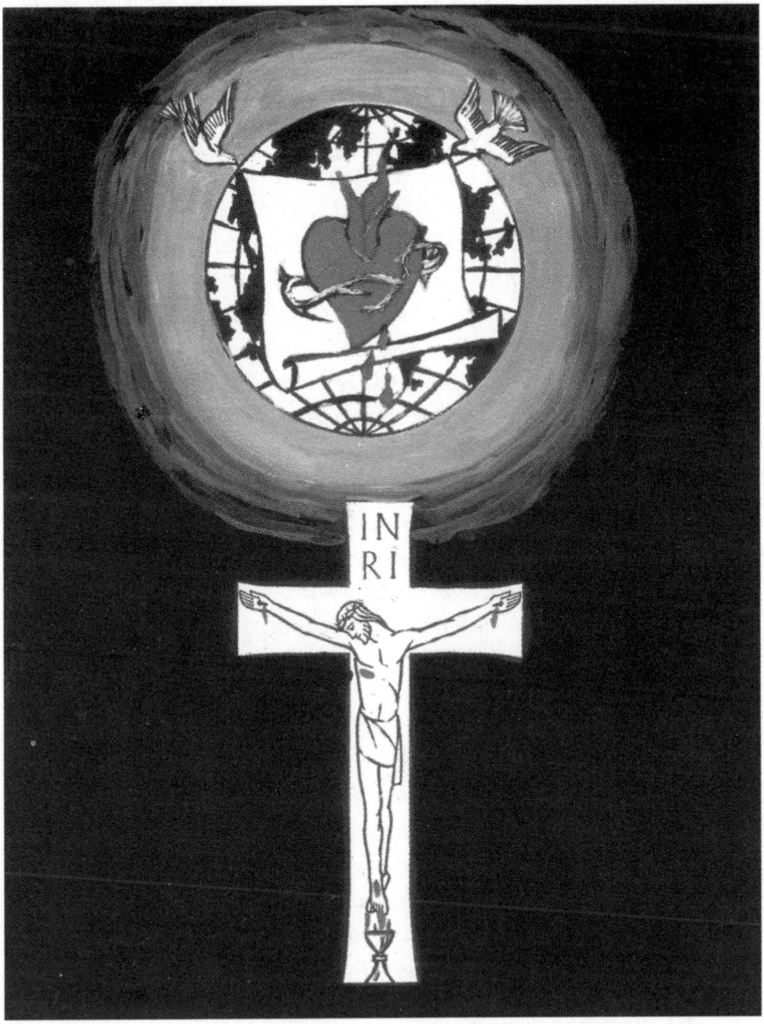

what is to come in My First Coming, but soon you will see a victory over evil and all those faithful will see with their own eyes the beauty I intended for all men on earth. When that comes, you will witness My love for you face to face. There will no longer be any doubt of My control over everything. I am your King of the universe and I intend to show My glory as never before. I give you this message, My people, so you will have hope and faith in Me to follow My way. My burden is light, but your reward will be great. Come forward now and accept your Lord. Follow My will and become a part of My living self. Experience Me in My oneness as you receive Me in Communion. Give praise, honor and thanks to your King."

Sunday, January 8, 1995: (Epiphany)

After Communion, I saw a picture of the people in the pews and then a picture of a white cloud and Our Lord enthroned in heaven. Jesus said: ***"Today, you are witnessing My Kingship in the glory of My people. For a moment I ask you to think truly how you came to be and how your parents shared in creation. My children, I am the one who instills a living soul in each one of you. It is I who gives you the breath of life through the Holy Spirit. Without My supporting your being every second, you would cease to be and return to dust. Give praise and glory to your King who sustains you in your every breath. Do not think you live and give life on your own, it is I who makes it so, and never forget it. For the same reason, since I have truly authored life, you must not destroy any life I have brought forth. My people, live for your Lord and follow My way and your immortal soul will one day enjoy the true glory of My Kingship in heaven."***

Later, at church, I saw a red carpet leading up to the tabernacle. This was a preparation for our King in the Eucharist. Jesus said: ***"My people, the Three Kings have brought Me gifts but I have bestowed on you a greater gift of myself in Communion for you to receive. In fact, I am a treasure which will last forever. Think of Me as a part of your body, for this is how close I wish to be with you. You have a King who gives gifts you cannot fully comprehend. Be thankful, My children, and you can give Me a gift of yourself to Me. Together, if you accept Me, we can be one in spirit. With Me at your right hand helping you, you can always*** *be safe. Work, My children, at enriching your interior life by praying to Me and helping your neighbor. You must have love in your hearts both for Me and one another. When you try to please Me in what you do, you will be following the plan I have laid out for you. Continue to keep your focus on Me and your spiritual life will grow all the deeper."*

Monday, January 9, 1995: (Baptism of Jesus)

After Communion, I saw a dove and it had a radiant glow all around. The Holy Spirit said: ***"I am the Spirit of Love and you see Me taking My place in today's reading as part of the Blessed Trinity. It is appropriate that I be at Jesus' Baptism, since I am present at all baptisms. In fact, My indwelling is given even at conception. My Spirit of Love becomes synonymous even with your spirit of life. It is this spirit which moves and keeps your body with life. When you are called back to God, it is this spirit of life which leaves your body and stays with your soul. Jesus has told you that you are one with Us and this is one intimate reason, since our beings are intermingled. Come, My people, to a better realization of the importance of God in your life and give praise and glory to your Blessed Trinity."***

Later, at church, I could see several single flames of fire. Overlaid with this image were pictures of little children and their parents. Jesus said: ***"My people, I am the author of life. My flame of love burns deeply in all of you. As new life is brought forward, it must be nurtured not only with earthly food, but with heavenly food as well. It is so important, My parents, that you help teach the faith to your little ones and create an environment of holiness, such that the seed I plant in each new life may grow up with the needed nutrients of the one true faith. It is up to you to bring these souls to Me, so they can be exposed to My love and graces through the sacraments. Each has a free will and must make their own commitment, but see to it that you fulfill your responsibility in their religious upbringing. A holy family of believers will be such a blessing to you that all will want to share in your joy. Giving back to Me your gifts of life that I have given you is the most treasured prize I desire of you as parents. Pray, all My little ones, that you will come to Me as little children—humble and innocent—so I may embrace all of you with My everlasting love."***

Tuesday, January 10, 1995:

After Communion, I could see a small spring with a little pool of water. Jesus said: ***"I offer you, My friends, living water as you come to Me in Communion. The promise of eternal life with Me lies in wait for all who are faithful to My word. This is the most precious gift which awaits those who accept Me into their hearts. See the value of this offering, My people, and choose life over the world and all its temptations which lead to death for the soul. By accepting My living water, you will live on in the spirit and know My true love in heaven."***

Later, at church, I first saw some feet walking outside. Then I saw a white cloth on a table and a priest preparing to say a home Mass. Jesus said: ***"My people, during the tribulation you will be most ecstatic to have a Mass where the priest could consecrate some Hosts. This will be another of your necessities to take with your Rosaries—that is some hosts and one for your monstrance. Once in these times, it will be good to keep Me in a holder to bolster your spiritual strength. During your trial, with Me sacramentally in your midst, you could draw on My love at an appropriate time. Be prepared, My children, as you will see events lead up quickly to the time of persecution. Know that I and others have suffered before you. You have had many trouble-free years, but all My faithful must be tried and tested before they can receive their crowns with Me in heaven."***

Wednesday, January 11, 1995:

After Communion, I could see a bright light from above and then I could see below on the earth what looked like a huge mirror. Finally, the mirror was positioned to face towards me so I could see my reflection. Jesus said: ***"I am asking all of you to take time out of your schedules to reflect on your individual spiritual lives. You need to recollect how you have been behaving, measured against the way I led My life on earth. Before complaining about others, look to yourselves where you can improve first. Once you realize your weaknesses, take time to pray and build up your spiritual strength. Form a plan how you can combat the evil one when he comes with his temptations. With your plan in place, you will be better prepared what to expect and be ready to keep yourself in check from repeating your former sins. By striving to***

please Me in all you do instead of yourself, you can be more perfected for Me."

Later, at the prayer group, I first saw a parakeet and Jesus said: ***"I have told you how your heavenly Father watches over the birds of the air. You are more valuable than a flock of birds, so do not worry that I will see to your protection. Do not worry what you are to do or say. At the appointed time, I will direct you so have no fear and have much hope to see the glory of My triumph."*** Then I saw some colorless roses and they were not allowed to have a full life since they were representing aborted babies. Jesus said: ***"My children, it is nearing the time of the anniversary of your allowing abortion in your country. This decision to give up your little ones in the womb is doing the work of Satan. He wants to destroy you with his hate for mankind and you have been helping him. Until you turn around this heinous crime, you will continue to reap the whirlwind of My wrath. It cannot last such much longer so prepare yourselves for the coming judgment."*** I saw some printing presses rolling. Jesus said: ***"Your media praises all the things of man and has little to say of My involvement in life. Man has received many of his gifts from Me but he only thinks of his own skills. There will soon come a day when all will bend their knee in honor of Me whether they believe or not. Then man will truly see how insignificant his accomplishments are. Pray to store up heavenly treasures."*** I then saw a vision of an infant. Our son David's angel said: ***"David thanks you for remembering the anniversary of his death. He is praying for all of you and especially for his immediate family. He asks all of his family members to remember to ask favors from him and he will take them to Jesus."*** I saw a vision of a mother protecting her child. She was in a darkened house looking out of the window. Jesus said: ***"The Anti-Christ will be much like Herod since he will demand all the infants of the faithful two and under to be brought to him. These little ones will then be offered up at black masses to kill them. This evil tyranny will last only a short time and then all those with the beast will be judged and cast into the eternal fire. This is why I have let it be known that it will be a harsh time for those with young ones at the time of the tribulation."*** I then saw Our Lady carrying the infant Jesus. Mary said: ***"My dear children, you must remember that my Son and I were the first to go into hiding because of His name***

and His Kingdom. We fled to Egypt to flee Herod's attempt to kill my Son. You too may endure some persecution much as your Lord did. He is giving example how He is in control and only allowed evil its time for His better purpose of saving man. Be prepared to suffer for your Lord, but His promise of heaven will be your triumph with Him." Finally, I saw an ancient man from an early civilization. Jesus said: ***"Before man came to be, I could see ahead how I would offer Myself as a man for your redemption. I did not preempt man's free will but I did foresee the events as they followed My plan of salvation. Know, My children, I am with you always and I will never leave you since I have shown My love by dying for you on the cross. Cling to My ways, My people, and you will enjoy the place I have reserved for you."***

Thursday, January 12, 1995:

After Communion, I saw Maria E. and she said: ***"May the Lord keep us together."*** I then saw a covered wagon full of possessions being carried around. Jesus said: ***"Many of you, My people, are dragging around a lot of excess baggage with the love of your material possessions. By letting things get in your way, you have a hard time keeping focused on Me. Remember, it is on Me you should depend and not your creature comforts. You are called to suffer and train for heaven in this life. It is not a place to waste your time on resolute living. Your time is too precious to waste on pleasures with no spiritual meaning. Instead, direct your prayers to changing your life to one that closely follows My way of the cross, for it is My way that will lead you to heaven, not the ways of the world."***

Friday, January 13, 1995:

After Communion, I saw a person standing with a light such that it cast a long shadow behind them. Jesus said: ***"My people, you do not always realize the effect one person has on others. When someone dies, it is in your reflection that you realize what good or evil influence that person has had. You, My friends, by your very living out each day in your daily contacts can be a tremendous influence of good in the world. Take My word and spread it by your example to all who will listen and notice your message. My love I give to you is all consuming and never offen-***

sive. Live your lives with love for all those around you. This love will be contagious and spread to all those who see you. You may not realize this but others will learn from you and peace will be increased by your very presence. So take care, My children, to give good example to others since any adverse behavior will also destroy the harmony of the world."

On our way to Angie's prayer group, I received some aches and pains like a fever without the temperature. I received the word ***"Pain"*** very forcefully. Jesus said: ***"My children, you have seen how much I have suffered for you. If I ask you to suffer pain, be willing to offer it up for the expiation of sins. Be willing, also, to offer up your prayers with a regularity that will continue to perfect your love for Me."*** I then saw a vision of Jesus sitting among a bunch of folding chairs in the back of the church. It had yellow walls and a lot of light. Jesus said: ***"Would you act any different if I was in your midst in bodily form? I tell you I am always with you in My Blessed Sacrament, so be always prepared with Confession to greet Me and keep your soul ready. I shall come again at the appointed time to judge all mankind."***

Saturday, January 14, 1995:

After Communion, I was looking up out of a hole like a grave and there was a ring of people around the top of the hole looking down. They were all dressed in white robes. Jesus said: ***"The transition from your earthly life to that of heaven will be much like when Levi was called to follow Me. He gave up everything to follow Me as each of you at death will have to sever your ties with all your earthly comforts and pains, but once you experience My deep peace and profound love, you will never want to return to earth. You do not realize the joyful life which awaits you. If you keep yourself in My ways, even though painful at the time, you will more than make up for it when you see My glory. So do not fear death, My friends, it will be a release of your bondage in your body. Look forward and desire My day with great hope and faith."***

Sunday, January 15, 1995:

After Communion, I saw a blue sky with a few high clouds. Then some dark clouds moved in and there were pillars of rock growing out of the earth towards the sky. Jesus said: ***"The clouds***

of an evil time are growing on the horizon. The appointed time of the Anti-Christ draws near. This will be a time of unparalleled evil as yet to be seen. You will see the demons come up out of the ground from hell to roam and torment those on the earth, but fear not, My faithful, believe in Me and call on Me for your strength to endure this time. All those who are with Me will be protected, but those who are not, will be claimed by the demons as their own. That is why it is important now to prepare with your Rosaries, crosses and holy water on hand. After a short time, My friends, you will see My victory over evil and you will be welcomed into an era of My peace. Pray much, My people, for your deliverance."

Later, at church, I saw an agonizing Jesus hanging forward on His cross in bitter pain. In another scene I could feel myself being pushed to the edge of a cliff and then time stopped and I did not go over. Jesus said: ***"My son, you have had a little taste of pain in your sickness. Know that your future trials will test you as well. Remain faithful to Me no matter what may befall you. I am ever present to protect you from harm. Even though Satan's forces may seem to be winning, I will come at the most timely moment to take victory away from the evil forces. You will see My triumphant glory sweep forward guided by My Archangel, Michael, as the demons will then be thrown into hell and sealed for a millennium. My people, I am making you ready for this last Battle of Armageddon so you may see the fulfillment of My promise. Do not give heed or any credit to the Anti-Christ for all that he will do. All will be a testing time which I will give you strength to come through. You will see My glory and your life thereafter will be ever fulfilled in My love."***

Monday, January 16, 1995:

After Communion, I at first saw an hour glass which turned into a volcano, that was spewing out rocks. Jesus said: ***"My people, you will see an ever increasing number of signs as the end times draw near. Many will suffer calamities that will befall you. You will see earthquakes and increasing volcanic activity as the evil time approaches. Some chastisements will occur in areas of greater sin to give witness to the people's behavior. Even though there will be awesome omens, take heart, My people, and keep***

faith in Me, for My coming draws closer as well. Pray much in this time that My protection will see you through your worst fears."

Later, at church, I could see myself being dragged through a muddy aisle and feeling very humbled. Jesus said: ***"My son, I am asking everyone to carry their crosses to Calvary, no matter how impossible the task may appear. My love wants to envelop you with an understanding of your tasks on earth. If you wish to be perfected, then treat this life as one of sorrow and not looking for success and consolation on earth. In this way you may spend every moment in My service. If you are healthy, help your neighbor in his need. Even those you dislike, suffer for Me by being kind to them. When you are sick, offer your pain and suffering for sinners. Even though there are pleasures in your life, the more you suffer for Me, the more merit and spiritual advancement will be yours. Come to Me always, My little ones, and you will see doing everything for Me will join Me in My one Divine Love. This is the level of love I wish all of you to come to."***

Tuesday, January 17, 1995:

After Communion, I saw some black fibers woven together as a rug draped over a chair. I saw a view as near dawn with a light near the horizon but dark over the land. Finally, I saw a stairway to heaven with this black rug all the way up. I felt myself being drawn up the stairs effortlessly and passing the moon by. It was an exhilarating feeling. Jesus said: ***"Peace be to you, My people. Do not be alarmed at what you are seeing. If it be in My will, I may take some people to a safe refuge during the trial. I have told you I would protect you. Did you have any doubts? Know that indeed those faithful to Me will in fact be protected. Their souls shall not be taunted by the demons, for I will assign their angels to be vigilant in their protection. This is why I have told you often to be in close union with your guardian angel during the evil days. Seek My help and your angel's help and you will not be fearful. I will grant you My peace until My triumph comes."***

Later, at church, I saw a circling flame approach me. Then I saw some raging fires over the land. Again with no fire, I saw the ashes of what once were someone's possessions. Jesus said: ***"My people, I am again showing you the futility of placing your trust in your possessions instead of Me. I am the one you should have***

your focus on at all times. I am the one who provides you with what you need both spiritually and physically. Remember, you are here only for a short time compared to eternity for your final destination. Would you not prepare now for where you want to be after this life? You will see as time goes on how precious little time you have. Spend it wisely, My friends, in My service. It is better to build up heavenly treasures than relying on your comforts and pleasures in this world. Everything here is fleeting and will not last but a moment in time. Do not be surprised if even the things of this earth are taken from you since you have no authority over their future, so I tell you now to pray for discernment in how to lead a life directed only at bringing My Kingdom to everyone. For when you build My Kingdom, you are building your own future with Me in eternity."

Wednesday, January 18, 1995:

After Communion, I saw a young woman in need but I could not see her face. Behind her was a vision of Jesus standing with His hand on her. Jesus said: ***"I am giving you an example in this vision that you may understand how everyone of My children you help, you are helping Me as well. You must look at My human family in the big picture as My own hands and feet. As one part is in need, it is up to you to provide your loving care. As much as I reach out in love to help each of you, you must find room in your hearts to share your love with others also. In doing your acts of mercy I will see what is done in the secret of your heart's intent and reward you in My own way more than you can imagine. Continue, My friends, to take care of your brothers and sisters until the day all of you can share in My glory in heaven."***

Later, at the prayer group, I first was looking through a wheel and I saw a small motor running. Jesus said: ***"You remember how I talked to Martha and said how she was busy with many things of hospitality. You, My people, are also busy many times with this or lesser consequence and often for satisfying your pleasures or desires. I tell you still as Mary chose to spend her time loving Me, it is the same I wish of all of you, that you see the spiritual blessings as most important."*** I then saw someone going into a humble adobe house. Jesus said: ***"Make your home where your heart is.***

Welcome all those who come to you in their need. Pray with them and comfort them and you will be welcoming Me also." I saw a gold cup as one for a Mass with some wine in it. Jesus said: ***"I have drunk from the cup of sorrows that I may offer up My blood for the forgiveness of your sins. In this I give an example to you that you too may offer your suffering to help sinners. You are asked to drink of this same cup, but through your sorrows you will find life eternal with Me."*** I then saw a satellite orbiting the earth. This was followed by a scene of many asteroids floating through space. Jesus said: ***"I have sent many messages to you through various prophets asking you to reform your lives especially concerning abortion and killing. Man has not heeded My warnings and yet your sins cry out for judgment. I ask you, My faithful, to lessen your chastisements with constant prayer to atone for the many sins of the world. If enough prayer is not forthcoming to counter the scales of evil, My hand may allow these heavenly objects to strike your earth. Have no fear of losing your souls, My faithful, but there may be much physical anguish."*** I saw someone getting killed with a spear, which possibly represented Cain killing Abel. Jesus said: ***"Man has been killing each other over vainglory since the time of the fall. Your wars and man's inhumanity to man has continued even in your world today. If you expect peace, you must start with peace in your own homes. Peace must be My peace and held close to your heart in order to lessen the anger of your wars. You must change your hearts if you expect men to want peace."*** I then saw a little child playing. Jesus said: ***"My heart goes out to all the little children who now more than ever deserve your protection. Pray, My people, that no harm comes to them or those perpetrators will be challenging even God's wrath. See to it these precious lives be valuable in everyone's eyes."*** I finally saw Mary come in a dim lit scene with candles on either side. I sensed she was honoring those killed by abortion. Mary said: ***"As your Mother, I ask you to pray for all the unborn and their mothers. These poor children are being badly misled by Satan and those in your society trying to enforce their warped mentality on others. Pray to educate these future mothers to the proper value of bringing these gifts of life to term. I am taking your prayers of petition to Jesus and I am giving you***

my blessing. It is your Rosaries I need many of to fight the advances of Satan against your people. Stand and fight in the battle of good and evil which is coming to a head at this time."

Thursday, January 19, 1995:

After Communion, I saw Maria E. and she said: ***"Lift up your Lord."*** I then saw a vision of graduates from school in their graduation gowns, but I could not see their faces or above their shoulders. Jesus said: ***"You, My friends, are students of life and are striving to know more about Me. Do not try to laud it over others that you are smarter or have more gifts than another. No matter how much you learn, you can still learn more. So be humble in life to your fellowman and give good example to others, never insulting them or questioning their intelligence. Do evangelize others of My word if they are open to hear. Be careful of your own failings and pray much to keep close to Me and you will be rich in My blessings."***

Friday, January 20, 1995:

After Communion, I saw a vision of a nun and it was St. Theresa. She said: ***"Yes, my son, the Lord has sent me to help you in your spiritual life. No matter what demands are made of you, you must keep your balance in regard to your time management. Give the Lord His proper time for prayer and communication and if you are having difficulties, remember to call on His help. Continue to develop patience in your activities, especially with those around you. Do not be worried or prideful that you will not always accomplish what you desire. Many times humans try to do more than they are able. The main lesson is not to lose your focus on God no matter what earthly demands come to you. Dedicate your prayer time and stick to a strict regimen."***

Later, at church, I saw jets of fire separate from a rocket. I was then traveling free in space with little motion. I again came upon some asteroids that took on a reddish brown color. Jesus said: ***"My people, you are witnessing the events as the great chastisement will come. I will call My faithful to a safe refuge before My triumph comes to purify the earth. You will see parts of heaven will fall to wipe clean all those unworthy to go before the Lamb of***

God. I will then renew the earth and you will see the glory of My triumph. After this time, the faithful will be joined again on earth for an era of peace. All who live to see My day, will rejoice always and give thanks they were chosen to be with Me. It is to give you hope that I show you these events. All will come to be in My time, but it is coming soon. Pray much, My people, to fulfill My tasks for you in this time. Do not waste your time on non-spiritual things."

Saturday, January 21, 1995:

After Communion, I saw the outside walls of a church and a priest was standing in his Mass vestments. Jesus said: ***"I tell you, My people, pray for your priests. Encourage them in their work and support them for they need your help. My priest sons need to stay close to Me to be sincere in their work and obedient to My will. Your priests are important to you since they bring Me to the faithful in the sacraments. They are the spiritual lifeblood for My faithful. Pray also for vocations in a land which desperately needs more priests. It is only through prayer and your turning around that more vocations will be allowed."***

Later, at Nocturnal Hour, I saw a woman kneeling in prayer in candlelight. Jesus said: ***"It is possible, My people, that some of you will soon be without your electricity. As you remember your previous experience, you can see how frail your precious society is and how reliant you are on your electricity. Put your trust more in Me, for your things will fail you when you need them most. They are passing away and you will have to answer before Me in the end with no one else's help. You must see your heavenly gifts and treasures are more worth saving than all the things you could buy on this earth. Realize, My friends, that you are in spiritual warfare, so pray for My strength to help you endure it."***

Sunday, January 22, 1995:

After Communion, I saw a vision of children with their parents in the pews of the church. The next scene was a row of empty pews to represent those that were not yet born. Jesus said: ***"My people, as much as you either deny it or not there is a battle of good and evil going on. The powers of those who defy My law are advocating abortion. This, as I have told you before, is one of the***

most serious sins man can commit—the taking of life. You can understand I have a plan for each soul conceived in the womb. To treat this lightly is the devil at work. Those who would thwart My plans for these lives in essence are doing battle with Me. Do not listen to the evil one's cunning in committing abortions for convenience or any other reason. Pray, My people, you will understand My ways and not violate any life. I am the giver of life and I am the one to call souls to Me at My appointed time. The cry of this injustice is the biggest price of sin over your country today. Wake up, America, before it is too late or My justice will visit you in ongoing chastisements. You cannot violate My love and My law without expecting some retribution. I will not let this continue much longer."

Later, at church, I saw a huge tidal wave come up and envelop New York City. It seemed to be higher than most of the buildings. The Lord led me to believe this was during the Great Chastisement. Jesus said: ***"This time of year marks the anniversary of your allowing abortion in your country. This is a sad testimony on your country, yet few realize the importance of this issue and most do not want to fight this injustice. I tell you lawmakers and judges will be held accountable twice as much for being able to overturn these laws and doing nothing to stop it. You people are concurring in this act of killing by your inaction and will also be held liable. Unless you are willing in public to stand up and defend My laws, I will not witness for you before My Father. You must be more active in deed and prayer to try and bring this injustice to an end. You will be seeing more chastisements for not heeding My words. I will continue to bring you to your knees until you acknowledge My law and My will. I love you, My people, but justice must be done."***

Monday, January 23, 1995:

After Communion, I saw spots of white light center on different people at Mass as if the Spirit of the Lord came down as they received Him. Jesus said: ***"My people, I want you to see that My spirit rests upon each of you since you all belong to Me. I am showing you this so you will realize the value of each human soul and why each soul is so precious to Me. I ask you to recognize this gift of life and give it its rightful respect in all of its***

forms even to the unborn. Each soul is made to My image and likeness and is an extension of My ongoing creation. See the reason therefore in the evil of abortion or any killing. Pray, My people, that you understand My love and share it with each other instead of killing each other."

At church, I could see very ornate pictures and lanterns like those seen at the foot of the Cross in the Holy Sepulcher Church in Jerusalem. Jesus said: ***"My people, I wish to bring you a message of comfort but also one of duty. I call on you, My people, to look on Me in the crucifix and try to understand the way of the cross. I ask each of you to take up your cross and follow Me. Follow the path which leads you to Me on Calvary. Pray, My people, that you will keep your eyes fixed on Me so you will not lose your way. Do not be distracted or follow other paths which the world calls you to. Instead stay on the straight and narrow path which will lead you to your destiny with Me in heaven. You may suffer here a short time since you must place your will at My service, but as you will see, following My will for you is the best you can hope for in this life. So give yourself over to Me willingly and you can share in the peace and joy of My love. Keep close to Me in My Eucharist and I will hold you close to My bosom. It is that deep love and committment which I search for in every one of My faithful souls."***

Tuesday, January 24, 1995:

After Communion, I saw someone's neck and they were wearing a crucifix and a scapular. Jesus said: ***"My children, I come to you and ask you to recognize Me in the symbol of My cross. Wear My crucifix, My friends, as an outward belief in My saving act for all mankind. By wearing this sign of My love, it will be a protection for you from all the demons. Have it blessed by a priest as well. Again, I ask you to wear My Mother's scapular as well. In this way her mantle will protect you also from Satan's attacks. She has promised you, you will be protected from hell if you keep your allegiance to Me through her. I mention these sacramentals because they will be even more important in the coming trial. Use the Rosary and these sacramentals, My friends, and you will have spiritual armor against the evil time of tribulation."***

Later, at church, I saw a wide river covered with snow. This was a dividing line between the evil people and the righteous. Jesus said: *"My people, as the time of the trial draws near, you will see a polarization of good and evil people. As evil will appear to gain strength with the coming of the Anti-Christ, My faithful will need to gather in groups for protection and hiding. You will see things gradually come to a head at the Battle of Armageddon. At that time, My angels will win the battle and all the demons and their prizes of evil souls will be cast off the earth to hell and the earth will be purified. Prepare now for this time since the evil in power will cause much grief to My faithful. Draw on My protection at this crucial time and avoid all worldly cares and comforts. There will be great temptations by the demons to join their ranks. Do not be misled and keep close to My will in prayer. It is only by your steadfastness to Me that will allow you to get through the tribulation. Pray and trust in My power and you will be overjoyed with My triumph over evil."*

Wednesday, January 25, 1995: (Conversion of St. Paul)

After Communion, I could see an outline of the earth and it was all aglow around the edge with a white and blue light. Then gradually I saw a blue light come from the earth and it traveled into space and appeared as Mary coming to greet me. Mary said: *"You are witnessing the glory of my coming triumph when the earth will be renewed. It will begin as my foot crushes the head of Satan and He will be held captive for an era of peace. This is an exciting time for all of you to live since you will live to see the promise I have foretold would come at the end of the present age. Evil will be vanquished and God's true peace will reign once again over the earth. No longer will the effects of evil restrain you from giving all your love and praise to God. For those who remain faithful to my Son's word, your reward will be well worth any suffering you may endure. Keep close to my Son at all times and soon you will experience His glory."*

Later, at the prayer group, I saw some green water in a fish tank. Jesus said: *"I will make you fishers of men for My Kingdom. This is an acceptable time to come to Me in repentance. Those who are led by the spirit, go out to those who are hungry for My word. Let them receive My grace through your instrumentation."* I then saw some fuel tanks with flames and black smoke eminating from them. Jesus said: *"You will see an increase in accidental fires*

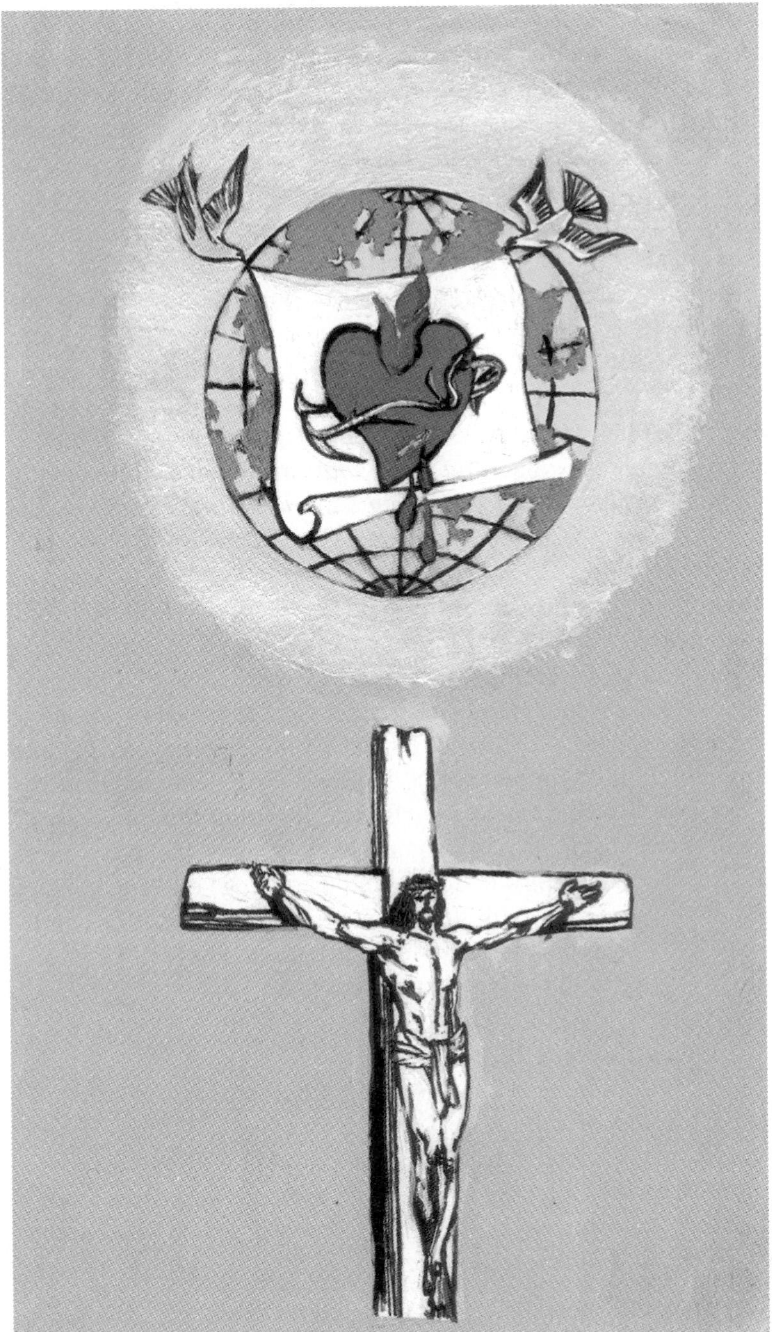

partly as a chastisement since many sins are being committed, but few come to Me for forgiveness. I tell you, My people, unless you admit to being a sinner and ask forgiveness, you cannot be My disciple." I saw an amusement park with many rides and games. Jesus said: ***"I want you to pray more, My children, and not be so concerned with having to have recreation for all your free time. Every moment you can spend with Me in meditation brings you that much closer to Me in heaven. Concern yourself more with pleasing Me than yourself."*** I then saw a king sitting on a throne and soon he turned into a statue. This represented the false king you will seek in the Anti-Christ. Jesus said: ***"I am giving you a warning before the tribulation. Do not follow the Anti-Christ or honor him in any way. He is part of the father of lies and he will have a strong power of suggestion. Pray and avoid him and especially his false peace. Only I can bring true peace, he will be an imposter."*** I saw a vision of Mary come slowly before me. Mary said: ***"Peace be to you, my children. I am coming to give a message of hope. I will go before my Jesus to intercede for Al's father, since I have heard your prayers. Continue to pray for His soul."*** I saw several flames flickering on some candles. Jesus said: ***" I am asking you, My people, to pray a constant vigil of prayer to atone for the many sins of your world. Especially, keep intentions in your prayers to atone for the many abortions being committed. Pray more people will come to their senses and stop this carnage."*** I finally saw what looked like some men walking on the moon. I was led to believe our spirit bodies would take refuge either near or on the moon during the earth's purification. I asked Jesus for a confirmation of this as being true and He gave me an image of Our Lady of Guadalupe with the moon under her feet.

Thursday, January 26, 1995:

After Communion, I saw Maria E. lifting up her hands and she said: ***"Be joined with your Lord."*** I then saw a gold medallion with someone's body struck as a raised image. Jesus said: ***"The world measures success in gold and money and possessions. I measure your success by My standards which are opposed to that of the world. I look into the heart at the intentions of your deeds.***

A good person reaches out to others not worrying over one's self inconveniences, but is happy to help even with financial help. An evil person is one who is selfish and inflicts hardships on others as they spew deeds from the evil intent in their hearts. Live your lives in My service and your neighbor's and all good things will be given you besides."

Friday, January 27, 1995:

After Communion, I saw concentric circles of increasing darkness. I then saw a long porchway on a big building and someone was running in fright. Jesus said: ***"My people, you will be entering a time of persecution, a time when you will no longer be able to walk about freely. As the evil days close in on you, you will be sought out for torture or martyrdom. Do not worry what you are to say or where you are to go for I will provide for you. You will be asked to give up your possessions and the things of this world so you can serve Me only. This will be a time when you will need to put your full trust in Me and My word. It will be a time as in the Exodus when the Lord provided food, shelter and the direction for travel. Pray now to build up your spiritual courage, but live in hope for the day you will see My glory."***

Later, at church, I first saw some wooden fences at night. In the distance were some lights as torches and people were in search of someone. Jesus said: ***"My people, have no fear even in the trial of evil to come. I will be at your side guiding you and showing you the way. No longer can you rely on your own devices. Instead, you must place your full trust and faith in Me. In doing so, you will find peace even at a time of turmoil. For when you have Me with you, you have all your soul desires. If you should be tortured or martyred, offer it up to Me. It will be only a short time that evil will have its appointed time. I will protect the souls of all My faithful till the time of My victory. At that time, death and evil will lose their sting. If you keep close to Me in prayer, this will be your foundation of protection. Keep focused on Me each day, then all your work will be easy. Share My hope and peace with others and explain My promise of good will to all those who listen to My word."***

Saturday, January 28, 1995:

After Communion, I saw Our Lord standing there and then I saw seven people materialize from the same space. There was an arrow moving from right to left. Jesus said: ***"I am with you always, My people. I have given you prophets even in your own day to realize My help for you is ongoing. In all of your cares be focused on Me only so that you will follow My will for you at all times. You must have faith in where I will lead you. At the same time, you must make yourselves good examples to others in leading them to Me. You are placed next to those souls who need your help to inspire them to follow Me. I use all of My faithful as instruments to spread My Gospel. They see in you pillars of spiritual strength to give them hope in My word. Pray My friends to guard your interior spiritual life so you can continue to help the spiritual poor."***

Later, at church, I pictured myself in a boat and I was using both oars to move. Jesus said: ***"My people, you need to be consistent in your words to Me. Strive to keep My promises and I will keep the promise I have made with you. It is important to count the costs to give yourself over to Me. For those who understand the beauty of My peace, no explanation is needed. For those who do not want to give up their control over life, no explanation will be possible. You either believe in Me and love Me or you will reject Me in favor of these temporary comforts. If you could see and understand My glory, it may be enough to persuade some to change their desire to want to be with Me. Blessed are those, though, who believe on faith alone and do not need to see Me to believe. In any event, those who choose Me will receive a just reward. For I long to bring everyone into My Kingdom since I wish to share My love with all of humanity, but I will not force Myself against your will. You must choose Me freely or I will not enter your house and soul. Pray to fully understand the gravity of your eternal life's decision. Being in heaven should be everyone's desire since I have created you to love, serve and adore Me. Coming to Me should be your soul's goal."***

Sunday, January 29, 1995:

After Communion, I saw a man get up before a huge crowd of people to read the Word of God. Jesus said: ***"My people, I give*** *you many prophets to spread My word of love, joy and hope. I ask you, my son, to go forward and proclaim what I have given you. Be not afraid to tell those awaiting My word. Take courage in a time that is not always listening to Me. Through you as an instrument, they can see your sincerity and believe My word is coming through your hand as you have prayed. Be confident in Me that I will give you the right words to say at the proper time. I am rich in graces and I wish to bestow them on all My faithful. Have them know I wait to hear their response to My invitation to know Me better. Pray, My children, and keep listening for My words of love."*

Later, at church, I saw a very old and battered wooden house and then I saw a long corridor that was very dark. Jesus said: *"Many times I have preached to you about the uselessness of owning possessions on earth. They would serve you better if you gave them away to the poor. By selfishly hanging on to them or piling up more wealth, you will be doing nothing toward gaining your salvation. If you do not discard your possessions, they will soon be taken anyway by the evil people who will soon roam your world. Look to Me My people and see how My love reaches out to you. See that the heavenly things should be the most sought after. Love your neighbor and witness to My love with your prayer and your praise before My Blessed Sacrament. By showing Me you truly love Me in all you do, you will be satisfying My desire to bring Me closer to your heart. It is everlasting love I wish to bestow on all of you that drives Me to seek you all out to the last hour of hope. I have faith in you, My people, that you will keep Me in your heart. I know your love burns and yearns for Me. I am giving you hope, My friends, that your trial will not last much longer."*

Monday, January 30, 1995:

After Communion, I saw a map of the Pacific Ocean including China, Korea and the Japanese area. Jesus said: *"My message this day is an ominous one since the vision of this part of the world (Asia) will affect all. The earth will shudder from the events of this region. Do not be overly concerned but be forewarned as the events I have spoken to you about often, will be quickening. All will occur according to My plan as the events will soon culminate in My victory over evil. Know that an end to this age is not*

far off. Many have looked forward to this time. My justice will come and My love for you will fulfill all of My promises."

Later, at church, I saw a woman's arm with a gold bracelet on it. Then I saw a scene of an ornate fireplace with a huge fire in it. Jesus said: ***"My people, see in this picture of fire a means for purification. In order to purify metals a strong fire must be used to burn off the salts and debris. So it is with you, My friends, each of you must be purified before you can be received into heaven. All your earthly desires and cravings for wealth and fame must be taken out of your heart and replaced with a new fire. A flame of faith must burn in your hearts free from all earthly cares. Once you have focused on My love, the desires of your soul will crave to be with the love who created you. It is when your love becomes selfless and you lose your old selfish ways, that is the love I am seeking most. I am jealous of each of your souls until you can give them freely to Me. It is when you have raised yourself in love to Me that your love melts into My one infinite love. It is then that you will truly experience Me in heaven. So be perfected by your love for Me in all you do, then life will be glorious and new."***

Tuesday, January 31, 1995:

After Communion, I saw a huge circular clock which changed from a vertical position to lying down. I was walking around it as it moved. Jesus said: ***"My people, you have been given a precious little time in your life. Use your time wisely for the most spiritual gain possible. Once it is spent you cannot retrieve it. You will see time apparently speed up as events will fall on one another. Remember to manage your time to include your prayer time and never think worldly things are more important. The care of your soul and your talking with Me is most paramount in this earthly life. See to it that your spiritual life is your first priority in life and you will indeed ready yourself for the next life."***

Later, at church, I saw Christ standing in robes with a crown. I then saw our planet as it circled the sun and there was a white glow that came all around the earth. Jesus said: ***"My people, I bring you great hope as you are nearing the dawn of a new era of peace. A new life will be awaiting My faithful. For those who have longed to see Me, you will have your wish fulfilled. You will experience love and peace beyond anything you can comprehend on earth***

presently. You will see a new dimension in spirituality which you have yet to experience. Being a part of My oneness in the divine will, you will no longer have to discern that which I desire for you to follow. You will then be doing My will intuitively without any question. You will not even contemplate your own desires but you will want to do everything to please Me. Once the earthly blinders have been removed from your heart and soul, you will understand full knowledge of Me and My love will make everything so obvious. Truth even now is still the same, yet now you have an imperfect knowledge of Me. Pray to keep strong in your blind faith and one day soon you will experience Me so deeply that you will wonder why I was so hard to understand."

Wednesday, February 1, 1995:

After Communion, I saw a man dressed like the pope wearing some kind of head piece. His face looked very sinister and resigned. Jesus said: ***"My people, I am giving you a second warning to be wary of as this evil age comes to its height. When My Pope son, John Paul II, is removed from his position, know that his replacement will signal the coming entry of the Anti-Christ. This successor will not be true to Me so be prepared for turmoil in My Church. Some will be consumed with the wine of temporary power and fame. This new leader's power will not last long since he will be smote by My angel. He is the one referred to in the Scriptures of Revelation. So be wary of his reign and do not follow him since he will be an imposter trying to lead the people astray in worshipping the Anti-Christ."***

Later, at the prayer group, I saw a witch doctor performing some kind of ritual. Jesus said: ***"As the level of evil increases, for a time you will see more satanic masses and more open worship of Satan and the coming Anti-Christ. This will be another sign to you of the time of tribulation. Pray to Me and your guardian angel to protect you from the powers of darkness."*** I then saw some people at a bar drinking. Jesus said: ***"Do not seek drugs or alcohol as a means to forget your troubles. These and other obsessions only make your life more difficult. Instead, come to Me for help and let Me walk with you through life's problems and comfort you. None of these things on earth should distract you from Me. Seek Me first and all you need will be given you."*** I saw some pictures of Valentine hearts. Jesus said: ***"It is good for you to love your neighbor as yourself. An atmosphere of love should pervade every day of your life. This will be a good preparation for the love you will see in heaven."*** I then saw a large building with open windows. Jesus said: ***"You must keep your soul open for Me to come and enter and dwell with you. As you seek Me in prayer, this will orient your heart to receive My blessings. It is through prayer that I can work spiritual miracles through you. By being open to Me, you can understand My plan and carry out My will for you."*** I saw someone typing a letter. Jesus said: ***"You have received many messages which are a training for My faithful. Share My word of Scripture and the messages with those willing to listen. Through your instrumentation, I mean to visit as many souls as possible before the tribulation."*** ("Crucifixion" decade) I then saw Our Lord suffering on the cross and He had His gaze fixed on heaven in prayer. At the same time, I saw a lot of little flames burning all around Him. Jesus said: ***"Be ready, My friends, to suffer your trials with Me, as I have suffered for you. I have given you an example to purify yourselves and make reparation for your sins and those sins of others. As you understand how sin so offends Me, please pray to counter the great evil around you."*** Finally, I saw Mary waiting patiently for her children to listen to her. Mary said: ***"Pray, pray, my children, for all those experiencing the increasing chastisements. Man may try to explain away all of the damaging events, but know it is my Son's hand of justice which is visiting you now. Sin is so prevalent, I can no longer hold back His hand. So I ask you to increase your prayers to restrain these punishments and help others to stop sinning with no regard to hurting my Son."***

Thursday, February 2, 1995:

After Communion, I saw Maria E. with her eyes closed and she said: ***"Yes, Lord we believe."*** I then saw a picture of a pine tree with its branches pointing heavenward. Also, a picture was seen of praying hands with the fingers pointing heavenward. Jesus said: ***"There are many signs in nature and even in the human mind and body which show evidence of the creator's hand. All creation should be praising and giving glory to God in their own way. You, My people, are also a part in this thanksgiving that you***

should thank the Lord for your life and all you have been given. See, My people, that in everything you do that you direct yourself back to God since He asks for your respect."

Friday, February 3, 1995:

After Communion, I had a vision of a cemetery and there was a wooden casket that was red in color and it opened up. I then saw a woman's face and it seemed to be Mary. Jesus said: ***"You are perplexed my Son by recent events. Do not be troubled but keep My peace with you in all you do. Be not afraid to speak out and witness to My word and My Second Coming. It is important that the people hear My message. It is an opportunity to bring My word to souls who may not have any other means. The warning and the evil trial ahead is important for people to understand. These things are drawing near and it is appropriate to witness them as My Holy Spirit will lead you. Pray and keep close to Me, my son, and you will be led what to say and do."***

Later, at church, I saw the United States flag and behind it was a scene at dawn. Jesus said: ***"My people, you will see the dawn of a new age of evil."*** I then saw a picture of some fires in the streets of a city. ***"You will see fires in your streets as vandals and chaos will be striking your cities. You are seeing the demons coming up from hell as this trial of evil worsens. They literally will be seeking the ruin of souls. All those who are not close to Me or thinking of Me or their guardian angels will be subject to the demon's torture and suggestion for sin. This will be a time when you will need to trust in My grace for you. You must rely on Me to bring you through this short struggle. After My triumph you will glory in the revelation of the renewed earth. Life then will be the true peace I alone can bring. It will be marvelous to behold and well worth your fight against evil in the trial. This time will sift the true faithful loyal to Me against all odds. Remember to stay with Me through the fight even if you must suffer persecution and death. It will be your faithfulness that will win your salvation. Stay close to Me in My sacraments and My Mother's Rosary."***

Saturday, February 4, 1995:

At the Hotel Hilton in Caracas, Venezuela, after Communion, I saw Our Lady come in white and blue and she wore a crown.

Mary said: ***"Come, my children, to your Mother who awaits you at my shrine of Betania. There are many places of apparition and messages and I send out graces to all who visit my holy places. Your pilgrimage is special each time you come since the spiritual blessings are always better than any material feeling. Be sincere and humble when you come and keep my Son, Jesus, always close to your heart. I bring you closer to my Son so you may see how to follow His will for you. Give me your petitions and offerings and I will place them before my Son. You must have faith in what you pray for and my Son will bless you in your need. Come, my children, and do not hold back your feelings but pour out your heart and troubles to me. I, as your Mother, will comfort you and lead you on a path to please my Son."***

Sunday, February 5, 1995:

At the Betania Shrine I saw a picture of Our Lord on the cross. The scene then changed to Our Lord preaching to the people. Jesus said: ***"Beg the harvest master to send laborers for the harvest of souls. I have called many to My service, but many walk away without helping Me. Even now I must call other bearers of My message of love to train the people and prepare them for the evil age. I do not want to leave My people orphans, to the wolves in the demons who will torture those on the earth. Pray, My people, to become one with My word. See the love in My arms as I reach out to protect you. You must give up your worldly pursuits and strive only to do those things spiritual. In the end it is most important to direct your spiritual lives to Me since I am your salvation. I am the one who brings you My heavenly bread which unites you to Me in My oneness. Believe in My word and come to Me now. You will not have much more time to choose since I will come in judgment shortly at My Second Coming. Pray constantly, My faithful remnant, and you will share in My glory in heaven."***

Monday, February 6, 1995:

At the Betania Shrine after Communion, I saw Our Lady come down an aisle with lights all along it. As her face came closer to me I then began to see the faces of many people. Mary said: ***"My children, I am happy to greet you here at my shrine of Betania. You are seeing in your vision all the faces of people united in my*** *mantle of protection. You are seeing also how all my children are united with the one Body of my Son, Jesus. This Mystical Body includes everyone. It is you who choose to be a part of His Body or reject Him, but you are part of His Body embraced by His love. He can never deny you because you are a part of Him and He cannot deny Himself. So, also, when one part of His Body is ill or in trouble, He shares in your pain. He asks you when you are in need to come to Him with your troubles and petitions of prayer. If it be in His will, He will answer your prayer to the best spiritual benefit for that soul. Have faith and trust in Him, for the way He answers your prayer will be even more glorious than you could hope for. Pray, my children, and stay close to both of us through your daily Rosaries."* Note: Maria received us for five hours at her summer home.

Later, before the Blessed Sacrament I saw a picture of a blue globe and it emanated a great light. Jesus said: ***"My people, I feel the love from your hearts reaching out to Me in the Blessed Sacrament. You are deeply in love with Me and I reward you in many ways for your faithfulness. I love you dearly, My beautiful souls, for you are very close to My heart. I know that you are in earnest to live your lives just to follow My will. In the vision I am showing you My triumph in the renewed earth. You will see My promise fulfilled when I restore the earth to its former beauty before the fall of Adam and Eve. This will be your joyous peace which I will share with My faithful souls. This is My best message of hope in the face of the evil days which you must still endure for a time. Please see that living each day to carry out My will is the best you can do to please Me. When your will walks with mine, you will see the beauty and harmony I meant for all creation to share. When you share My love in your interior life, you will have no fear of any of the events that will come. For all is in My plan and your acceptance touches My heart with a joy of satisfaction."***

Tuesday, February 7, 1995:

At the Coromoto Shrine Chapel after Communion, I at first saw Christ on the Cross. I then saw a picture of Mary holding the Child Jesus and caressing Him. Mary said: ***"My children, I come to advise you on the sin of pride. You must realize it is the most subtle of sins if you praise yourself before my Son. Understand,*** *my children, if you do not consider yourselves sinners, you cannot require my Son's forgiveness of your sins. Again, if you do not see your sin, you will not require my Son's redeeming act of salvation for you on the cross. Do not worry about your status on earth, or how successful you are, or how much money you have. In the end, this will count for nothing at the judgment. Instead, love my Son and see that without Him you could do nothing. It is His grace which brings all you have. So ask my Son's forgiveness for all your iniquities and understand how you must ask His help to perfect yourself spiritually. When you see my Son's love for you in your life, put your trust in Him to save your soul. It is through love of God and neighbor that you will be saved, not by love of self only."*

Wednesday, February 8, 1995:

At Merida Cathedral I saw an entrance gate which opened up into a beautiful cemetery. I then saw a beautiful glow all over the cemetery as the spirits of all those who had died in the faith rose heavenward. There was a beautiful feeling of peace and joy. Jesus said: ***"This vision is one of beauty and one of hope for all My faithful. All those who have endured hardship and have professed My word will receive their reward with Me in heaven. Anything you will go through is nothing in the face of My promise which awaits My faithful. You will become a part of My true love. You will be in ecstasy at My sight eternally, for you will experience My beatific vision. How could you consider any other choice, but being with Me forever? All your soul could ever desire or imagine will be fulfilled in the instant of your spirit's release from the shackles of this life. You have such beauty of My love awaiting you. Pray, My faithful, and keep close to My heart. You will experience love and peace as an integral part of My being. No longer will you have any more earthly cares or temptations. You will praise Me and be in awe of My glory. Your spiritual life will be forever with your Savior."***

Thursday, February 9, 1995:

At the Church of the Sacred Heart (Fr. Moreta's) in Venezuela, I saw Maria Esperanza praying and she said: ***"Be with me and Jesus."*** I saw a picture of empty churches. Then I saw a vision of tunnels and darkness in the tunnels. Jesus said: ***"My people, why can you not attend My Mass? Many are claiming to believe in God, but few attend regularly. Are you more concerned with your materialism than Me? Must you rush around and spend your precious time with earthly pursuits only? You must understand how My call goes out to all of you to come to Me and drink of My blessings and graces. You now see how some of the poor are so helpless, yet they are rich in faith. You too, in the coming days will be stripped of your possessions and you will be forced to choose between faith in My Name or that of the world. Once you can rid your heart and soul of the loves of that which is earthly, only then will you have room in your hearts to receive Me. You must prepare a place for Me if you expect to be spiritually purified. It is only when you can give your whole self over to Me, that you will be ready for entering My Kingdom. So perfect yourself in everything you do and give all over to Me, so that your faith in Me will be complete."***

Friday, February 10, 1995:

At the Cathedral in Maracay (Blessed Mother Mary of St. Joseph's incorrupt body), I saw a town of foreign faces and then I saw a huge stadium with an empty chair. The Anti-Christ was being praised like the admiration given to Simon Bolivar. Jesus said ***"My people, I bring you a message of hope. Do not be fearful or give homage to the evil one. This is not meant to scare you, but it is meant to be a test. You all must be purified of the desires of earthly things. You will see an appointed time for evil come upon you. All who are faithful to Me will be protected spiritually. Many of My faithful will be tortured and killed, but remain faithful to My name. My warning is offering you a choice as I have mentioned before. Choose Me or the world. Do not worry about your relatives. Pray for them to choose wisely and all will be treated equally. All must freely choose Me and accept Me if they are to be saved. Time is short, since after My warning evil will have a stronger power, but the time will be shortened to save My elect. If you do not ask My help, you will be surely lost. If you do not accept Me as ruler of your life, you cannot enter My Kingdom. Pray, My children, I want to save all of you. Come forward to Me and open your heart. This is all I ask of you. You will see in time,***

My triumph will then purify the earth of all evil. Only then will you all be called back to witness My glory on a renewed earth. My love for you is everlasting. Continue in your prayer and fasting to give Me honor and to strengthen you for these coming days. Have hope in Me always and do not be fearful. My glory awaits you and My arms are always open to receive you."

(At the Convent at Los Teques -The Miracle of the Eucharist) I saw Our Lord being nailed to the cross. Then I saw His head bleeding with the crown of thorns and a lance piercing His side. This hole in His side became closer and closer until I was absorbed into His wound. At one point, I saw a jaw of vicious sharp teeth as a ravenous animal approached me representing the devil. It was then taken away. Jesus said: ***"My people, My message today is one of suffering. I have gone before you to give you an example in My suffering. As I have suffered, so you must suffer, if you would be My disciple. I tell you to prepare especially before My warning. Give up taking pleasure in your earthly comforts. Instead, offer up your sufferings and penances for your loved ones, so they may come to Me with repentant hearts. I ask you to make many penances of fasting and prayer to make reparation for sins and for the conversion of sinners. This is an important time not to waste, but offer up all you do to My Sacred Heart. Be willing to suffer for Me all that I ask of you out of love. It is your perfect love for Me that I desire since this will be your salvation. Love one another and pray for the spiritual health of all My souls."***

Saturday, February 11, 1995: (Our Lady of Lourdes feast day)

In Betania, after Communion, a lady physically gave me a statue of Our Lady. I saw Our Lady in many glimpses of different positions and dress. Then I saw a beautiful garden with much green vegetation. Mary said: ***"Good morning, my children, I bring you my light in the sun after the rain of suffering. I am here, your Mother, waiting to receive you and encourage you in your faith in my Son. I give you my water in the spring as your protection from evil spirits. You must reach a state in your life where material things have no value to you. You must give your heart and soul over to me and I will present you before my Son. I will lead you to Him so that you will be perfected. I love you my people and I will bring you my Son's spiritual comforts which are more***

meaningful than any earthly comforts. Believe in me and pray my Rosary as often as possible and you will grow closer to my Son. Keep searching, my children, for a deeper understanding of my Son —He will bring you to your spiritual fulfillment as your reward. All the faithful will enjoy my Son's peace and love both now and after my triumph. At that time, your soul will burst forth with a joy and praise of God you cannot imagine."

(Night at the chapel in the hotel in Caracas) At first I saw Jesus hanging and suffering on the cross. Then it seemed that the

cross was rising upward to heaven. I then saw Jesus laid out in the tomb and finally, I saw Him arise from the dead in radiant glory. Jesus said: ***"My people, I have kept My promise from the time of the fall that I would come to redeem all of mankind. Through My death on the cross, I have freed you from your sins. If you would come forward with a contrite heart and ask My forgiveness of your sins, surely you will be healed, for I am the healer of all broken hearts. Please see the grace that awaits you in Confession and My Eucharist. You cannot survive spiritually without My sacraments. They are the food of the soul which will nourish you and heal your sins. Be close to Me in prayer and visits to Me in the Blessed Sacrament. Those who seek to be one with Me will find their consolation with Me in paradise. Know that I love you and I will forgive you. Do not stay away from Me out of fear, but come to Me with your burdens and I will refresh you. Stay with Me always in all you do and communicate with Me daily. You will see My glory in a short time. Be ever faithful."***

Monday, February 13, 1995:

After Communion, I saw a long cylindrical tube which seemed to lengthen to a considerable distance. There was some rotation inside and a movement in things at the end of the tunnel. Jesus said: ***"My people are always in search of signs. Yeah, I have given you many signs of My Second Coming, yet still you do not believe and understand. You will see a sign that will be hard to deny and it will be a supernatural event. My children, I love you and I will go to the last minute to try and save all of you from your false gods and idol worship. You will see that I am the Lord over everything and you cannot ignore My effect on your lives. Come to Me, My people, and prepare with prayer and the sacraments, or your souls will grow so stony cold that you will be unable to return to Me. I wait patiently for your conversion, but each sinner must come to Me freely asking for forgiveness of their sins. Unless you worship Me only, you cannot come into My Kingdom."***

Later, at church, I could see myself drifting into a dark space. There were several small point sources of light shining down on the earth. This appeared as a light of protection during the evil days. Jesus said: ***"I will send My angels to guide and protect you during the tribulation. You will see My grace of protection en-***

velop you and make you Mine. Then the evil one will claim those who have rejected Me. Even though these days will be a trial, know that I will never leave your side. Cling to your Redeemer who has triumphed over evil once and for all on the cross. My saving blood will fall on you and wash away your sins. Keep faithful to Me by asking My help and using your sacramentals of holy water and the Rosary. These will be your signs to Me that you will accept Me and My protection. With My help ever available to you, you must have no fear of these coming events. My people, keep your love for Me and your neighbor strong, and the evil one will not be able to break this bond of unity."

Tuesday, February 14, 1995:

After Communion, I at first saw a football goal and then I saw the two hearts of Mary and Jesus intertwined. Jesus said: ***"My people, love one another as I have loved you. My infinite love wraps you close to Me as I am eager to be a part of your life in every respect. See My heart is always open to receive you. Take an example from My Mother's Immaculate Heart of love for Me. You must see Divine Love is another dimension above human love. You must come to Me in your simple earthly humility and ask to become an integral part of My being. Love Me in My Blessed Sacrament and you will have your closest experience of My love for you. To have your will one with Mine is all I ask. Walk with Me in prayer and give all your sufferings over to Me. Be at peace in all you do and keep focused on My love at all times."***

Later, at church, I saw a picture of light colored tanks. They were quickly moving into position from hiding to take over our government. This was a picture of the One-World government taking over power. Jesus said: ***"My people, it is not long that the reign of Anti-Christ will be thrust upon you. These evil men have planned a long time to bring the world under their control. I will allow a time of persecution to test the souls who are faithful to Me. There will be a military takeover of power that will send all of you into hiding for survival. They will take over your possessions and you will flee for your lives. It will appear for a while that evil has won the battle, but then the time will be shortened and My angels will carry out My triumph as the evil one's power will collapse on itself. At this last battle of good and evil,***

the evil people and the demons will be purified from this earth and cast into hell. At that time, all things will be made new as I originally had planned. You will see the Son of Man coming on a cloud to lord over the earth. At that time, the men of this age will be judged whether they are worthy of being a part of My new Kingdom on earth."

Wednesday, February 15, 1995:

After Communion, I saw a triangle representing the Trinity. Jesus said: ***"You, My people, will indeed see how your sins have offended Me. As I show you how your life has progressed, you may be enlightened to change your ways and come closer to My heart. In all I do, My children, you are the ones I care for and love. You are the ones I draw close to My heart. You must pray in earnest over these evil times for you will need My help and full trust in Me. I will lead you and protect you if you would continue to be faithful to My name. Repent, repent, My children, for your testing time draws near."***

Later, at the prayer group, I saw a statue of Our Lady in the side of a hill. Our Lady of Betania said: ***"My children, I want to receive all of you tonight, especially those who could not visit my shrine. I am your Mother at all my holy places and I come to share my graces and blessings with each of you. Continue to pray your Rosary, for this is how my people will remain united through all adversity."*** I then had a vision of Our Lady coming towards me with her arms outstretched and her heart glowing. Mary said: ***"My love reaches out to you, my children, as I desire to absorb all of you into my heart, so you can be one with my Son Jesus as I am. See my call for you as a guide to bring you to my Son who desires all of you to love Him from the bottom of your heart."*** I saw some headlights in the darkness and Jesus said: ***"You must search to be with Me at all times. You will find Me in the faces of other souls and in My Blessed Sacrament. I am not hard to find, if you desire to be with Me, but continue in your efforts to find a deeper meaning for Me in your lives."*** I was looking out from a sewer up to some huge buildings. Jesus said: ***"You will be brought low and despised by men. Fear not, for I was rejected before you. Do not fear those who mistreat you, but only fear the***

one who can send your soul into hell. It is mercy I desire and not just sacrifice." I then saw Mary holding the Infant Jesus. Mary said: ***"Our two hearts desire to be joined with your heart. Receive the blessings we bring to your prayer group this night. We love all of you dearly and I spread my mantle of protection around you."*** I saw a monstrance with the Host in it. Jesus said: ***"I invite all of you to visit Me in My Blessed Sacrament whenever it is possible. Come to Me, so I can radiate My love to you with My rays of grace. I wish to communicate My love to you more intimately by being face to face with you in My presence. Adore Me and give praise for all I have given you."*** I finally saw a picture of darkness in a cave and a dove as the Holy Spirit came to shed His light on us. The Holy Spirit said: ***"I come as the Spirit of Love to give you My blessing and guidance in the trials to come. I will lead you and show you the way, even though evil will be all around you. Keep Me close to your heart and My flame of love will always burn with you."***

Thursday, February 16, 1995:

After Communion, I saw Maria E. and she said: ***"Share Jesus with me and others."*** I saw a huge spotlight come toward me. Our Lord was on the cross right in front of the bright light. Jesus said: ***"You must witness Me publicly before men, if you expect Me to present you before the Father. As in the Gospel, man is always seeking the easy way out of every situation. It can not be this way with My disciples. I have suffered for you and you in turn must be willing to suffer for My Name. No longer can you follow earthly ways, but you must direct your will to follow My will and My ways. Follow My spiritual direction and all My glory will be shared with you."***

Friday, February 17, 1995:

After Communion, I saw the moon and it took on a different shading or a new color giving a sign. Jesus said: ***"I tell you, My people, a big event is imminent, but this is all I wish to reveal to you at this time. You must prepare with prayer and fasting. Offer up all your sufferings to Me and I will apply them to the reparation of the sins of the world. Much is needed to offset the scales***

of My justice. Soon the world will no longer doubt My presence nor My dissatisfaction with the weight of your sins. Pray constantly for My and My Mother's intentions."

Later, at the Crucifixion decade I saw a vision of St. Therese dressed in a brown garb and she was holding some red roses. She said: ***"My son, I am happy to come to you once again. You must remember that your daily Rosaries should come before any of your daily duties. Do not put your prayers off until later, since time may not be sufficient for both. Jesus has told you now is an important time for prayer. It must be constant, for much prayer is needed. In this vein then, see to it that your prayers be first before all else. You must repent and prepare for the trial which awaits you. Pray, pray, my child, for you will not always have the luxury of this time you now have."***

Saturday, February 18, 1995:

After Communion, I saw shadows on a stage and finally a man stepped forward into the light. The next scene was a glorious showing of light coming down to earth and a dove representing the Holy Spirit descended. The Holy Spirit said: ***"I am the Spirit of Love and I come to strengthen you and empower you in what to say and do at this time. We are asking you to be our ambassador of the truth. Give witness to those around you of the glory of God. This is the time most important to save souls. You cannot hide this gift of faith or do what you would like only. It is your duty now to witness Our love and grace in all you do and especially at this time of grace. Come closer to Me and accept My help in fulfilling God's plan. You and all messengers must come forward to save souls by your witness. I send My gifts and virtues upon you, to lift you all up in these coming days."***

Later, at church, I saw a map of Europe and part of Asia and Jesus said: ***"My people, I enjoin on you today that you be ever prayerful for the evil times which I have foretold to you are about to unfold. You will soon see events in the world speeded up, so that you will not understand how they can happen so quickly. I tell you to have faith in My word beyond all other pursuits. Thank you for coming this day and sharing My love with you. My people will soon understand the joy and power in My presence at the Blessed Sacrament. My children, I ask you to come to Me now***

more than ever since it may be difficult in the future to receive Me in this manner. Love one another is My message to all of you and evangelize My message of love to others. Your prayers will be lifted to Me by the angels. Your prayers are beautiful indeed and will be more so if they come straight from the heart. You cannot rest with ease just now, but rouse yourselves to follow Me every moment of every day. As your efforts are pleasing to Me, I will see them and reward you accordingly."

•

Sunday, February 19, 1995:

After Communion, I saw a crown displayed on the side and the words came ***"Your King reigns"***. Jesus said: ***"My people, you have been praying for many years in anticipation of things to come, but do not be concerned when things will happen. They will happen in My own time, when I feel the time to bring them to completion. I have warned you much to pray for this age, but do not think you will know when things shall happen. It is not important to know the dates of My events. You will surely know them when they happen. Be more concerned with your prayers and pleasing Me. That will be enough for you. Everything in My plan will come at the proper season, so live each day as one of preparation for My Second Coming."***

Later, at church, I saw a man lying in a bed with many bright lights overhead. Jesus said: ***"My people, each one of you will be appointed a time to die in this life. If you are fortunate to have a slow death, you will have time to make amends to God. This will be a time of great struggle, for it will be the devil's last attempt to steal your soul from Me. At that time, pray to Me and ask help from My Mother and the angels as well. It is at that time that you can give Me your final witness and choose to be with Me in eternity. Your whole life is culminating to make this decision. I want to walk with each of you into My Kingdom. I have prepared a place for each of My little ones. Your reward awaits all who are faithful to My Name. During life you must come to the realization that your goal awaits you at your death. Therefore, it is proper that you use your available time on earth to prepare for your eternal journey. Your time on earth is very brief, yet enough to see what glory lies ahead. Do not be like the foolish virgins who did not prepare for the master's coming. Be like the wise***

virgins and be ready so when your time comes, I will say, 'Come into My wedding feast, for you are truly one of your master's faithful servants.'"

Monday, February 20, 1995:

After Communion, I saw some cars parked in rows at night at some secret meeting. Jesus said: ***"Beware of those things that men do in secret. Those things which men do are sometimes for their own gain rather than things done for God. These are the men to fear, for they are directed more by evil than good. The plottings of men in secret are such, since they want to control the whole world for themselves. You will see an increasing separation of good and evil as the final battle will continue to build up. Have faith in Me and My word."***

Later, at church, I had a wonderful feeling as Our Lady came with all of her graces. She appeared very peaceful and just moved about slowly. She said: ***"My dear children, you have been praying and fasting so beautifully this last week. Now, I direct your attention to the beginning of my consecration prayers which foreshadow the feast of my Annunciation. Learn to perfect yourselves by making my consecration. Give all you have freely over to me so you can die to self and lose your craving for the things of this world. When you make your consecration, you are uniting yourself with me and Jesus. By perfecting yourself, you are readying yourself to receive my Son. He is the one calling you through me. He has asked me to gather all my children under my mantle, so I can gather you to meet Him at your completion of this life. Pray dearly these prayers and make each day glorious for His triumph. When all can see and understand the love of my Son, you will be a part of His peace."***

Tuesday, February 21, 1995:

After Communion, I could see feet moving forward in a line at ground level. Jesus said: ***"Follow Me in My footsteps if you expect to be My disciple. I have been rejected and despised by man because My ways are not your ways. Even though you must suffer for My Name's sake, continue in your efforts to imitate My life of love. It is in doing My will for you that you will find eternal life. This is the narrow road I ask all of you to follow and you will not***

be disappointed. Love your neighbor as yourself and work to bring souls to Me by your good example. I love you, My people, and I will always stand by you."

Later, at church, I was in a room with bright lights. Jesus said: ***"I am calling you to Me for strength against the attacks from the evil one. You must realize, when you witness for Me, that Satan will not let this go unnoticed. You must prepare now, for He will unleash every attack to bring you doubts and all manner of disturbance. Expect this and with My graces you will be at peace. You must show no fear as I am with you. I will give you confidence in what you are to say through the Holy Spirit. You must be firm in your faith and trust in Me. Your life in these events may change dramatically. You will find it harder to pray and be alone. Do not be taken up with any temptations to feel important. In all of this keep your humble spirit calm in My love. Be gracious, you have an opportunity to witness to My Name. You will receive some harassment but keep faithful to My Name. I love you so much and I want you to follow My will for you no matter what you must put up with. Cling to Me in My Eucharist. This is My witness you will always understand. My presence is always here to keep you close to My heart. Pray much, My child, and you shall have no fear."***

Wednesday, February 22, 1995: (Chair of St. Peter)

After Communion, I saw an outline of Mary come with her mantle and next to her was a picture of Pope John Paul II. Mary said: ***"You are seeing how I protect my priest son from all adversity. He is the joy of my heart and he is fulfilling the will of my Son in leading His Church. I care for him as a Mother and I help him in his tasks. This is your faith—that you follow your Pope in his leading of the faithful. Listen to his pronouncements and know that his hand is being guided by heavenly inspiration."***

Later, at the prayer group, I saw a young lady at a table and it appeared to be Sister Mary Carmine (a nun in Venezuela). Mary said: ***"I come to many of my children in vision and locution. In these days I am coming to enlighten many of the Second Coming of my Son. I have been sent as His herald and bequeath this gift to those special ones I have chosen."*** I then saw a gold horse as on a merry-go-round. Jesus said: ***"My little ones, you have worried about***

when My warning shall come. It is indeed coming soon, but keep it in perspective for when it will be. It will happen when My plan comes to fulfillment and not a day sooner." I saw a crowd in a stadium and then a picture of bread and wine. Jesus said: ***"As at the time I fed a vast crowd, I am calling all men to Me in My heavenly bread in the Eucharist. I am the life and the resurrection. You cannot come to heaven unless you come through Me. Prepare yourself spiritually so you may be more worthy to receive Me."*** I then saw a loaf of bread amongst a prayer group. Jesus said: ***"I am always in your midst where two or more are gathered in prayer. Have no fear, My friends, of coming together in prayer. Those who would discourage your praying are the same ones who need prayers the most. If you are meant to share in prayer, continue on, for at this time much prayer is needed in groups especially."*** I saw some government buildings as they were white and tall. Jesus said: ***"Pray for your leaders, that in their proceedings they will see how much I am needed in their lives. Your country's testing hangs in the balance on what actions they take. Pray they will follow My ways more than that of the world."*** I saw and felt Mary's presence. Mary said: ***"I come, My children, to give you my blessing and encourage you to do my consecration prayers."*** Finally, I saw a hard wintry scene of snow and cold. This was followed by a scene of a school gym where people were coming to seek a warm shelter. Jesus said: ***"You will see a continual testing of the elements, My little ones, for your pride will be humbled. The things you depend on are far from Me. You must see that you must depend on Me only or I will bring down your comforts. Again, I say, look to Me for your trust and not in men or things of this world."***

Thursday, February 23, 1995:

After Communion, I saw a Host on a patten on the altar and the Host seemed like it turned into flesh. I then saw Marie E. as it commemorated the Last Supper. Then I saw a covered bridge which looked like a tunnel. Jesus said: ***"As you approach the evil days know that you will be tested more and more for My sake. Keep faithful to Me through all your adversities. I will send you extra graces during these days so you can endure any hardships. You will be trusting in Me from day to day as I would like you to do always. When you truly follow Me, you will see how life's road***

will seem easier. Then you will wonder why you did things on your own without Me. Pray, My children, and you will see the light of My knowledge."

Friday, February 24, 1995:

After Communion, I saw a priest reaching out with a handshake. Then I saw Mary standing as a helping Mother with her arms outstretched. Finally, Jesus came to console me with His tender way. Jesus said: ***"I come to you through My priests. Love them***

as I love them, but I am with you even more intimately in My Blessed Sacrament, which you receive often, for it truly is the Bread of Life. You are more than just a friend to Me, since you are truly a part of Me and a reflection of My goodness. See the beauty of our union so that you walk with Me as a part of your life. Through all life's trials keep focused on Me as your guiding Redeemer. See that this life is a training ground to learn what true love is all about. Marriage is a human experience which closely expresses My love for My Church. It is the everlasting faithfulness which I seek from each of you that brings joy to My heart. When My love touches you in that indescribable beauty, I relish your understanding of what I mean to you. Grow in My love, for your perfection lies in a deepening of My love for you."

Later, at church, I saw a bright light on a column of trees in the snow. Jesus said: ***"My people, do not always try to be someone special that you are not. In everything, be at My peace and live for Me. Be yourself and do not be swayed to do that of others. Follow the prompting of the Holy Spirit and this will be enough to lead you. Do not worry how things will happen, especially for events you have no control over or proper concern. Instead, live each moment for Me. Concentrate on those things that please Me as prayer and fasting. Gather your strength from Me in your visits to My Blessed Sacrament. My love flows out to you and I expect your love in return. It is beautiful for two spiritual lovers to come together. We seek each other and I enjoy sharing My peace with you. Bury your fears and troubles in the love I pour out on you. I love you, My children, and I want you to appreciate all I do for you. Come and enjoy My refreshing Spirit of Love. Thank Me for all you have and all the graces I am giving you. Live on in My peace and you will know Me in My love for you."***

Saturday, February 25, 1995:

After Communion, I saw a picture of a small cross insignia as on the Host. Then I could see pictures of just people's eyes. Jesus said: ***"My people, you must be at ease more and open to receive My graces. Do not let daily events so take over your life that you do not leave any time for Me and prayer. Your prayer life is too important to not leave enough time for it. This is a time to open your eyes to your soul, so I can enlighten you about your interior***

life. You will have a hard time to understand My love if you are not in the right disposition to listen to My word of love. In all you do, think of Me and how I would do things and try to imitate Me. When you live like I want you to follow, all will be in harmony and you will continue to have My inner peace among you. Do not let anger or impatience enter your life, for this causes discord and hard feelings. Live like everything depends on you and share My love and good example with all you meet."

Later, at church, I saw a big town with many lights at night. Then I saw a horrific sight of many demons passing overhead and the people were cowering to the ground. Jesus said: ***"You are being privileged to forewarn the people of the plight of the coming evil days. This is not meant to scare My faithful since I will protect those who seek My help. You should know for the rest though, it will be a time of evil influence never before seen on the earth. The bowels of hell will be opened and the demons will torture those who are against Me. It is those who will be threatened without My protection that you should pray for and try to convert. Those who have denied Me or are too lukewarm to love Me, will be the victims of the demons. They will see for a brief moment in My warning, a chance to repent and convert. If they do not seize this final opportunity, woe unto them, for their last state will be worse than the first. Those who still deny Me will be condemned to hell forever in eternity and will be tortured by these demons. They despise humans and will indeed make both life and death into an eternal nightmare. Wake up those who do not believe, or your end will be so horrific that it will be indescribably hideous. Choose Me instead and your life could be eternally blissful."***

Sunday, February 26, 1995:

After Communion, I saw a vision of some helical ribbons from top to bottom as an image of DNA with roots back to creation. There was a picture of the reenactment of creation with God the Father pouring out a beautiful gold light at the top and filtering down all over everything. God the Father said: ***"When you see a sunny day, you are being visited with the radiance of creation. As you understand some of the scientific roots of the origins of man, you have learned some of the beauty of creation as well. It is the image of our likeness which we have instilled in all of mankind.***

You all are spiritual beings, less than the angels, but still with immortal souls which are called to give praise and glory to God. All men should witness this faith and knowledge of God to all ready to listen. The spreading of the faith through evangelization is what all My disciples are called to. Have a firm belief in Me and pray to guard your interior life so that you may persevere to your prize in heaven."

Later, at church, I saw the name "Jesus" spelled out in the form of lightning. Then the name appeared as flames. Jesus said: ***"I am showing you this vision so you will see Me as the central focus in your life. No matter what adversity or confusion will come over the earth, you must see I am your help through it all. Prayer and fasting as during Lent is a good practice to keep your body's desires under constraint. In order to maintain a good spiritual life, you must be in daily communication with Me. Talk to Me at any moment of the day and I will be attentive to your call. Keep yourself nourished on My Bread of Life and you will be close to My heart. Do not be fearful of anything of earth, for I will always protect you. Keep My peace in your soul at all times and you will desire Me only. As your love for Me deepens, you will long for the day to be with Me in heaven. Even now, this life is a burden for some, since some would rather be with Me in paradise. You each must struggle through life, though, to show your endurance of faith through all obstacles. Pray for the strength to persevere to your goal with Me in heaven. Your struggle will not be in vain."***

Monday, February 27, 1995:

After Communion, I kept getting visions of snow scenes. Jesus said: ***"You see the new fallen snow as pure white. It has a purity which is similar to how you should have your soul pure from sin. In this way you are more pleasing to Me if you are dressed in the proper wedding garments. If you need to be cleansed of your sin, then make haste to My Sacrament of forgiveness in Confession. The priests are ever willing to bring you back into the flock of the faithful. It is when you have your robes washed as with rain and snow, that you become a new creation ready to go forward in sharing My love. Remember, it is a contrite heart which I most desire."***

Later, at church, I saw a spinning cylindrical tunnel and at the end of the tunnel was a very bright intense light which represented God in all His love and peace. Jesus said: ***"This is a most important message which all My children should know. There is coming a most spiritual event where I will communicate openly to each individual soul. This will be a most spiritually awakening moment which all must endure. It will be glorious to behold My close visitation. To those who are in deep sin or far from Me, you will indeed be humbled to see how you are offending your Lord. This will be a time of grace in giving everyone a practical opportunity to either choose Me or the pleasures and gods of this earth. Satan will always hide his wickedness to tempt many through the bodily senses. Pray, My people, for constant discernment so you may follow in life the example I have given you. It is important that you prepare yourself spiritually, for the coming evil time will try even the souls of My faithful. Continually pray for My help and I will be your everyday spiritual protector—your shield against the evil one who is making his last struggle for souls. You will have to be ever vigilant in your prayer life, for your spiritual endurance will be required of you."***

Tuesday, February 28, 1995:

After Communion, I could see many vacant chairs at the morning Mass. Jesus said: ***"Where are the people to receive Me? I make myself available in My Eucharist everyday but only few avail themselves of My many blessings. I am offering you the bread of strength to carry out each day's battles. Encourage others in Lent to take advantage of these graces. You will not have such an offering as easy during the evil days. So make the most of your precious time now. Now is the acceptable time for conversion and repentance especially through Confession."***

Later, at church, I saw some headlights on some rocky hills. I then saw some people coming out of some caves. Again I was walking through a carved tunnel and the walls gleamed with a bright light as it was being formed. Jesus said: ***"As you draw near the evil times, do not be fearful for I will protect My faithful. As the Anti-Christ comes, I will direct you where to go and stay. You must avoid him and his agents for they will be leading souls astray by***

their evil powers. I will even provide dwellings hewn out of the rock by My finger. I am telling you as before not to take the mark of the beast even though you may not be able to buy and sell. If you take this mark, you will know that with it you will be asked to praise the Anti-Christ and not Me. If you knowingly give in to this, you will be in the book of the living dead and not in My Book of Life. You cannot be with Me and still belong to the world. You must choose between faith in Me that will last forever or a temporary comfort which will end up in eternal torture. Your future is yours to decide, but pray you choose Me for I will lead you to a land of milk and honey which no demon can promise and fulfill."

Wednesday, March 1, 1995: (Ash Wednesday)

After Communion, I saw the priest giving out the ashes. Jesus said: ***"My people, as you receive your ashes today let it remind you of the mortality of the body. This life is only a short stopover on your way to preparing for the afterlife. Remember, also, you have an immortal soul which will live on past the grave. It is your direction of life that will determine whether you will be in heaven with Me or with the demons in hell. This is a proper time for purifying your soul with prayer and fasting so that you can please Me by your acceptance of My plan for you. It is only those who refuse My invitation that will not taste My dinner."***

Later, at the prayer group I first saw a head and rays of light shone outward. Jesus said: ***"My people, I want you to have eyes of faith so you can discern the coming events. Use this Lenten season as a spiritual preparation so you will be better able to withstand your future trials."*** Then I saw a pen set at a desk from varying positions. Jesus said: ***"I send My messengers to you so they may write My words for all of you to hear. I am sending a constant message of love and hope which should keep you at peace and shed your fears of the unknown."*** I saw a large telescope looking into the sky. Jesus said: ***"Look to the heavens for the signs of the coming events. You will be given many signs, some permanent so that they will witness My glory to you. Even though there will be fearful omens, you can look to the heavens for your consolation."*** I could then see some books open in a library. Jesus said: ***"You should spend your time reading good spiritual books which will enlighten your spirit to see Me more clearly. When***

you meditate on these words, you will see how My presence in your life is walking you through your spiritual training." I saw some large signs as if they had fallen from some buildings. Jesus said: ***"You will continue to see earthquakes as scourges of the people. Many victim souls will suffer as their sufferings will atone for the many sins in the world. I have told you before that these events will occur more where rampant sin flourishes."*** I then saw an Indian maiden as Kateri Tekakwitha standing before me. She said: ***"Saturday will be a moment of testing for you. But the Lord will see you through it with His graces. You are to witness His love, hope and peace as well as His warnings. In all that happens, keep His peace foremost in your proceedings."*** I then saw Mary as at many places of apparition. She said: ***"I bring you my blessings this evening and I thank you for your sincere Rosaries as your pleasing gift to my Son. Continue to pray my three Rosaries each day. The time you spend away from the world is much more powerful than those earthly things you are about. There is much need of prayer in your sinful world, so pray much for my intentions and I will share your merits with others."***

Thursday, March 2, 1995:

After Communion, I felt joined with Maria E. and she said: ***"Share with Jesus."*** I then saw a large stained glass window and there was a picture of Jesus acting as a judge. Jesus said: ***"I set before you the blessing and the curse. Choose life so you may come to My abundant graces. I am here waiting for you to follow My commands. I do not force them on you since I am a loving and forgiving God, but you must realize I am a just God as well. Those who choose rightly to follow My will have chosen the better portion and will not be denied their reward in heaven. Those who know My laws and still turn away from My love, are making a decision they will eternally regret. So choose carefully, but choose life with Me instead of a terrible punishment with the demons in hell."***

Friday, March 3, 1995:

After Communion, I saw a pool of water and there was a rock wall in a semi-circle where I could see My reflection in the water. Jesus said: ***"During this Lent it is good to meditate on how you***

can best improve your spiritual life. Fasting, as mentioned in the readings, is a way to hold the body's earthly appetites and passions under constraint. Use your fasting to purify your intentions each day to do My will for you. Do not be like the hypocrites who do things on the outside for show, but inside they are plotting evil deeds. As you also have seen the vision of water, think of how best to cleanse the guilt of your sin and confess your sins with My Sacrament of Penance. As with the water, look at yourself as others see you and do what you can to mold your behavior to My example. Be caring of others and help where you are needed. Even put yourself out to help others so that you go the extra mile as I did. In the end, increase your love both for Me and your neighbor."

Later, at church, I found myself in the middle of a whirlwind where things were spinning around and being tossed all about me. Jesus said: ***"I bring you a message of hope for all to understand. You will see Me shortly when I will bring My warning to My people. All will see their lives pass before them much like before death. Only this time everyone will be given a second chance. You will also sense My love drawing you to be at peace with Me. You all have a free will and are being asked to choose life. For those who have forgotten Me and those who have refused Me, I am offering you one last opportunity to straighten out your life and follow Me. For those that do accept Me, you will see I offer you by My death on the cross a chance for salvation with Me in heaven. O happy fault which I have atoned for, now you see the gates of heaven available to you if you would follow My will. You have seen My love and peace in My visions to you. Share them with others to show I am the only true choice. My justice must still be meted out, though, to those who will still refuse Me. Tell them that the jaws of Hell's torture is an eternal horror which they must avoid at all costs even if they must suffer for Me to be saved."***

Saturday, March 4, 1995:

After Communion, I saw a shape of a heart. On looking further it was a shape of a heart recessed on an empty box. Jesus said: ***"My people, this is My Lenten message to you that you must empty your hearts to receive Me. I am asking three things of you. First, to accept Me as your Lord and Savior. Second, that you empty*** *your hearts of your earthly desires and your selfish wants. In doing so, you will make room for Me to occupy. Then third and most important, you must admit you are a sinner and ask forgiveness of your sins as part of your conversion. In this way you can invite Me into your hearts and I will bring you My love and peace. If all men could do this, your world would have instant peace. As it is, My disciples, you must bring this message to all who are willing to listen and act on it."*

Later, at church, I saw some statues of the apostles. Then I had a vision of how St. Peter witnessed to the people the truths of Christ's Resurrection. Jesus said: *"My faithful disciples, you are the ones I am calling forth to witness My word before all men. As I left this world I asked My apostles to go and teach all nations of My love and My death on the cross for the salvation of all mankind. This message is repeated now to all the faithful that it is their responsibility to go and evangelize those willing to accept My invitation. This is your mission to bring souls back to Me before it is too late. My son, it is important that you make the people understand the infinite dimensions of My love. I am all-loving to the point that I reach out to all My creatures with a tender hand which is held out to you to guide you to your eternal reward with Me. My love is given freely to all as I allow you freely to love Me in return. I will not force you to love Me, but if you hear of the witness of the beauty of heaven and how I wish to share the glory of My resurrection, then you will be drawn to desire Me all the more. Come to Me in the Blessed Sacrament so I can share My love with you. See that loving Me will consume you so much that you will have no fear and will desire Me only over earthly things."*

Sunday, March 5, 1995:

After Communion, I saw in church a row of people and they all had their heads bowed and they were kneeling. Jesus said: *"My people, I am giving you an inspiration about purgatory. During Lent is a good time to purify your spiritual intentions. It is a time when prayer and fasting helps correct the body's appetites. You should know, My people, that during your life I forgive you your sins in Confession, but still there is due the temporal punishment for your sins. Your prayers and sufferings and good deeds can be applied against the punishment due for sins—such that when you die and approach judgment the things you have done during life will be the heavenly treasure I have asked you often to store up more than earthly riches. Now I am saying if there is sufficient merits for you at that time, some have been allowed straight into heaven and have avoided the purification of purgatory altogether. So I tell you, My people, through more prayer, denial of sin, and all of your good deeds and sufferings, you too can alleviate that time in purgatory while you are still here on the earth. I am a gracious and merciful God. It is love I desire from you and all of these heavenly treasures will help you at your time of judgment. Come to Me, My children, and I will give you your heavenly rest."*

Later, at church, I saw a white object hurl through space. Jesus said: ***"My people, you must be able to read the signs of the time. Know now that events will be speeding up. Also, you will see that each event will become more serious than the one before it. It is important to prepare your spiritual well-being before these events overtake you. By doing My will every day you will grow closer to Me in love. Do not fear and be peaceful at this time for you will not be able to do anything about these happenings. It is good enough for you that you remain faithful to Me no matter what befalls you. This will be a great leap of faith to trust in Me at all times, but you must ask My help to keep strong during the trial. After this testing time, you will see My glory will shine as My triumph will bring an era of peace where you will be able to share in My victory. Pray, My people, to understand My way is the plan I give you."***

Monday, March 6, 1995:

After Communion, I saw a grave stone in white with a large ornate cross on it. Jesus said: ***"My people, it is good for you to contemplate on how you will face death. For those who have been faithful, you will be looking forward to sharing My eternal love with you. For those who have refused My invitation, they too will receive their just reward. You will see this as a judgment time when the faithful come forward and I will claim you as 'mine'. And when the accursed come forward Satan will claim them with his 'mine'. It will be a time when the tares will be separated from the wheat or the goats from the sheep. Prepare yourselves to be on the right side."***

Later, at church, I could see the Host in a monstrance and there was a bright light which shone from the front and back. I also saw angels kneeling and giving glory and praise to God. Jesus said: ***"My people, I would like you to imitate My angels. They are in union with My divine will and they have joined their wills to Mine. They go about and do My every bidding without question. They are ever at My side to give Me praise and glory. They do a constant vigil in perpetually adoring Me. You, My people, must take a lesson from them for you too can be faithful to Me. My people, ask your guardian angel's help in keeping close to Me by follow-***

ing My will. You can give over your will to Me as well. Each day walk with Me and follow in My footsteps so I may lead you to heaven. Without Me you are nothing, so come to Me so you can be whole in both body and spirit. Pray much this Lent to keep vigilant yourselves in your constant adoration of Me."

Tuesday, March 7, 1995:

After Communion, I saw several views of galaxies and great pictures of stars. At the bottom of all these views was a man and a child. Jesus said: ***"I am sharing these visions of the heavens with you so you can realize the God who created the universe is still paying close attention to each individual. You all are a part of creation and you should see how you fit into My plan. Everything has been created to give glory to God and serve Him. I have loved you so much that I have brought you into existence to share in My love. Even further, I did not leave you here to forget you. I have seen fit to die for you on the cross so that your sins have been forgiven. I love you so and I direct you this Lent to return your love to Me. Understand how beautiful life can be when all men are in harmony with Me. Continue to give glory to Me and you will be rewarded with My many graces."***

Later, at church, I saw a vision of a solitary table and light shone around it. I sensed people were giving more respect to the altar than the Blessed Sacrament in the tabernacle. Jesus said: ***"You see before you the termites who are undermining My Church as I instituted it. You must pray My people for discernment of the truths of your faith. Know your Scriptures, for some will come as false witnesses trying to mislead even My elect. It is you, My faithful remnant, whom I will rely on to hold up My one true faith which I have taught you. You are indeed among the times of the coming apostasy where false witnesses will abound. You will see factions in My Church which will try to destroy it from within. There will be prideful people trying to change My laws to fit their convenience. Beware, My friends, when some advocate change for change's sake or want to modernize My Church. Most all of these feeble attempts are not God-inspired but inspired by men's warped minds. My laws are changeless and I will be eternally faithful to all My people. See to it, My loving people, that you stay in love with My Eucharist and follow My commandments. In the***

future, you may be deprived of My churches as you know them. But pray and keep faithful, My graces will protect you."

Wednesday, March 8, 1995:

After Communion, I saw a vision amongst the clouds and an image of Jesus came forth. Jesus said: ***"It is true that you have a greater than Jonah here each day in My Blessed Sacrament. Receive Me and be a part of Me through each day. I call on all My messengers to give witness of My name before the people. Listen to My prophets that you may hear My word and take it to heart. I give them the responsibility to show My people that knowing Me and My love is ever important. You must reform your lives this Lent and follow My ways if you expect to come to Me in heaven. I am here all-loving, waiting to receive you and grant you forgiveness of your sin. Repent and confess your sins and you will prepare yourselves to receive Me into your hearts. In a word be contrite in heart and love Me dearly. Then I will see your sincerity and accept you as one of My faithful."***

Later, at the prayer group, I first saw a picture of some people gathered in prayer. Jesus said: ***"Where two or more are gathered together in prayer, I am there in their midst. Keep close to Me in your prayers. I tell you to guard your interior prayer life. For if you should forget your prayers, you will be more susceptible to the temptations of the evil one."*** I then saw a man in vestments and I saw some papal insignias. Jesus said: ***"Keep your faith strong in My name and follow the leadership of your pope. My priest son will lead you correctly on faith and morals. Listen to him and study his teachings so he may watch over My flock."*** I saw a ship and it represented our country. Jesus said: ***"Pray for your leaders that their proceedings will be in accord with My ways and not just fruitless selfishness. Your leaders must see clear to be responsible in their leadership to My faith and morals."*** I saw many red, orange and bright colors come rushing towards me like a fast train. It was a picture of the life review as I have seen the warning. Jesus said: ***"Prepare to receive Me at any time. For you know not the hour of your visitation. I could come for you at your death before the warning, so be ever ready. For those who live to My warning, do not be frightened. Only those not in My grace need fear. My faithful will be protected spiritually."*** I saw two candles and a picture of some priests who have passed on. Jesus said: ***"I have taken home many of My priest sons and those left will be under much pressure from their daily tasks. You will see fewer priests since there are less vocations and those teaching in the seminaries again are teaching errors. So pray for your priests that they may lead My people properly."*** I saw an old plane and a new jet. Jesus said: ***"Do not let science or technology be a god for you. What little you know only will scratch the surface of all knowledge. Do not be prideful in your accomplishments for you can be humbled quickly by the elements or sickness."*** I finally saw Mary coming as bright sunlight. As she drew closer I could see twelve stars around her head. She came still closer and I could see her weeping. Mary said: ***"Why do you offend my Son constantly with your sin? Why do you continue to occupy yourself mostly with this world's desires? Please prepare yourself with prayer, for my Son's Second Coming is not long off. If you could pray in reparation for your sins, my Son would be much more pleased with your change of heart. Look to Him for your goal and all else will be given you besides."***

Thursday, March 9, 1995:

After Communion, I saw Maria E. and I felt the words come: ***"I love you, Jesus."*** as we both shared in that message. I then had a vision of a boat hauling in fish. Jesus said: ***"My faithful, I am calling on you as I did My apostles to be fishers of men. You are to follow My will in your own vocation but always put forth your example of My love. When people see your love for Me and neighbor, they will be drawn to the source of your strength in Me. Help others in their need and you will be helping Me in them also. Live a life of service for your Lord and I will reward you for fulfilling your duty. My message today is to bring souls back to Me."***

Friday, March 10, 1995:

After Communion, I could see some lilies in the distance down a long narrow corridor. This seemed to indicate the coming of Easter. Jesus said: ***"It is good to set your goal in sight this Lent toward My death and resurrection. Before you can share My glory, you must go through a time of suffering much like I had to en-***

dure the cross. I have set an example for you, if you are to be resurrected with Me. That is why you must be tested and purified by your dying to self. All your prayers, fasting and sacrifices are being offered to purify your soul and so your spirit may come to new life through Me. During Lent you must be sorry for your sins and confess them. By repenting you will then be born anew and will be waiting to celebrate My glory on Easter and at the time of your entrance into heaven."

Later, at church, I saw at first a casket with people all around it worshipping. The casket opened and there was a dark hideous demon inside. This appeared as Satanic worship. Jesus said: ***"My people, I am warning you not to be frightened but to be aware that there will be increasing worship of the devil in Satanic masses and rituals. They will become more apparent and known publicly. Even more to note is how many people even today worship the things and people of the world as gods in themselves. Is it any wonder that I am concerned if I will find any faithful on My return? I must rely on My faithful remnant to preserve My one true faith. Keep Me in your midst through your prayers and your worship of My Blessed Sacrament. For you are the ones I will protect and you must pray much to make up for the evil going on in your world. Many people are being led astray because they are concerned too much over the pleasures and comforts of the world. These things were never meant to be an end in themselves. It is time now to wake up these people to the reality that they are spiritual beings made to give honor to Me and serve Me. If people lose a sense of prayer and holiness in My presence, how can they be saved? Invite them back to Me by your example and your teaching."***

Saturday, March 11, 1995:

After Communion, I saw a parapet with icicles dripping. The feeling was that of the Lord looking over a precipice when He was being tempted by the devil. Jesus said: ***"I am telling you My people you must pray and prepare yourself for the coming evil days much like I prayed forty days in the desert before I went up to Jerusalem. In prayer, meditation and fasting you hold the body in check and raise the strength of your spirit. It is important to build up your spiritual strength for you will be entering an age of tempta-***

tion beyond your previous earthly experience. You must pray for My help during this time for you will not be able to endure it on your own. I will be at your side for protection if you would only seek My help. Pray and spread this warning of preparation among the people. Go to Confession regularly and keep close to My heart and you will be saved from this trial."

Later, at church, I was seeing a highway. I then was driving and I saw large barriers on the side of the road. Jesus said: *"You must see your life as on a highway with your final destination coming to Me. Throughout your lifetime you will be challenged by detours which will test your faith in Me, but with your hope in Me you will be able to struggle on and make the best of your situations. It is important to take time and reach out to those looking for a helping hand. With your faith you can uplift the spirits of those around you who may be down on their earthly fortunes. You can be the Good Samaritan in helping others as I have given you an example. Be loving to all you meet and be willing to go the extra mile for those in need of your help. Much has been given to you and much will be expected in return. My love reaches out to lift you up in all you do. As I help you in spiritual matters, you too must help others with the example I have set before you. Continue to love Me and your neighbor and keep your prayer life as the center of your life from which you can gain your salvation."*

Sunday, March 12, 1995:

After Communion, I saw a scene of Jesus walking on the road to Emmaus and the disciples did not recognize Him in His resurrected body. Jesus said: *"You will see that those worthy of coming to heaven will enjoy My glory as you have sampled in My Transfiguration, but many times you do not recognize My presence in those souls around you. Much like the disciples on the road, they reveled in hearing My words from the Scriptures, but you must put these words into action and do works of mercy and spread My message of love. It is only when you accept your crosses and follow My will that you will indeed recognize Me in the breaking of the bread. For when you share your gifts with others, you are sharing them with Me."*

Later, at church, I saw a lot of lights in a city scene and then there was an old man holding an hour glass. Jesus said: *"Time is running out for your cities. Many times I have called you to repentance, but many have a deaf ear to My requests. If you refuse to listen to My words of faith, there will come a time when temptation will overcome you and your soul will hang in the balance. Your cities are reeking with sin and violence which will only get worse. My children, come to Me for forgiveness and repent of your sin before it is too late. Now is a time of grace before the evil days are upon you. Trust in Me or your cities will be lost to the evil one. You must have prayer in your life or sin will corrupt what little good is left in your cities. Please pray for these people or the evil one will take them."*

Monday, March 13, 1995:

After Communion, I saw a picture of people greeting each other at Mass. Jesus said: ***"My people, I love you and I want you to forgive one another as I forgive you. If you can develop a spirit of love for Me, I will help you in extending that love to everyone. When you have love for My creatures, it is much easier to forgive them if they should offend you. It is easy to love those who love you but I am asking you to go one more step beyond in loving those who displease you as well. By showing acts of kindness to those who dislike you, you can begin to melt any hate in their hearts. So be all-loving to everyone and your faith will be a witness to all."***

Later, at church, I saw a huge statue of Mary and then I saw a very touching scene of Mary holding her dead Son as in the Pieta. Mary said: ***"I am here, my children, your loving Mother who comes to nurture you in your spiritual life. My Son has given me this task of helping you to receive Him. I want to encourage you my little ones to be humble as lambs and join me in prayer as much as possible. The more you pray my Rosary, the closer you will be to my Son. It is through this heavenly communication that you can be joined with His Spirit. He calls you to be one with Him in all you do. It is a joy to call on Him in prayer so He can talk to your heart. Empty yourselves of your earthly desires and you will be open to receive Him. It is this union with Him that should be your life's perpetual longing. Pray this Lent since it is an excellent opportunity to renew your love with my Son."***

Tuesday, March 14, 1995:

After Communion, I saw a picture of a lady's purse hanging. There was a little sense that this was a representation of one's personality. Jesus said: ***"Be yourself. This is My message that you should not be a contradiction or a hypocrite. On the one hand, do not put on airs as if you were rich or very intelligent. For on further inspection, people would see through your facade. Again, do not act against your faith in unChristian-like activities. Be true to your Father in heaven and He in secret will credit you accordingly. Also, follow your Christ-like living in all you do. If you are to be seen as an imitator, imitate Me and others will profit from your example. Learn from watching other's faults that you, yourself, are being watched as well. Let them not find you wanting or unfaithful to My laws, but shine forth, My love, as the morning sun and you will spread My peace all around you."***

Later, at church, I saw an ornate room where many cardinals were seated around a big table. It appeared as a conclave to elect a new pope. Jesus said: ***"My people, you will soon see some events leading up to My Pope being replaced by a strange election. There will be a power struggle among My prelates and My Pope, John Paul II, may be silenced or exiled. Then they will deliver up a new leader who will eventually usurp power and lead My Church astray for a while. This will lead up to the time of the Anti-Christ, who will have the new pope helping him. My Church will be in disarray at that time and will splinter into several factions. Many of My faithful will then suffer persecution for not following the new pope's agenda. You must pray to preserve My remnant Church. Come to Me in hope and trust and I will help you bear up during your future trials."***

Wednesday, March 15, 1995:

After Communion, I at first saw someone laying on the floor and then others walking while I was looking at ground level. Jesus said: ***"Many will be involved in the coming religious persecution. You, my son, must endure suffering for speaking out in My name. You will be brought low and subjected to harassment for My name's sake. For a prophet is never accepted in his own land, but people around you will become more wicked and they will taunt and deride all those who would criticize their lifestyle. In telling***

the Gospel message and preaching repentance, you will suffer as a result. As with My early disciples, count yourself fortunate to be chastised in defense of My witness. I will protect you from spiritual weakness, but pray to Me for strength in this time."

Later, at the prayer group I saw a picture of Santa Claus. Jesus said: ***"I give you a gift of Myself all the year round in My Eucharist. It is by your reverent reception of Me in Communion that I can shower on you the graces of this sacrament. Receive Me as often as you can and you will be welcome to the bounty of graces I have available to all who seek them. You, in your turn, can give a gift of yourself back to Me in return."*** I saw a car-hitch connecting a trailer. Jesus said: ***"Prayer is your connection which keeps us linked together spiritually. Pray often so that you may keep linked to Me and even strengthen this bond of life so that it may be your eternal union with Me."*** I then saw a porch entrance to a house. Jesus said: ***"Your heart is the entrance way to receive Me. When you pray from the heart, you are being sincere in asking Me to visit you. With your hands full of good deeds, you will be ready to open your heart when I knock on the door of your soul."*** I saw a drainpipe with a U shape. Jesus said: ***"I am asking you for frequent Confession so I can wash away your sins and blot them out of My memory forever. As things are seen no more when sent down the drain, so your sins will be forgotten. Please come forward, My people, and ask forgiveness of your sins with a contrite heart."*** I again had a vision of Kateri Tekakwitha standing at the shrine in Auriesville. She said: ***"I welcome all of you to visit my place of honor and come closer to understanding my life. I would ask that you pray especially for Maria and all visionaries who are being tested and sacrifice for others."*** I then had a vision of the blue globe of the Earth and Jesus was on a throne representing the "King of All Nations". Jesus said: ***"I am Lord and Master over all things created. By My sacrificial death on the cross I have conquered sin and the evil one. I am pouring out My graces on you at this time to strengthen you for the trials to come. Have no fear and hold on to My peace and I will see you through to My triumph."*** Finally, I saw a vision, very clearly, of Mary as a young girl and she was present on a sunny day in the world as it appears to us. Mary said: ***"You are in the world but you cannot be of the world. In other words, follow my Son's will in your walk through***

this life, but do not be taken up with the world's distractions such that you forget your prayers. See the beauty in all of my Son's creations and give glory and thanks to Him for your blessings. I receive your prayers and I thank you for your sincere Rosaries. Keep dedicated to me through my consecration. All you give to me I will pass on to my Son. He is the one who has asked me to be mediatrix of all graces. Listen to my Son and He will reward you with His infinite love."

Thursday, March 16, 1995: (Story of rich man Dives in Gospel)

After Communion, I saw a smiling face of Maria E. she said: ***"Thank you, Jesus. You have the words of everlasting life."*** I then had a vision of being in a pit with beings looking down on me. Then it was as if someone threw flames down on me. This was to give the impression of what hell was like. Jesus said: ***"I will not leave you orphans in this world, but you must look to Me and My words through the prophets for your direction and help. For those who seek Me, I will give the grace of understanding. With the light of faith you will see your path clear to Me through a life of prayer and suffering on this earth. Do not be like the rich man and search for comfort here since he found torment in the after-life. Instead, seek out storing heavenly treasure that you may store up for your comfort with Me. It is better to prepare for your judgment day than to forget why you are here and not be ready to receive Me."***

Friday, March 17, 1995:

After Communion, I saw an image of a man with a staff which represented St. Patrick. He said: ***"I share your heritage from the country I evangelized. You yourself have taken on this faith in Jesus. There is a responsibility in this gift that this faith be passed on to others. Do not be too comfortable in this world for you all are asked to evangelize the people. It is important that the Lord's blessed word reach as many as possible so they will have a chance to accept Him if they so desire. This is your mission as you know, so pray to keep on your destined path."***

Later, at church, I saw a hill and there was a lot of molten lava coming down the hill. I then saw many visions of computer CPU chips. There was a sense that the powers of hell would abuse this technology. Jesus said: ***"I am sending you a warning, My children, on how computers can be easily used to manipulate people and their money. Be watchful when too much power with computers are in the hands of a few. You will see increasing centralization in respect to control over food and money. As these forces converge, they will be laying the groundwork for control by the Anti-Christ. When he comes into control do not seek his peace nor his devices to buy and sell. No matter what he offers, have nothing to do with him for his control will seem overwhelming for a while. Avoid him as best you can and pray for My help to withstand him. Then soon I will triumph over him. Let Me leave you with an emphasis on the one message I want spread. Do not worship him in any way or take any mark or electrical device to buy and sell. It is in this way he will control the people and try to win over their souls. Give yourselves over to Me and worship Me only above all earthly things and creatures."***

Saturday, March 18, 1995:

At church, I saw an old book sitting on a table. As the book was opened and I expected to see pages with print, I instead saw each page was a moving live picture of a person. Jesus said: ***"The Book of Life contains all those faithful who are by their choice devoted to Me and destined to be with Me in heaven one day. Those whom I recognize as My children and who have accepted Me into their lives, are written in My Book of Life. You are the ones who determine by your free will whether you will be with Me or not. For those who are written in the book, on judgment day I will receive you, but for those not written in this book I will say to them: 'I do not know you. Cast them out into the darkness where they will wail and grind their teeth.'"***

Later, I saw Our Lady as at Fatima and I saw her looking up to heaven. She had her arms stretched out to all of us. Then as if on a wall I saw a very bright light come and I could sense Jesus was coming to bless us. Mary said: ***"I come, my dear children, to bless this house for receiving me this day. Thank you for your Rosaries. I know how much you want to please me and I am happy that you are overjoyed to receive me. I love you my children with a warm Mother's love. I will offer up your petitions to my Son. As you grow closer to my Son, I will join with your hearts so you will***

follow my Son's will for you. Pray my Rosary often and offer up your sacrifices especially this Lent so you can purify your bodies. Trust in my Son's love and He will watch over your every trouble."

Sunday, March 19, 1995: (Reading on the Burning Bush)

After Communion, I saw a cup and an image of God the Father was apparent as rays of light spread out all over the earth. God the Father said: ***"My people, 'I AM' is coming to you to show you how fortunate you are in My sending my Son to you. You have been saved by His becoming man and dying on the cross. This act of salvation has restored all mankind to His former standing before the fall of Adam. You still have free will and are still in a weakened state, but the gates of heaven are now open to receive those who seek us and want God in their lives. You must see it is My plan and My will that will be carried out regardless of what man thinks and does. Your choice is to accept God's love or reject Me. Those who love themselves more than God will see the gates of heaven closed to them again. For those who do not believe in how the Scriptures portray My word, you should know that God is not to be mocked. Nothing is impossible with God even though you do not understand My ways. For what has been written by the inspired writers of My word is not to be changed or misinterpreted. Those who refuse this teaching should not confuse the people and should not be listened to. My people have been led by Me through My prophets throughout history. Listen and heed My words or you will accept the consequences of your disbelief."***

At church, I could see some military vehicles moving. I saw some mountains where armaments were secretly hidden in our country. Jesus said: ***"Many secret dealings are going on in your country. There are evil men planning a military coup in your country. Secret armies and caches of weapons are all in place. Many of your bases are being cut back so it will be easier for a takeover. There are people in high places in your government willing to sell out to those who want a one world government. Many plans are in place to help the Anti-Christ to assume power very shortly. It will be soon after the warning that these events will come to a head. These powers will not last long since I have planned their downfall soon after they come into power, but you will see a major persecution of My faithful during a testing time.***

Know ahead that My plan of conquest will frustrate all the evil one's plans. My angels will win the battle and the wicked and the demons will be chained up in hell. At that time, I will bring you to My era of peace and My love will conquer all. Prepare for this trial and have hope that you will soon enjoy My glory. Many will be lost, though, since they love the world before Me."

Monday, March 20, 1995: (St. Joseph's Feast Day)

After Communion, I could see a man in a tunic with a staff and it appeared to be St. Joseph. St. Joseph said: ***"My son, I was called to protect the Holy Family in my quiet way. You too have been called to speak out for God to His people. You must help in sheltering the faithful by giving them hope and courage to carry on. Continue on your mission to evangelize and bring souls back to God. All of you by Baptism are called to this, but you especially must fulfill the Lord's call. Pray, my friends, that God will guide your every step and walk with Him in His will."***

Later, at church, I saw some high bushes against a tall building. It was given to me that this was like the judgment seat of Pilate. Jesus said: ***"My friends, life for you is like a trial. When you are brought to the judgment seat, how will you be judged? Will witnesses come forward to attest to your worthiness to be My disciple? Will people know by your actions and deeds that you love Me dearly? Will they say you helped your neighbor in His need? Will they say you cared more for Me than the world? These are the thoughts you should contemplate this Lent. Examine your life and where you are on the road to heaven. Pray to Me for help and secure for yourselves My graces through My Eucharist. In this way you will have the spiritual stamina to endure the race for your crown in heaven. I have loved you always from the beginning. Witness your love for Me in all you do. Then when the final judgment comes, I will say to you: 'well done My faithful servant, come and enter your Master's rest.'"***

Tuesday, March 21, 1995:

After Communion, I saw a wall and I could see where the mortar held the bricks together. Jesus said: ***"My people, I have formed you and knit you in your Mother's womb. You must see I am the keystone of the structure of life. I am the one who is the mortar of***

love holding all of you together as one faithful people. I am the one who shows you the blueprint or plan for each of your lives. Follow My will for you and listen for My instructions to you through My word. I find this structure of My Church beautiful to behold. See to it that you too know how you fit into My plan and feel blessed that I care so much for all of you at all times even when you disobey Me. Pray, My children, and keep faithful to the path of life which leads you to Me in heaven."

Later, at church, I saw houses in the foreground and a red lit sky above. Then I saw people traveling in desert country. Jesus said: ***"My people, you should realize you are living in the end times. You are seeing a representation of the famine and pestilence that will come upon your world. Many will recognize these omens as the time of the tribulation. You will see your food supplies gradually tested by floods and droughts. A famine will be spread over your land and it will be manipulated to force you into the hands of the plans of the evil one. You must have faith and trust in Me that I will provide for you with food and drink. I will provide even manna for those in need to survive this test. Keep faithful to My word and do not listen to or worship any one else. My love will envelop you and protect you from the evil men and demons who will test you. Your faith and hope in My word will be your salvation."***

Wednesday, March 22, 1995:

After Communion, I had several visions of the elevation of the Host at Consecration time with different priests each time. Jesus said: ***"On Holy Thursday night, I instituted My Blessed Sacrament in the Eucharist for all of My faithful. This is My memorial and living gift to you so that My presence may be among you until the end of time. This is an extension of My love for you so you can partake of Me more intimately. Even the angels are not given this grace of intimacy but are still close to Me. So I say to all of you, believe that I am personally present to you under the appearances of bread and wine. For those who do not believe in this dogma of faith, I am still present none the less. I come to you each Communion to be accepted into your hearts and I bestow My sacramental graces upon all who receive Me. For your part,***

live My message of faith and follow My will and you will soon share eternal heaven with Me."

Later, at the prayer group, I first saw a vision of some green and pink candy. This was my penance for Lent. Jesus said: ***"It is good to take the opportunity during Lent to offer up something you like as an act of self denial to purify the cravings of the body. You must keep in perspective how the spirit should control the body and not the reverse. The worldly let their passions and desires run freely, but it cannot be that way with My faithful who must restrain your earthly desires in favor of a higher spiritual life."*** I then saw a chain hanging from a wall. Jesus said: ***"You know how a chain is only as strong as its weakest link. You must watch closely over your spiritual weaknesses so that you can control them with prayer. In doing so you will be that much stronger in your time of temptation."*** I saw an announcer on TV and a picture of a potato. Jesus said: ***"Do not be lulled to sleep spiritually in listening to your TV programs. Many such programs teach a wrong morality by comedy. While they are seemingly amusing, they are subtly destroying the morality of your country. You would better use your time in prayer than to weaken your faith."*** I then had a beautiful vision of Mary wearing a crown in heaven with a dazzlingly bright light around her. Mary said: ***"I will soon be celebrating my feast of my Annunciation with you. I am asking each of you to share the graces received from saying my Rosary together. Please say yes to my Son as I did in following His will. You will have a fulfilled life if you let Him lead you down life's path."*** I saw a woman with an unwanted pregnancy. Jesus said: ***"Pray often for those women contemplating abortion that they may choose life for their babies. No circumstance should be allowed to directly kill one of My little ones. Each life has a plan and some place to help society, but it cannot come to fulfillment if this life is snuffed out for selfish reasons. Tell all who will listen how important each life is both to Me and those who will share with this life."*** I saw a bright light strike the bottom of a single yellow rose. Then I saw St. Theresa in the light ready to give a message. She said: ***"All those who are making their consecration to Mary will be sharing in the perfection of their life's work. When you give yourself over to Mary and follow her Son's will,***

you will be following the path of life with Mary's protection. Follow her example of a humble life and live for Jesus and not for yourself." Finally, I saw an open door to a tomb at the bottom of a hill much like at the Dormition Abbey where Mary was placed. Mary said: ***"My children, I am calling your attention to my Son's resurrection and His victory over sin and death. You must have faith in Him so that one day you too will be resurrected with Him. He will raise up all His faithful from the grave to be renewed in a spiritually new body to give Him praise and glory forever. No matter what troubles you may experience, always keep focused on Him as your goal."***

Thursday, March 23, 1995:

After Communion, I saw Maria E. in prayer and she said: ***"Lift up your hearts."*** I then saw a table with a monstrance and Host on it. Jesus said: ***"My people, will you continue to stay close to Me through adversity? Will your faithfulness stand the test of time? Will I find My faithful waiting when I come again to call you to Me? These are your choices as in the Gospel to keep close to Me or to scatter. My dear children, see how deeply I love you and I do not wish to lose even one of My souls. You must in the end show Me how much you love Me. And will you love Me in good times and bad? I am your Savior. Ask if you are in need and I will help you in your need. When you are focused on Me, little else matters since your spiritual union with Me will be enough to get through any difficulty. I will not disappoint you and I can be always trusted to be at your side. You, for your part, must do the same to be one with Me in heaven."***

Friday, March 24, 1995:

After Communion, I kept seeing beams of light coming in the windows. Jesus said: ***"As you see the sunlight, think of Me as the source of all light at every moment for eternity. Things of this life pass away but with Me all is in the eternal now. I have given you everything you are, your life, your goods and all that is in the world. Be thankful and give Me praise for all you have received. Realize that nothing is truly yours since you are My creation in every sense of the word. You are only temporary stewards over your souls, bodies and your possessions. At the judgment you***

will have to make an accounting of how you have managed your affairs. For those who have been gracious and shared with Me and others of your time and all you have, these will enter My Kingdom, but for those who have been selfish and abused what they were given, these face My rejection. Pray, My people, that you live wisely and follow My will. Then your future with Me will be guaranteed."

Later, at church, I saw myself driving through tunnels on the road and then through the hills covered with pine trees. This was the type of terrain the Lord was pointing out for a good hiding place from the evil one. Jesus said: ***"My people, know that no matter what events may befall you, never lose your interior peace with Me. Always put your trust and faith in Me to protect you. All you need do is call on My help in prayer and I will come to your aid. You will see much persecution in the coming tribulation. This is why many times I have told you to go into hiding to avoid the Anti-Christ and his agents. Seek out the wooded mountains for cover and protection. I will provide for you if you would just believe in My help. Many dire events will come but fear not, I will triumph and you will be gathered into My flock. I will shepherd My people, for you will need Me to lead you. Continue to have hope no matter what the odds are against you."***

Saturday, March 25, 1995: (Feast of the Annunciation)

After Communion, I could see only statues of Our Lady holding the Infant Jesus. Later, I could see a vague picture of the angel Gabriel and Mary kneeling before him but I could not see her face well. Mary said: ***"My dear children, as you consecrate yourselves to me and my Son through me, be sincere in your words and actions. Do not let it be just for one day. You, my faithful, are blessed to understand the meaning of this consecration. It should mean to you, to cast aside all fears and cares of this world. Instead trust in me and my Son that we will guard you down life's path. In short, you must be a people of constant prayer. In this way you can see your heavenly goal more clearly and love both of us more dearly. Continue your devotions to Me in your Rosaries and other prayers and you will be blessed with many graces for your protection."***

Later, at church, I saw several wolves roaming around showing their teeth. This was a sense of spiritual warfare increasing. Jesus said: ***"My people, you should prepare with prayer and fasting to be ready for the spiritual battle ahead. You will see many come forward to ridicule your ways. This will be only the beginning of your persecution. These same people will eventually see you as an annoyance to their consciences. They do not want to admit they are doing anything wrong. So consequently, they will try to silence My faithful. Because of this harassment, I will lead you away from them and protect you spiritually. Many will come in My name but do not follow them since they will be false witnesses. Instead, test those that come with the fruits of their labors. If they be of God, there will be peace and harmony. If they are not from God, then there will be hate and confusion. Pray for discernment but do not judge them. Let their fruits decide the case."***

Sunday, March 26, 1995:

After Communion, I saw a landscape picture but part of it was seen through a green filter and the top part was seen through a red filter. Jesus said: ***"You are seeing the different colors that contrast the different ways you can view life. On the one hand, you can look at things as the world views it as a more selfish attitude of enjoying the pleasures of life for your own gain. Many people do not realize this part of life is only temporary and that you are to learn about how to please Me more than yourselves. On the other hand, you can see life through the eyes of faith, love and hope. In this way you have an appreciation of the beauty of creation and the potential for love in people. Helping others and doing things to please Me now takes on a new meaning. With the eyes of faith, much like the prodigal Son, accept that you are a sinner and ask for My grace of forgiveness. Do not be self-righteous to the extent that you are jealous of other's generosity and judge others more harshly than you judge yourself, as the older brother. Be ready also to witness for Me to others so more of My people can be evangelized. You will be following My will if you spread My word."***

Later, at church, I saw several toddlers running around with their toys. Jesus said: ***"Let the children come to Me for they are My little treasures. They are the picture of innocence which I***

would like each of My faithful's spiritual lives to imitate. The children are your future so it is important that they be trained properly in the faith. You must help them with the sacraments and let them come to an understanding of Me in the Scriptures. Children have played an important part throughout history. Keep them close to Me and do not allow others to abuse them or abort them. Many abortions occur for financial reasons which are overshadowed by their worth if they were allowed to grow up. All My plans yearn to be fulfilled and are frustrated when man acts on his own to alter history. Pray for the children and their protection. I long to see them mature to become part of My faithful."

Monday, March 27, 1995:

After Communion, I saw a lady's purse. Jesus said: ***"I bring you today a message about money. It is only a means of exchange. You cannot seek it out for its own sake. Those who seek riches are chasing shadows. You must realize how fruitless it is for the soul to seek financial security. For riches are fleeting, they can be lost easily to theft and corruption in many ways. Do not put your trust in wealth since it is not lasting. Instead, seek Me in everything and I will give you an everlasting security in heaven. Fear not the one who takes your money, but fear the one who endangers the loss of your immortal soul. For if you should be cast into hell, your eternal loss would be far worse than any other misfortune. Understand the important things in your life and keep them solely with a spiritual perspective. You cannot have two masters—God and money. Seek Me first over all earthly things and all will be provided for you."***

Later, at church, I saw a large building where boats were built. Then I had a vision of a large wooden boat being constructed. Jesus said: ***"My people, I am asking you to prepare yourself spiritually to withstand the coming events. Much like Noah prepared the ark for the physical storm in his day, I am asking you to prepare a spiritual ark of graces to protect you in the tribulation. I have asked you many times to maintain a constant prayer vigil. In this way you will build up your strength against the evil days. In another context your body is a physical ark which houses My spirit in everyone. I have made a covenant with you by reason of My death on the cross to open the gates of heaven to you. You for your***

part can fulfill your part of the covenant by following My will. In this way, each of you will become an ark of the covenant who will carry My word to those willing to listen and be evangelized. At the time of the trial I will be there to protect you. Call on Me whenever you are in need of My help. I am always present to you offering My loving hand to lead you to your destiny with Me."

Tuesday, March 28, 1995:

After Communion, I saw several crosses laying on the ground. Jesus said: ***"You are always being given a choice whether or not you want to pick up your cross and follow Me. If you love Me and want to please Me, accept your cross lovingly and be willing to suffer whatever I ask of you. In carrying your cross you must be willing to work with those you dislike and to even help them. You must treat everyone equally no matter what their station is in life. Many times you will be asked to do things which you would not like to do, but I say be willing to come out of your comfort zone to do difficult things for My glory. When I see you are willing to make sacrifices for Me, I will reward you with heavenly graces. You must reach out as Simon did when he was asked to help carry My cross. You are helping to shoulder others' crosses when you pray for them or do good deeds for them, and when you help others, you are helping Me also. Learn to love your daily crosses since through them, you will gain your eternal salvation."***

Later, at church, I saw a long street with a little picket fence along one side. There was an old man walking along in some black clothes. Then suddenly there was a flash of bright light which almost blinded him. It was revealed later that this was not a bomb but an experience of the warning. Jesus said: ***"My people, I have in many ways been preparing you for My warning. It will still be a foreign experience to you and even some may die of fright. A loving person will quickly understand how this experience of seeing your life will help you focus on improving how important loving people is. You will learn from this how I see you and what is expected from you by My standards. You still will eventually have to choose in your life which way you want to go—either towards Me or away from Me. If you choose to be My disciple, you must see what I expect from each of you. In other words, you are making a life's commitment to do My will. In this way you***

must cast aside the world and accept all I ask of you. You must give Me praise and thanksgiving for all you have been given. You must also accept Me on your own with a freely chosen decision to please Me in all you do. Stay faithful to your faith's discipline and keep Me before you in prayer."

Wednesday, March 29, 1995:

After Communion, I saw a crucifix in the shadows and only a tip of one side was hit by light. Jesus said: ***"Come to Me, My children, for I am the source of eternal life. You have seen the witness of My life in the Gospels and how I rose from the dead. This resurrection of body and spirit is the promise I give each of My people who accepts Me and lets Me become part of them. Those from the grave who have been judged worthy have their spirits already with Me in heaven, but at the final judgment all will be reunited with their body and you will be whole in both body and spirit. For this is how you were created and this is how you will be for eternity. Pray, My people, that you will understand My call to your glory with Me and live lives according to My plan for you. For My burden is light but My glory is abundant. For all are welcome to enjoy the beauty of heaven which is the prize you all struggle for."***

Later, at the prayer group, I saw some new flowers spring forth from the ground. Jesus said: ***"Look to nature in the new growth which is announcing a new season. As you see these signs look to the signs of your times and you will see those which are indicated in My Scriptures of My Second Coming. Be ever ready for you know not the time of My arrival."*** I then saw a mailbox with a light on it. Jesus said: ***"Many of you are eager for news in your newspaper or what may be in the mail. I tell you to magnify that desire to hear My good news in the readings at daily Mass. You will have food for your soul and an opportunity to live what you are understanding as your faith is enriched."*** I saw several belts on some people. Jesus said: ***"Be ready to gird yourself spiritually so your faith may be steadfast. Wrap yourself firmly in faith and My word and guard yourself each day from the evil one's temptations."*** I then saw buds come forth on the trees and flowers were blooming in their radiance of beauty. Jesus said: ***"You also must bloom where you are and burst forth with your talents so all may***

see the glory of God. Let My love and your faith shine forth from your face so your joy may be contagious to all. Share My peace with others and bring your cheer to help others that may be losing heart." I saw some scales as the symbol of justice. Jesus said: ***"I welcome all of you with My infinite love and mercy. I wait for each of you to come to Me, but you should know that I have been given to be the judge of all mankind. Pray and show your love for Me and I will have you with Me forever."*** I saw the inside of a dark church and I could see some old stained-glass windows. Jesus said: ***"Protect and guard the heritage of your precious faith. My faithful remnant, keep close to Me in your fervent devotions. Be ready to pass My word on to the younger generations so the torch of My love may live on in them."*** Finally, I saw a dove come out of heaven down to us and it became very large. I could see a gold light and white rays shine and flow down on all of us. The Holy Spirit said: ***"I am the Spirit of Love and I bring My blessings and graces on you tonight. I want to share My gifts and virtues with you to strengthen your faith to withstand today's challenges from the world. Pray your litanies and keep close to Me and My love will burn in your hearts."***

Thursday, March 30, 1995:

After Communion, I could see Maria E. praying in her chapel. She said: ***"Share with the Lord."*** I then saw a vision of a separation between two people. Jesus said: ***"It is in a sense of sharing with your neighbor that I come today. Do not let the opportunity pass by to help those around you with your time, talents and finances. This world is fleeting by and it is better to have good deeds in your hands when you come to Me on judgment day. So make an extra effort to help those around you and you will feel a joy in return."***

Friday, March 31, 1995:

After Communion, I saw several pictures of Pope John Paul II. Jesus said: ***"My people, you have seen throughout history that prophets who brought forth My word have always had to face the rejection of the people. The true word as even I brought it must still be told since My words are everlasting and are the words of eternal life. So whoever proclaims My laws and My***

will in My name shall be close to heaven and those who hear and obey My laws also will be saved, but woe unto those who hear My word and do not believe for they will face the fires of Gehenna for all eternity. Even today as My priest son, John Paul II, proclaims My laws of life, these are changeless and in keeping with My commandments. Many prophets suffer persecution for speaking out in My name but it is their duty no matter what befalls them. You, My faithful, will also be persecuted for believing in My name as well. Pray for My help that you may struggle against evil men that will put you to the test for belief in Me. You will see in the coming times how men will flaunt My law in favor of their own selfish attitudes. All who are not with Me will be accursed. So stay strong in your faith and you will win your eternal peace with Me."

Saturday, April 1, 1995:

At St. Patrick's in Harvre de Grace, Maryland after Communion I saw a dark aisle in a church. As I gazed down the aisle, a bright light was shining where Jesus was appearing, but there was a shadow blocking my complete vision. I could only see half the vision. Jesus said: ***"You must remember Me at every moment of every day. I am with you by your side and I wait patiently for your attention. Remember, I am here and do not allow yourself to get so distracted that you forget about Me. Ask Me to help you in all you do each day. Offer up all your actions as a prayer to Me. When you get taken up with only your thoughts and desires, you leave no room for Me. Remember, I love you so much that I died so your sins may be forgiven. So during the day say some little prayers throughout to show Me how much you love Me and do not forget Me. Go now and be on your way, but always keep your gaze fixed on Me and your love intertwined with mine. For a lover does not let his beloved out of his sight for one minute."***

Sunday, April 2, 1995:

At St. Patrick's in Maryland after Communion, I at first saw a memorial spot where someone had died. Then I had a vision of the tomb like at Holy Sepulcher Church and I saw Jesus come forth in radiant glory. Jesus said: ***"I am the resurrection of life. Many have longed to see My day, but you now are the heirs of My glory. For***

all who live and die now have eternal life if they believe in Me. Many have said they would believe if one would come back from the grave. I have come back. Not that death had any hold on Me for I have shown you My resurrection to show you My triumph over sin and death. After this life, all who are faithful will experience true love and peace with Me, but woe unto those who do not believe, for their fate will be sealed in a living hell forever. Believe in Me, My people, and you too will be with Me in heaven. Join with Me in the sacraments and you will share in My love. Share My living bread and I will be with you always. Your life is always directed towards Me since I want to share the day when you also will be resurrected. I have conquered death so have no fear since I will save you."

Later, at church, I saw a vision of some animals and a bright blue sky with plenty of sun. It was like a picture of the beauty of creation. Jesus said: ***"My people, I am asking you to look with the eyes of faith at everything in your world. When you love Me, you see a special richness of color in the flowers and trees. Everything in life sparkles with the glory of God. Each moment of life will never be repeated. Enjoy and live life to the fullest with Me in every part of your day. You must see My presence in the people you meet. Take every opportunity to spread the Gospel***

and give encouragement of faith and hope in Me without glum faces. Do your best to bring the sparkle and vitality of My glory as the rest of nature. Learn from My creation how the harmony of nature can be among the human condition as well. Share My peace and love with all you meet and your auras will mingle with My graces and joy."

Monday, April 3, 1995:

After Communion, I saw a huge stone and received the word ***"Capstone"***. Jesus said: ***"I have brought My people forth from Egypt. Then again, by My witness of walking the earth, I became the capstone of the Church. The stone rejected by the builders has become the cornerstone of the structure and I find it marvelous to behold. By My death on the cross I have brought you forth, My faithful, from the bondage of sin. This is even more hideous than Pharaoh's abuse. See, My friends, that I have formed My Church with the apostles and that what I have established through their successors is true and valid. Follow the teachings of My Church through the guidance of My pope and you will be led down the road to your salvation. Do not dispute this teaching lest you defy even My own authority and be subject to My justice. Pray, My people, that through My love and peace, My Church will bear good fruit in abundance. All those who believe will receive a prophet's reward."***

Later, at church, I could see a bird's nest and it was empty. Jesus said: ***"You are My precious people whom I am forever watching over. You are like the young in the nest reaching out to Me for My heavenly food in the Eucharist. My love is so consuming that you yearn to receive Me as often as you can. Come to Me, My people, so I can strengthen you with My graces. Give your heart over to Me so I can bring you to My heart and you can be one in My love. I embrace you whenever you come to Me. I will love you always. You can depend on Me when everyone has rejected you. I will then raise you up so you can fly on your own with Me guiding you. When you see My plan, you will be able to walk through life knowing I am beside you. As you soar toward heaven in your quest for Me, keep focused on My love and peace which is waiting for your eternal reward. My love will then absorb you into My being and your joy will know no end."***

Tuesday, April 4, 1995:

After Communion, I saw some damp rocks large enough to walk on. It appeared they were sloped and hard to walk on. Jesus said: ***"My people, many times in life you are faced with situations which look impossible to handle. In these desperate times call on My help, for nothing is impossible for Me. Let Me guide your steps so you may not falter, but if you should slip and fall, you can always return to Me with Confession where I will forgive your sins. So have hope and courage that with Me you can accomplish many hard tasks. You are not alone so call on Me often and My help will be ever ready to receive you."***

Later, at church, I saw a picture of a shepherd's staff several times. Jesus said: ***"I am calling all the time for My shepherd bishops to lead My people back to Me. Many of My bishops are more occupied with what men think instead of what I want. My people need to pray for discernment over their pronouncements. Keep close to Me through the teachings of My pope and you will be following My words. My flock needs to be tended, but those given that work have not always been faithful to Me. Listen to those bishops who bring My word and not those spouting the way of the world. My people, you must be ready to evangelize others to the faith where the proper instruction is not being given. Pray, My children, that you may understand your mission and carry it out."***

Wednesday, April 5, 1995:

After Communion, I saw some priests and then a picture of a small plane to signify we would be in flight. Jesus said: ***"As you have read in the Scriptures of those persecuted for believing in Me rather than other gods, so you also will see in the evil days to come. As the apostasy of this age advances, you will see more severe religious persecution. The priests will be the first to be attacked. Then all who seek God instead of those things of the world, will be tested. The evil authorities as directed by Anti-Christ will also try to punish and kill those who do not worship him. These readings are your prediction of things to come, but you should know that these persecutions of My people have gone on throughout history. This time will be even more evil and hideous in My sight. Pray for My help and be confident I will save your souls if you put your trust in Me alone."***

Later, at the prayer group, I first saw a light on an empty white cupboard. Jesus said: ***"Many of My people have empty spiritual cupboards. Those who are not following a life of prayer and are not helping others with good works will continue to be barren until they hear My word and live by it. I preached to the hypocrite Scribes and Pharisees who did not live what they taught. You, My people, also must give good example by honoring My request to imitate My life of prayer."*** I then saw someone sitting in a chair next to an old stained glass window. Jesus said: ***"I beg you, My faithful remnant, to hold fast the one true faith which has been carried on by My apostles. Read the Scriptures daily and learn from Me how you can grow in your faith. With My grace struggle to advance in faith rather than fall backwards by indifference and apathy."*** I saw a picture of Jesus being nailed to the cross and then He was lifted up. Jesus said: ***"Prepare yourselves for the coming Holy Week so that you may have a deeper understanding of why I suffered for you on the cross. Understand that this was My greatest act of love I could show you. Learn from My suffering how you can use suffering as well to help your friends."*** I then saw an old black car. Jesus said: ***"You must remain faithful to My word and stay with your devotions which have been tried and tested by time. Do not fall victim to those who want to have something new to follow just to show their intelligence. Remain solid with the preaching of Paul and the Gospels and you will be at peace with My love."*** I saw Mary come with a very sad face. She said: ***"I am your sorrowful Mother who comes to show you the infinite love of my Son. I am sad to remember how my Son's own chosen people abused Him and would not accept Him as the true Messiah, but my sadness is turned to joy when I see His saving act which has enabled all men to reach heaven. His gift of His life was the supreme sacrifice most worthy to forgive all sin before the Father. Be ever grateful and thank Him for giving you this grace of opportunity."*** I saw the rock of Gethsemene and I saw Jesus experiencing His agony. Jesus said: ***"Many agonize over life's decisions but know that I have gone before in such suffering. Call on My help so that I may lead you through life's difficulties. Remember to ask My help for I am always ready to listen to your prayer."*** I finally saw a negative image of Jesus as on the Holy Shroud in Turin. Jesus said: ***"How easy it is for people to***

question the truths of the faith. Even Thomas doubted My resurrection, but once he placed his finger in My hands and side, he believed. Some of you have evidence from Scripture and science and still you will not believe. I gave many witnesses of eating before My apostles and many testimonies of My apostles spoke of My real body present after My death. Even science has shown you a miracle in the holy shroud which gives evidence of the light emitted at the moment I resurrected. No mere man can rise from the dead on His own. It is only My grace that will raise all My faithful to heaven. Believe in the light of faith in Me or you will be faced with cursing the darkness of disbelief."

Thursday, April 6, 1995:

After Communion, I saw Maria E. and I felt the words come: ***"Let us all share with Jesus."*** I then saw what looked like a landing of a space shuttle. Jesus said: ***"Man has found another god in his technology. Some are so prideful of the advances in science and space that they look to science to answer and verify all knowledge. This knowledge, even though it only scratches the surface of what can be known, has been put on a pedestal for man to think he knows all. My friends, do not fall into this trap of pride that you have all the answers. There can only be one God in your life and unless you accept Me as creator and ruler of your life, you will not taste of the glory in heaven awaiting you. I have made a covenant with you by My death on the cross. I have ransomed you from your sin, but you must humble yourself by living up to your part of this covenant in loving Me in return. You must swallow your pride and admit you are a creature of mine created to love and serve Me. You must desire conversion in giving up your will so you can become a part of My divine will. In submitting to My heavenly invitation, you will truly gain all knowledge in the end. Pray, My children, to understand this lesson and your joy with Me will be without limit."***

Friday, April 7, 1995:

After Communion, I could see dark cold water and a bright light appeared in the sky. Jesus in white radiant robes came down from heaven and He went to put His hands on some people to console them. Jesus said: ***"My people, I call on you to stay close to***

Me. I have given My message to be spread by many of My messengers. Those are blessed who have been asked to serve Me, but you will see all those who preach My crucifixion and My word will be despised by men. In man there is always a conflict between the spirit and the flesh as a result of the fall. That is why some cannot accept facing the true purpose they were put here for; to love and serve Me. Unless men renounce their own will to follow My will, they cannot be My disciples. Know now that My messengers will thus be persecuted much like Me and all the prophets before you. Reach out to Me, all who are distressed and I will comfort you and protect your souls from evil men. You may suffer for Me but continue to witness Me or I will refuse to witness you before My Father."

Later, at church, I saw a large orange fireball which looked almost like the size of an atomic bomb. Jesus said: ***"This is one of the events you will see as the evil times draw nearer. Man has prided himself on his accomplishments, yet he fails to realize how fragile his existence is on earth. All your strivings for wealth will be fruitless, as they may be destroyed or taken away. Man in his greed fails to see that the true purpose of his existence is his spiritual well-being. This earthly life is but a test to see if you love Me enough to seek and follow Me. You will see all your own desires will gain you nothing. Therefore seek the life and graces I will give thee for the asking, and I will grant you many blessings besides. It is only when you seek Me first, that you will find peace in all you do. When you live to please Me and not yourself, then you will be on the road to heaven. So worry not how much of this world's goods you need, but look to store up heavenly treasures instead, for these are everlasting."***

Saturday, April 8, 1995:

After Communion, I saw a shiny marble floor and someone in a grey robe was seated in the first seat of what may have been a church. Jesus said: ***"Do not look for places of honor in churches or banquets. Do not seek riches or honors for your own benefit for you must be humble in My sight. For those who puff themselves up with fame and popularity will let their pride overshadow their real purpose on earth of serving Me only. You cannot serve money and Me equally. The things of this earth are passing away.***

For those popular today, tomorrow's dust will erase their memory. Be humble and seek to be in My graces. Look more for lasting value in My Father's house. You must serve the rest, if you are to gain esteem in heaven. Be faithful in leading a holy, humble and prayerful life and you will be close to Me for eternity."

Later, at Nocturnal Hour, I saw an Egyptian person in old attire and the people were worshipping some God. Jesus said: ***"The evil from 'of old' will spring out of Egypt once again. As My people came from Egypt and as I came out of Egypt, you will see the same possibility of the Anti-Christ coming out of Egypt. As the evil of your age increases and becomes more worldly, so the time of the Anti-Christ approaches quickly. His reign will be brief, but many souls will be drawn to him. Pray constantly and with My help, you will overcome this trial. My triumph also is not far off, so lift up your hope."***

Sunday, April 9, 1995: (Passion Sunday)

After Communion, I saw a few small clouds and then I saw several people standing in the dark of an eclipse. Jesus said: ***"My people, I have endured My trial when I died on the cross. So you also will endure your coming trial as you face the evil time. Just as the eclipse darkened that afternoon in My trial, so you also will see darkness at your trial. Know, My friends, that My warning will be like the beginning when evil will have its hour. You will know that the darkness will be as a loss of love and light. As the hour of evil comes, you will pray and await the coming of My light and My love. As the light of My resurrection will burst forth with joy for mankind, so My Second Coming will be announced by My light and love as well. My presence will curse the darkness and the light of My knowledge, love and peace will permeate all things forever."***

Later, at church, I saw myself in a dark space and I could see a bright blue globe of the earth. It appeared to be illuminated by a brilliant light with a renewed look of lush vegetation. This seemed to be at the time of the triumph on earth. Jesus said: ***"My people, I mean to give you a message of hope in all of life's distress. I go to prepare a place for you especially at the time of My triumph. Do not despair over any of the coming events. Know that I am in control at all times over the events which occur. Do not think I***

will abandon you even during this trial of evil, for I am here to protect you. You must know you cannot do anything on your own. You must ask My help both in life and in protecting your soul. I am all merciful and I hear your prayers. Be patient and My answer will bring you to your destination with Me. I love all of you so dearly, but you must have faith in Me that My plan for you is better than your own. You will see My day at My triumph and I will call all of My children forward to share in My joy and love. All I am asking is that you make a step forward to seek My help. Come to Me and I will reward your faith in Me on a renewed earth of peace."

Monday, April 10, 1995:

After Communion, I could see through a crack in the ceiling down on an office with many file cabinets. Jesus said: ***"The age of computers has become the age of control. When so much information is available on everyone, it puts the power in the hands of a few. At the same time, it enables abuse of that power for evil purposes as well. The evil one, through the Anti-Christ, will use these devices to his advantage. Beware, My people, how such control will force you to flee for your own protection as the evil persecution will come down hard on My faithful. You have seen over the years how religious persecution has been carried out. It is the ruthless leaders, who defy God, that will act in concert with the evil one to try and purge religion from the earth. They, in the end, will be unsuccessful and never fulfill their desires, since My intervention will thwart their plans. I will be here to protect you, but pray to understand how you will have to suffer for a time to be humble and acknowledge your true faith in My power."***

Later, at church, I could see into a deep well. Then, in another scene, I could see a huge shrine like a small pyramid with stairs. The people were worshipping some strange god. Jesus said: ***"My people, how quickly you turn your interests to the things of the world. I am your rock and I have given you a basis of faith in Me that should satisfy your every desire. But alas, the human condition is not always steady and faithful. Many allow distractions to take them away from My attention. I pray, My people, that you will see that you are weak and you will see that you need to be united with Me in prayer every day. I am pleased with***

My little bastions of My faithful remnant. They continue to lift Me up to others, as the rest of the world is steeped in evil as the foundations of the coming evil grow each day. I am asking My faithful to lead the others back to Me for you are acting for Me on earth. Keep fast to your roots in My faith and My glory will soon be upon you."

Tuesday, April 11, 1995:

After Communion, I saw a small home and then the words came: ***"The Son of Man has nowhere to rest His head."*** Jesus said: ***"You have followed Me through the Gospels and now I ask you to follow Me through life. Do not become too comfortable with your surroundings in this world. I have provided for you in your need, but your faith must be rooted in Me without any need for the world. You must be ready at all times to leave this place to follow Me wherever I lead you. It is this faith in Me and love for Me that keeps you focused on My will rather than your own. You will see a day when you too must roam about as I did, not tied firmly to any one home. For when you are ready to follow Me as such, you will be ready to loose your bonds to sin and the world."***

Later, at church, I saw very clearly a gravesite with a head stone and I was meditating on the meaning of death. Jesus said: ***"My people, as you approach My commemoration of My death on the cross, you should be in fervent prayer. If you knew more of My judgment, you would even be on your knees praying every available moment. Come to Me with many good deeds and prayers in your hands. These heavenly treasures are your real prizes. So often men are taken up with their own desires. It is then, though, that you see how fruitless these endeavors are and your time is many times wasted. Concentrate more on My wishes for what you are to do. Then, your pleasing Me will bring you more graces. When you are strong in My love, you will be better able to block out the world's distractions. Keep close to Me in prayer and you will be guided on your path to heaven. Think more of your life as an extended pilgrimage in a foreign land and you will be ready to follow My will for you."***

Wednesday, April 12, 1995:

After Communion, I saw a woman holding a rose. This was a symbol for buying the perfume in preparation for the Lord's burial. Jesus said: ***"As Mary perfumed My feet with the aromatic nard, so all of My faithful should be in preparation for My death and resurrection. See My example in suffering that you too may be able to endure the test for My sake. As I was faithful to the Father, you too must be faithful to God for all you must do for Him. In a word, you must be made perfect through My ransom of the cross and your acceptance of your own crosses. Then My faithful will be ever ready on Sunday morning to share with Me in the glory of My Resurrection. Your glorious moment with Me in heaven will be awaiting you soon."***

Later, at the prayer group, I first saw a mailman delivering letters to people. Jesus said: ***"I send you daily messages of love to strengthen and console you. You must listen for Me in prayer and before My Blessed Sacrament. Then you can return your own message of love back to Me. Remember to keep this link of communication with Me to perpetuate your love."*** I then saw a sign with the word ***"Cars"*** on it. Jesus said: ***"As cars are necessary for transportation, so I rely on you as well to transport My message of love to those around you. Never cease trying to convert wayward sinners. Your words of encouragement and your example witness to My love for sinners."*** I saw Jesus as He was praying in the Garden of Gethsemene. Jesus said: ***"I share with you in your daily cross each day. Your pains, tensions, and troubles I take on as My own. So ask often for My help each day that I may walk with you through all your suffering. I suffered My agony and death on the cross to follow My Father's will. I am asking you also to offer your will up to Me so I can carry out My plan through you."*** I then saw a beautiful picture of Mary, but she had a very somber look on her face. Mary said: ***"See, my children, in the accounts of the Gospels how much my Son suffered for you in His last days on earth. See and try to understand how much Jesus loves each and every one of you. If you were the only sinner on earth, He would still have died just for you. I am begging you, my children, to refrain from as much sin as possible so that you will lessen the pain my Son must suffer for your sins."*** I then saw a glorious and majestic image of God the Father spanning over all creation. God the Father said: ***"I have made a covenant with Noah to never destroy the earth again with water as many of you witnessed in My rainbow today. Know also how I made another covenant with my Son that His gift of life on the cross would be an acceptable offering of Body and Blood to forgive the sins of all mankind. This is an everlasting and personal covenant with each of you. Treasure this gift as heaven was again opened for all of you to occupy."*** I saw a picture of many booths and walls in some offices. Jesus said: ***"Many of you like privacy, but do not build up walls of indifference between you and your neighbor. Be joyful and voice your Christian love with others to buoy up their spirits. Do not complain, but speak positively to encourage each other."*** I finally saw someone's pictures they were viewing. Jesus said: ***"As you look at a picture, it stops you at a particular moment in time. You must think of life with its many milestones of faith. See each advancement as one more step closer to your goal in heaven. If you are not improving much, take stock of how you could improve yourself. All improvement comes in giving over your will to Me. When you follow Me in prayer, My grace will help you in your spiritual growth."***

Thursday, April 13, 1995: (Holy Thursday)

At church, I saw a corpus on a cross and the cross slowly moved over toward the tabernacle. The corpus disappeared first and then the cross. Jesus was leaving His memorial to us in the Blessed Sacrament. Jesus said: ***"Remember Me forever in My Blessed Sacrament, since this is the gift of My presence among you. This is more than just a remembrance, it is your daily bread by which you have a viable spiritual life on earth. This gift of My presence awaits your visiting and praising Me. This is the beginning of heaven for you. It is like a training, since you can worship Me on earth as often as you like. My angels share in this worship, for which they also are eternally grateful. Share your all with Me."***

Later, at the Holy Hour, I could see a shiny new gold colored car. Jesus said: ***"My people, how many times must I remind you that striving for riches in this world is not your purpose in life. Many times, also, I have sent you this message that only heavenly things have any real value for you. Strive, My people, to please Me*** *only and you will then see at the end why I have directed you so. You cannot take your riches with you. They will not help you at the judgment and if you were selfish, they may even hinder your spirituality. Do not let this message of My love for you fall on deaf ears. Listen to My priorities for your life. Then you will see at My gates of heaven how much peace and joy awaits you. You must be patient in My love as I will prune all your worldly ways from you. When I have you all to myself, I will be able to lavish My graces and joy on you and you will wonder why you did not see My light of understanding sooner. My faithful, you will share in such glory that you cannot even imagine how beautiful life will be with Me. Have hope and keep straight on your path to Me."*

Friday, April 14, 1995: (Good Friday)

After Communion, I could see a very tall tree as if it went to the sky from its base. I then saw Jesus on the cross and I was drawn close to see His wounds. Jesus said: ***"Come to Me, My people, on this day commemorating My death on the cross. I have asked you to come closer to Me through prayer. Many times you find other things to do than pray as much as I ask you. At this time I wish you to look deep into My wounds in My hands, My feet, My side and My head. As you imagine just a little of the pain and agony I went through, think even now how your sins continue to aggravate that first pain on the cross. If you could refrain from your sins even for a moment, you could spare Me some suffering of what I must go through for you. I have died for all men and all their sins even unto the end of time. So My suffering is still on-going even today. My people, see the error in your ways and come to realize how My ways of love and peace will satisfy all your desires. Beyond your earthly wants, your soul craves to be with Me and rest in My glorious presence. So, give in to your spiritual aspirations and quell your earthly thoughts and you will rest in My peace."***

Saturday, April 15, 1995: (Easter Vigil)

At church, I saw an empty cross. I then saw an old person. Jesus said: ***"On that dark night, I descended into the bowels of the earth, as I went to those who had died. All at once, at the appointed time after three days, I led those spirits who were worthy up to heaven with Me. At that time, I defeated death and sin***

once and for all time. This is a celebration for good. In you, God has manifested the victory over evil. This is hope for eternal life to all who will follow Me. Come forward to Me, for now is the acceptable time to be forgiven and saved from Satan's clutches. Celebrate My Resurrection as the new life waiting for all who seek conversion. This is a blessing all should seek, to be with Me in My love and glory. Then at the second resurrection, once again you will be united with your body and you will be whole again as I intended it to be. Come with Me, My children, and glory in this jubilation."

Sunday, April 16, 1995: (Easter Sunday)

After Communion, I saw some angels kneeling in adoration at the Lord's Resurrection. Then above there was an all-seeing large eye of God the Father witnessing this event. Jesus said: ***"Alleluia, joy is in My heart this day for all My faith-filled people. Today is the high point of your faith. This hope which comes from My Resurrection is the pillar to grasp for to be saved. Since this is the celebration of My victory over sin and death, it is a glorious time indeed. This moment of love and peace I share with everyone. This is the instrument by which I will lift up all My people to be saved much like Moses lifted the snake on the staff. Come forward then and share in the happiness of My glory. By your acceptance of Me you will be sharing in your own resurrection. Be thankful and give glory to God for such a precious gift as life itself. Because now you can share in My eternal happiness in heaven."***

Later, at church, I saw a drive-in screen with a small picture being shown. The sense was that we should not just have a religion of convenience. Jesus said: ***"My people, you can only be faithful to Me if you let Me lead your lives. You cannot follow your desires and will and remain obedient to all My laws. In other words, you cannot have a religion of convenience for only one or two hours a week. You must live every day the faith I wish you to live. Do not be occupied with the things of this world to the exclusion of a good prayer life. Your free time should be spent equally for prayer and your desires. Anything less than that and you will be letting the world over influence you. Keep an open path to Me or your love for Me will soon grow cold. It cannot be this way for My disciples. I expect more from My faith-***

ful since you are My inner core of believers. Reform your lives now and you will enjoy your glorious reward for responding to My call for conversion. You cannot stand still in your love for Me. You will either grow or decline. See to it that it is for growth, for your own soul's sake."

Monday, April 17, 1995:

After Communion, I saw Jesus in some bright white robes and He was walking up a rocky cleft and called out ***"Follow Me"***. Jesus said: ***"My friends, you are an Easter people. If you would be My disciples, you must follow the way of My apostles. At first they did not understand what rising from the dead meant, but you have the honor of seeing both before and after My earthly appearance in the Scriptures. Take advantage of this knowledge and make it personal in your faith experience. Seeing My risen body gave My apostles hope and eventually calmed all their fears. This Easter message of salvation is such a glorious story that with the Holy Spirit the apostles were eager to evangelize the people and free them from their sins. You too must be touched by this excitement and renewal of your faith in Me. This joy is always available to you, if you would just make it a part of your life."***

Later, at church, I saw a picture of all manner of human spirits rising out of the ground. They were all traveling through the air horizontally head first and gradually they were lifted to heaven for the great judgment. Jesus said: ***"When the day of judgement comes, how will I find each of you? Will there be any faith left on the earth when I come for you? Some will ask if they saw Me in those in need. Yes, I say whoever clothed the naked, fed the hungry, or visited the sick, they did it unto Me. You must be accountable for your actions and how you love Me. You must see this life as a test of your faith's endurance. While you have the good life, it is easy to be thankful to Me. The real test lies when you must endure hardships and difficulties. You will learn you have to live life with My constant help. You will not win the battle on your own. You must give your life over to Me so you can lose your life to save it. Until you can give your will over to Me, your struggle in this life will be in vain. I am here to lead and help you, if you would just ask for My graces and blessings. Do not try to please men but please Me instead."***

Tuesday, April 18, 1995:

After Communion, I saw all the people in the pews with their heads down and kneeling as the Lord was standing on the altar in white robes. Jesus said: ***"I am the risen Lord and I ask your humble reverence in My presence. The faithful have indeed been true to My word. It is a time of splendor for you to remember the joy at the time of My resurrection. This is an example of the joy and beauty which awaits each of My faithful as you will follow in My footsteps to see Me face to face. You will then be a truly resurrected people, all a part of Me. See that this new life will truly be worth sharing. You must struggle now so you can be a part of us in this Communion of Saints. You will long to see this day, for it is your soul's strongest desire to be with Me. Pray that you will always stay united with Me."***

Later, at church, I saw a red and gold mural on the wall and then I saw a clock ticking with the second hand moving for about ten seconds. Jesus said: ***"I am being poured out like a libation for all My people. There is much joy at this Easter celebration, but you cannot forget that there are still many of My people suffering in this life. Remember to continue praying for peace and harmony in your world and have it start within your own families. You see much violence in your streets, in war torn countries and even abortions continue. I offer you hope amidst all this destruction. Until man realizes I am the supreme ruler of your lives, he will continue groping in the darkness. See My light of love and dispel the darkness by your own influence. It is mercy I desire and not sacrifice. In all you do, do it for love of Me. You must live your lives with a true Christian purpose or it will lose its meaning. Pray much, My children, for you have to endure much before you can be with Me in heaven, but keep your eyes trained on Me and I will lead you home."***

Wednesday, April 19, 1995:

After Communion, I first had a vision of a triangle representing the Trinity. I then could see a picture of Jesus lying in the tomb. Finally, I again could see Him in white robes walking about. Jesus said: ***"You have seen through vision and Scripture how the bulwark of your faith has been demonstrated. You have realized that even as a man, death had no power over Me. This is My***

example of love to you. It is also a vision of hope for all My faithful that God is always in control of events. I am the one you can trust to love you and help you in your need. Enjoy the beauty of this celebration and carry these thoughts with you throughout the year."

Later, at the prayer group, I saw a thick broad arrow pointing upward from the ground. Jesus said: ***"I have been raised from the dead to heaven to show you the power of God over death and time. Believe in My Resurrection since it is by faith that you will follow Me in this way as well. Remember your soul is immortal and death has no power over it. There will be a temporary separation of your body, but your spirit's dwelling must truly be planned for."*** I had a flashback to the sign ***"God is not mocked"*** at the picketing of the ***"Priest"*** movie. Jesus said: ***"The movie makers of this and other immoral films will have a heavy burden of guilt which will call down My wrath on their evil works. Time will show that those who defy My laws will be led to their own confusion and despair since they refuse My help."*** I then saw a clock and a person saying a Rosary. Mary came and said: ***"In time My Immaculate Heart will triumph in union with my Son. Your Rosaries will have great power over evil. So do not be discouraged if you think your prayers are not answered. In the end the answer to your prayer will be more beautiful than you requested."*** I saw a picture of the pope carrying the cross on a staff. Jesus said: ***"My pope son will have much to suffer at the hands of this world. Pray for him that he may have the strength to endure this trial for the faithful. When his power diminishes, your world will sink further into its demise."*** I saw some people suffering from today's disaster (Oklahoma). Jesus said: ***"You will continue to see the Arab element in much of the world's violence. Pray much for world peace and do not increase the hate in the world seeking revenge. This would cause an ever expanding circle of retribution as in other places."*** I saw a table with a Holy Bible on it. Jesus said: ***"Take the time to read My holy word and you will understand how the foretelling of My coming is central to salvation history. As with the disciples on the road to Emmaus, I would wish your hearts would burn for love of My word in you."*** I finally saw a pentagram and Jesus said: ***"Look for evil to gain an increasing hold on those who are subject to the world. They will grow in***

their harassment of you. Seek My protection and the evil will not influence My faithful."

Thursday, April 20, 1995:

After Communion, I saw what looked like a tomb where Our Lady rested and was raised up. Jesus said: ***"When you saw My Mother gloriously raised from the dead and My apostles more by the natural course, you are witnessing My first fruits of My resurrection. As in the readings you must really understand that it is truly I who raised body and spirit from the dead in your presence. This truly was My greatest miracle and so becomes a most salvific action for all eternity. Again, see that your salvation has been planned from the beginning of creation as witnessed by My prophecies in the prophets of old. See the beauty of this redeeming act to forgive all your sins. Now you have been made acceptable before the Father even despite your weaknesses. See this glory and be glad for your Redeemer loves you and is all merciful."***

Friday, April 21, 1995:

After Communion, I could only see a white Host. Gradually a scene of a priest lifting the Host at Consecration could be seen. Jesus said: ***"I am being lifted up before all of you as the one to have hope in. My very presence shows you how much I care for each one of you. My love is so pervasive that it reaches out to everyone completely, even the ones who refuse Me out of ignorance. You now can appreciate My loving act of instituting My Eucharist so that through the priest you can share in My ongoing spiritual meal each day. I offer you up My daily bread as a strength for and a closer share in the love of My oneness. If you should wander away through sin, know I am always here to forgive you. You are then welcomed back into My heavenly faithful community. Be all-loving to each other."***

Later, at church, I could see explosions of bombs with big white clouds. Then I could see faces of men overlaid on the clouds. Jesus said: ***"I have given you messages previously to warn you that events would be speeding up and eventually become almost simultaneous. You will see more of these terrorist activities and natural disasters coming more frequently. As man and nature both witness disharmony, you will see this as a result from love***

turning cold and away from My peace and harmony. As man wants to be left to his own devices and puts Me out of his life, all order will cave in around him. This is why the Anti-Christ will have appeal to quell the chaos and strive towards his false peace which will be his trap to gain control over the people's minds. So be attentive to these trends, but also take hope in My promise of true peace when evil will be overthrown. The Anti-Christ will be cold, calculating and unloving in all he does. Remain in prayer and continue each day with My help."

Saturday, April 22, 1995:

After Communion, I saw someone reading documents as in some kind of laws. Jesus said: ***"You will see, My friends, an increasing evil trend in your society as immorality will possess the people much like in the days of Noah and the days of Sodom and Gomorrah. As you see vile behavior in men, it will carry over into their laws and their behavior. You see even today people give excuses for promiscuous behavior and fornication. The sins of the flesh are rampant with artificial birth control and means of artificial fertilization. Even your abortion laws show the degradation of your morality on murder. Lawyers are allowed to manipulate the law for their own gains instead of real justice. You will even see this extended in the form of persecution as My faithful will be tested by evil men through many evil decrees. As My apostles suffered to defend My name, so you also will be tested for the increasing evil will soon attack the good in all manner of injustice. Even unnatural lifestyles are being promoted as acceptable behavior. I tell you there will come a day you least suspect when My justice will come upon these evil doers and My triumph will cast this bad lot into the eternal hellfire meant for the evil angels. Pray to Me for help, My faithful, to endure this evil time."***

At church, I at first saw some Easter lilies and then I could see some angels blowing long trumpets to signal the Lord's triumph. Jesus said: ***"My people, know that I love you all very dearly. You have witnessed My resurrection by word in the Scripture and in faith. Know that your faith in Me is not in vain and in essence I am your salvation. He who seeks Me and follows My ways, awaits Me at the gates of heaven. You know also that My mercy endures forever. As you prepare by novena for Mercy Sunday, you must***

reach out in faith to ask My mercy and pray for your needs. Those who have faith will receive My blessing and mercy besides for all your sins. Coming to Confession at this time is even more appropriate so you can have your robes clean to receive Me. I pour out My love on all of you as I share My glory in the spreading of My word. The more you are willing to grow closer to Me, the more graces I will lavish on those who love Me and give public testimony to Me."

Sunday, April 23, 1995: (Mercy Sunday)

After Communion, I could see the earth from out in space and there was a bright light all around it as all who were in heaven and all those in the universe were celebrating Christ's Resurrection. There was a sense we were honored by God's Son because the devil was on earth. Jesus said: ***"In your vision you are seeing Me more as King of the universe. You do not even understand how insignificant the size of your planet is to all of the Universe. This is why you all are indeed blessed to have your own personal Savior come to redeem you. Again, those who have been fortunate to receive the gift of faith, you too are even more blessed since your future with Me is assured with My help. This is indeed a celebration for those who have turned from their sinful ways to adopt My ways. Even though you cannot fathom an endless universe or infinite time, know that My love for you never falters and My mercy always awaits your return. When you have passed your test of life, you will see it is worth every minute of suffering to know you will be in the presence of My love and peace forever."***

Later, at church, on Mercy Sunday I saw Jesus with the rays of mercy and grace coming from His heart. I then saw a vision of a baby's birth. Jesus said: ***"Believe in My mercy and you will have eternal rest. I am showering My mercy and graces upon you, especially this day that you honor My mercy. I am with you all days and I ask you to continue this devotion to Me often. For those who accept My divine will as part of their own, this is the perfection I seek of all of you—to be one with Me. As you walk with Me, you will be as if reborn in a new dimension of love for Me. You will enjoy My peace and I enjoin on you to hold it fast since My love and peace is all your soul requires. You must live your lives of faith as little children. They have an innocence which should not***

be disturbed, as you should have. Again, you should have a strong sense of security in My taking care of you, as that of a child for its parents. You should be a peace-filled people, as I greeted My apostles. For fear should have no place in your lives. Believe in this faith and My mercy and you will be totally consoled."

Monday, April 24, 1995:

After Communion, I saw a man kneeling in prayer in a large European church which could have been St. Peter's. Jesus said: ***"Since the earliest days of My Church, there have been differing opinions which threaten the unity of the Church. Many could not accept the giving of My Body and Blood in the Eucharist for the faithful to partake in. Still others later created divisions over various beliefs in the faith. I call all My people to unity in one faith. Divisive clicks are from the evil one. Focus your attention on Me and believe in Me and do not be concerned that everyone should think exactly as you want everyone to think. But those who deny My laws, these will be dealt with. Do not follow false teachings and pray to the Holy Spirit for the proper discernment."***

Later, at church, I saw many beautiful flowers in a botanical garden. Then outside I saw a scene of green lawns and green trees. Jesus said: ***"My people, I have brought beauty every place you look in creation but what have you brought Me? My faithful please Me very much, but still I see many who are only bringing forth evil. You wonder why crime and killing is so rampant in your streets, but I tell you look how you are training your children. Today, your TV programming glorifies sex, killing and horror stories. Do you think this has an influence on children as well as the adults? The movie makers are most to blame, but it is the people who pay for this abuse and accept it, that makes it sell. With every passing day your society accepts a higher threshold of acceptance of this wickedness. Do you think that this will go unanswered? Now you must fight against this abomination in your media. Protest to the sponsors and better yet, turn it off and pray for these people. They have been so ingrained with this filth that they no longer see anything wrong. Is it any wonder why they do not come to Confession when they do not know what sin is? Pray much, My people, for My justice will be coming against this evil generation."***

Tuesday, April 25, 1995: (Feast of St. Mark)

At church, I saw a beautiful white angel and later I saw an angel with large wings leading me to an altar in a church. I asked the Lord for permission of my guardian angel, Mark, to give me a message. Mark said: ***"Greetings from your guardian angel, Mark. I am grateful you have asked for a message and welcome my counsel. Indeed, it is more important that you keep your thoughts on your Savior than being taken up with worldly distractions. Nothing should hinder you in saying your prayers. You have been told many times that your prayers should come first. Not only first but equal in time as well. Offer up all you do to the Lord so your every action can be a prayer. You are right in giving proper time to take care of these messages. They are worthy to have others benefit from them as well as yourself. Take these messages to heart and follow their intent for they are to help you as well. When you are outside of time, you will see why all creatures are so awed by God that we ceaselessly praise Him. When you are blinded by your earthly weakness, you cannot always understand this. I am telling you as Christ tells you to focus on Him more and desire to pray more so you are more prepared to please Him as when you will be in heaven. It is this desire and craving for Christ that sets His faithful apart from the accursed. So show your deep love for your Savior as often as possible and He will see your efforts and reward you with His blessings and guidance."***

Later, at church, I saw an adult dressed and acting like a child. Jesus said: ***"My people, many times you act like children as you complain and want everything easy and handed to you. Life, as you know it, is not easy. Anything worthwhile, as education or a good marriage must be worked hard for. You cannot just wish for something to happen without putting forth a considerable effort on your part. This is why life is a test and it does not suit the lazy and slothful. You must be conscientious in all you do, if you expect some good results. So it is with your spiritual life as well. Being holy and faithful takes some effort also. Your earthly bodies crave their own needs, but you must control your appetites and desires through your intellect. I have given you souls which crave nothing but being with Me. I have instilled a love in you for Me and your neighbor. It is still your choice by your free will to decide how much you will love Me and want to follow My will.***

For those who desire eternity with Me, you must pray much to overcome your weakened body's resolve. Ask for My help and grace to mold your spiritual life to please Me. Be willing to spend many hours in My service. If you can do this for love of Me, you will see and enjoy the fruits of your labor."

Wednesday, April 26, 1995:

At church, I saw a vision of demon eyes and black wolves with ugly faces. Jesus said: ***"My people, if you could only see how displeasing to Me your sin is. It is as displeasing to Me as it is for you to see these fallen angels tarnished by their stay in hell. If you could see also how evil appears even when you are tempted by the demons, you would run away from it in disgust, but even so, evil is portrayed to you more as a feeling satisfying some earthly craving. It many times is disguised as a good or some kind of rationalization. Deep down in your conscience, though, you know right from wrong. So no matter how appealing something may be to the body, follow My commands and do nothing to offend Me. If you truly love Me, follow My ways and think of sinful actions as a slap in the face to the One who loves you. You must be always on guard to fight evil temptations. Discern all your actions and thoughts and stay on the right path to following My will."***

Later, at the prayer group, I saw some generals and there was a sense that wars will continue to plague this century. Jesus said: ***"There is much love among My faithful, but others are still plotting takeovers and deadly force to win their objectives. Greed for power and riches drives many people who try to reach beyond their capabilities to control others. You will continue to see wars motivated by such obstinate people."*** I saw some people packing their belongings to make some kind of a move. Jesus said: ***"Many will be uprooted from their homes to travel away from certain cities and authorities. You have seen this in Africa and it will start to occur in other places all over the world."*** I then saw some tablets like the sign of the Ten Commandments. Jesus said: ***"Look to My commandments, if your society wants to correct itself. When you live in defiance of My laws, you will reap the consequence of a lawless chaos. Many want peace, but they do not want to make the sacrifices to follow My will."*** I could see the eyes of a terrorist with a mask on. There was an intent only to destroy any authority.

Jesus said: ***"Terrorism will continue to increase since this is one of the weapons of the evil one to kill and cause disharmony. It is intent only on disruption and is devoid of love or reason. This will increase as evil gains more of a foothold in your society. Pray for peace, My people. This is the only way to cure dissension."*** I saw some strange flying machines which looked like flying saucers. Jesus said: ***"There will be many unexplained sightings of mixed origin. Some of these forces will be exploited by evil. New technology will be used for evil purposes, rather than for good."*** I saw Mary come in the name of the Immaculate Conception as in Our National Shrine. Mary said: ***"This title of the Immaculate Conception is both symbolic of your country as well as my desire for all of you to imitate me. By yourself alone, you cannot do it, but with my Son's help you can follow me in a sinless life. Even though you may fail at times, never stop struggling for this ideal. With perseverance in faith, you will win your victory through Jesus."*** Finally, I saw some electrical devices and they were shrinking in size. Jesus said: ***"Your technology of miniature chips will enable stealth in the public to watch and control the people. Beware of these devices as they will be deployed in secret to monitor your very actions with your motives being questioned. Much of this will be done in the name of national security, but its real purpose will be to aid the Anti-Christ when he appears at his time."***

Thursday, April 27, 1995:

After Communion, I saw Maria E. on her porch and there was that same feeling as we were joined in God's love. I then saw a vision of a huge display of an eye. Jesus said: ***"My people, open*** *your eyes of faith and receive the Holy Spirit. Now is the time to celebrate My Resurrection and spread the good news of salvation. Man has been allowed again into heaven if he follows My laws, but I am a merciful and loving God as well. I receive all repentant sinners as the angels rejoice at their conversions. Even if a faithful one goes to Confession there is rejoicing over the rededication of that person back into My good graces. Come to Me and receive My blessing of forgiveness."*

Friday, April 28, 1995:

After Communion, I could see a figure of a pentagram. In the next scene I saw a rock as big as a small hill. Jesus said: *"My people, you see the results of much evil about you but do not be discouraged. For when I am with you and you call My name, all the demons will scatter before you. I am your rock you can depend on. This confidence in faith is at the root of My Church and is why it has been sustained through all these years. For as in the readings, this Gospel proclaimed by the apostles is based in Me and that is why it has survived. So be uplifted by My love, for you have been redeemed and your sins forgiven. This power of mine will help you succeed in life and bring you home eventually to heaven. This is the hope of eternal life with Me that all My faithful can look forward to."*

Later, at church, I saw a huge tornado winding its way of destruction. I could see multiple tornadoes as well. Jesus said: *"My people, I have warned you before that you will be tested by the elements. Indeed, you will see many disasters as the year draws on. This will be a way of humbling your pride in thinking you can control things. An errant storm can raise much havoc, and you will see how little you can do about it. As the big picture becomes clear to you, you will see how insignificant your control is over anything. It is with this realization that you will be brought to your knees in giving Me praise for handling creation. You will see how an evil generation will bring itself to disintegration so that I will have to intervene to make things new again. It is just a matter of time until evil will be overcome and the renewal of the earth will start a new era of peace under My control."*

Saturday, April 29, 1995: (St. Catherine of Siena)

After Communion, I saw a picture of St. Catherine. She said: ***"Many people of your time are troubled, especially spiritually, since they do not take time enough to be close to Jesus. I am***

asking each of you, especially the faithful, to teach others of the power of your Savior. Ask Him to help you evangelize those around you. I encourage all people to have a prayerful life, for this truly is the way of anyone desiring to be a saint with God one day."

Later, at church, I saw a Host in a monstrance and light was shining out from it as it was pulsating like a beating heart. I then saw the Host as if it was suspended out in space with the stars of the universe all around. Finally, it came back to earth again. Jesus said: ***"You are seeing how I am a prisoner for you so you can see Me under the appearance of bread. I chose to be present for you so you can see My heart beating with a deep love for you. You may have difficulty understanding how I can love the most ugly of sinners. Yet, I tell you I love each of you equally with the full infinite love I can express to you. As it is, you are the one who determines how much you love—I love you always to the fullest. As your love for Me is perfected through prayer, meditation and good works, you will be slowly drawn into My endless being. Those in heaven know Me without any limitation because I have absorbed their will into mine. You will be in such a spiritual ecstasy of love with Me, nothing else but praising Me will be your concern to please Me. This heightened state of awareness of God in full love and knowledge will give you such a peace that no words will be able to describe it. Live in My love and your heart will be complete."***

Sunday, April 30, 1995:

After Communion, I saw Our Lord with His hands stretched out before a huge audience sitting in a large theater. He was teaching the people. Jesus said: ***"My son, today I speak to all My messengers as in the Gospel to 'feed My sheep'. You have been given the responsibility to make My love known to all who seek My message. Even My faithful who have been baptized and accept My word are also called to publicly witness My name to the people. You will see in the coming days that you will be harassed for speaking of My name much like the apostles were maltreated, but I tell you, you will be joy-filled to be tested for the sake of My name. Even if you must suffer for proclaiming My word, it is better as Peter said to follow My ways than the ways of men. I will protect your souls, but your bodies may have to endure a future torture,***

but have hope in Me for I will triumph in the end and all who keep their allegiance to Me will receive a prophet's reward."

Later, at church, I saw the outlines of some newer cars and there were all kinds of electronic gadgets all over the cars. There was a sense that signals were going out from the cars. Jesus said: ***"This will serve as another warning to all those with newer cars. There will be detection devices in your cars that can be followed by satellite. For those going into hiding, other transportation as bicycles will be necessary for some distances. Many things of this world will be used against My faithful, but I will help you in your need to avoid the evil men. Stay focused on prayer and My Eucharist and I will give you hope to get through this trial. The time of evil will last only a short time and then My triumph will lead you to My glory. Fear not this time and keep My peace with you at all times."***

Monday, May 1, 1995:

After Communion, I saw a large white arrow pointing upward. Behind it I saw a triangular shaped opening to a tomb cut into the rock. Jesus said: ***"As I have raised from the dead, you too will do likewise. This is the faith all Christians have in Me that I will fulfill My promise of eternal life. It is hard for some to appreciate this gift of renewed life in the spirit, but it awaits each of you just the same. I eagerly await each of you to come into My presence after death. With this glorious day awaiting you, it should give hope to all who fear the unknown after death. Let Me assure you, those who follow My ways have nothing to fear. It is the souls who reject Me that need your prayers the most for conversion. Unless they change their intentions, they will suffer the pangs of hell for all eternity. Stay on the narrow road to heaven by committing your lives over to Me in a life of prayer."***

Later, at church, I at first saw a Host above with rays coming down on a man having convulsions. I then saw in an elevator shaft a chain being lowered to help someone. Jesus said: ***"My people, seek and you shall find. Ask and I will answer you. But in all of your endeavors never cease to remember I am right by your side ready to help you. Many times at the start of the day you pray for Me to help you through your day. I tell you, look close at everything you do during the day as well. Think of each action you are***

doing and offer it up to please Me instead of just satisfying yourself for accomplishing your agenda. As you look closely this way, some things you do, you will recognize as not pleasing to Me and this will help in correcting your motives and intentions. As a difficulty arises, think to ask Me for help right at that moment. I am always willing to walk with you through your every trouble. But learn to make Me more a part of your daily life. In this way, you will draw closer to Me and be stronger when temptation comes. Pray, My people, to live for love of Me and I will reward you with everlasting life."

Tuesday, May 2, 1995:

After Communion, I saw a break in the clouds which pictured a new world of milk and honey. It seemed we would encounter some future land of beauty as the renewed earth might appear. Jesus said: ***"The joy of being with Me would be to experience My presence in Communion for all time, but you, My friends, must first experience the suffering in this life as I had to endure it. The vision which St. Stephen had is your vision of hope knowing that heaven awaits you as well. All will not be martyred for the faith, but you each can witness your faith so that those around you can see the love of Me in you. Keep Me ever in your thoughts, so I can lift you up so you can endure this age. More trials will come on this generation for its rejection of Me. Keep My faith burning in your souls and you will soon see Me face to face."***

Later, at church, I saw a red carpet hanging on the wall and then I saw Jesus moving in agony on the cross. Jesus said: ***"I am showing the contrast between how I accept you with open arms to receive you and how many people reject My welcome. I am ever present to you in My Eucharist where I wait to nourish those who come to Me. Yet I am rejected not only by My name, but in the way many treat their fellowman. Realize that with wars, killing and anger when you harm your neighbor, you are making Me suffer as well. It is up to My faithful to encourage peace among all peoples so that harmony will reign instead of your deteriorating morality. Many prayers and good works will be needed to stem this evil, but alas, it will require My intervention to right this destruction man has brought on himself. Love Me and your neighbor and you will be following My will for you."***

Wednesday, May 3, 1995: (Sts. Philip & James)

After Communion, I saw a strong light as from heaven and there was a man with a beard that I assumed was one of the apostles. Jesus said: ***"You are seeing My true disciples who have proclaimed the faith I have given them. So it is with all of My faithful. You too now must go forth and spread My Gospel word to bring souls to Me. It is good you are at My daily sacrifice of the Mass, but you must share this gift of love with all who will listen. For I am your light and your life and you cannot go on without Me. I am by your side ready to lead all of you who ask My help. Put aside your pride and let Me control your lives. In that way you will be open to the gifts of the spirit."***

Later, at the prayer group, I saw a ship in a harbor and then later I saw it sinking. Jesus said: ***"You will see wars and terrorism increasing and many lives will be lost. Your testing time is coming and evil will have its day for a short time. But I will be with you to guide you, so have no fear. Have hope for My triumph is but a moment away."*** I then saw some people in the White House talking about terrorism. Jesus said: ***"I am asking My people to avoid participating in conflicts for the devil wants struggle to cause more killings. Instead, avoid taking up weapons and go into hiding to avoid the evil men. There is nothing on earth worth killing over, since all things will pass away. Look to the papal teachings on the proper disposition to warfare."*** I saw people wearing eyeglasses and a flame reflected in one of the lenses. Jesus said: ***"Your eyes are the light of your soul. Show your peace and love for Me in the way you greet others. Keep a joyful disposition because you are a resurrected people. By sharing your happiness with others you can witness a Christian love to raise their spirits."*** I could see a kitchen and a window being opened to air out the fumes of cooking. Jesus said: ***"Be open-minded, My people, to following My ways instead of just the ways of man. Let the breath of the Holy Spirit come into your souls to instill My love for you. You can improve yourself by emptying yourself of any selfish motives. Then you will be ready to receive Me and let Me lead your life."*** I saw an empty room which looked out of a window on a sunny day. I then saw the Lord coming to help me. Jesus said: ***"Do not let your earthly pride stand in the way of giving your will over to Me. You must lower yourselves before men instead of seeking***

fame and attention. As you shun the glory of men, then you will be ready to accept My glory which will make you whole in body and spirit. Mary wanted to come but there were many obstructions to seeing her. Mary said: ***"Your earthly distractions many times keep me from coming more into your lives. Pray my Rosary from the heart and slowly whenever you can. In this way I will be closer to you and you will see me more clearly."*** I finally saw some faces in great excitement over gaining money and things that glitter. Jesus said: ***"Do not be taken up with acquiring so much of this world's goods. They are only temporary and can be taken from you as easily as you acquired them. Seek My love instead. If you do not reform your lives, the Anti-Christ will sift you in your desire for his false peace and promise of riches for all. He will be cold and without love. It is My love in your life which should be the most important thing which you should seek."***

Thursday, May 4, 1995:

After Communion, I could see the little Host at Maria's chapel and we were joined in prayer. She said: ***"We will be joined with Jesus when I come."*** I then had a vision of a woman dressed in gold on a throne. She could have been some kind of queen. Jesus said: ***"At the Mass you are blessed with My heavenly presence. Be thankful for you have a greater than Solomon here. The queen of the south will come to seek Me for she will see My glory and be glad. Many on earth have praised Me, even those you least suspect. Rejoice in the glory of My Resurrection since now all of you are being invited to My banquet table. For many are called but few are chosen. Love Me with all your heart and show Me forth in all your actions. Then I will bless My faithful and bid them enter My Kingdom of heaven."***

Later, after Communion, I saw stairs as I was walking down into the tomb of Christ. Jesus said: ***"All of you, at one time, will face death and be anxious of the unknown. I tell you, have faith in My Resurrection for this is how it will be for you. You will see the first judgment as your body separates from your soul. At this time, those accursed will be sent to hell. Those that need purification will be purified in a place you call purgatory. While those who have suffered enough on earth to pay for the temporal punishment of their sins will enter My glory directly. The***

second judgment will unite your bodies and souls and there will only be those in heaven or hell for eternity. You are witnessing My mercy for those who love Me even a little and also My justice for those who totally reject Me. Pray, My people, to love Me to the utmost of your being and you can be raised to a higher level in My glory of heaven."

Friday, May 5, 1995:

After Communion, I could see a latrine at first, but I did not understand this vision since it was unusual. Jesus said: ***"My son, even though this vision is a hard one to understand, I am trying to show you that in every mundane task you do each day you see an opportunity to love Me. Offer up all you do each day to please Me. Even things you are obligated to do contain a blessing. So in today's readings, My offering up of My Body and Blood for your heavenly food was repulsive to the Jews and some of My followers. With many things in your life, you do not understand their inner beauty, but My Eucharist is your spiritual food with My presence and is your salvation. You must keep this testament of faith ever before you. This is My most loving act, to suffer for you, and it is My means of instilling My love in each of you."***

Saturday, May 6, 1995:

After Communion, I saw a carved out tunnel in the rock and I was passing through it. Then there was a light at the end of the tunnel and I came out into the renewed earth. Jesus said: ***"My people, you are called to suffer in My name. You first will have to endure this evil age by avoiding the Anti-Christ. He will be powerful for a short reign. It is at that time that you must go into hiding. This is why you are seeing the vision of caves, but you will be in the ground, as I was buried for three days. Then you will be raised at the time of My triumph and this will be the light at the end of the tunnel. The evil ones will all be placed in hell and you will experience a beautiful earth once again. This will be an era of peace and a reward for being faithful as well. So continue to pray constantly for this strength of spirit."***

Later, at church, I saw many city buildings with lights all over and then in their midst I could see a monstrance with the Host displayed. Jesus said: ***"Many people are in search of riches*** *in this world but they overlook the greatest treasure which is in their midst in all the churches. Come to Me, My children, and visit Me in My tabernacle or in exposition. Those that visit Me often can never get enough of being with Me. For when you are quietly in My company, I can talk to your soul, if you would just listen. There is a spiritual beauty in My presence which all your souls should crave ceaselessly. The more you praise and adore Me in My presence, the more My love envelops you. Ask Me in prayer to help you in your daily needs and I will walk with you through your difficulties. You need to pray with Me often to have a contrite heart and visit Me as well in My Sacrament of Penance. You need to renew yourself often to have your sins forgiven and keep your soul pure. It is humbling to admit your sins, but the more you humble yourself, the more childlike faith you will have. Love Me deeply, My children, for My love for you knows no bounds."*

Sunday, May 7, 1995:

At Fonda I asked for a message from Kateri Tekakwitha. I saw a long house and some flowers outside. I then saw a young Indian maiden and she showed me her cross. She said: *"As you entered this chapel, you have felt my presence. My lesson to you is one of suffering for Jesus. In your life you will suffer many hardships and even little daily struggles. Learn to use these as graces by offering them up to Jesus as a prayer instead of complaining. Go now and witness my love for you and your companions. I love you much in Jesus."*

Later, at the Auriesville Shrine Mass after Communion I very clearly saw a Bible and then some other books. Jesus said: *"My children, I am showing you a picture of My word in Scripture. It is important that you set aside a few minutes each day to read My word. It is inspirational for you to see My plan of salvation being fulfilled. For those who have a little more time for Me, it is good to read books about the saints and how their example may help you. By having others to act as role models for you, it will show you how to improve your spiritual lives. Those who are trying to perfect themselves, ask for My grace to help you see the proper priorities in your life. Once you see how beautiful your life can be following Me more closely, you will never want to cease grow-*

ing in your faith. Follow Me in spirit and word and your soul will have true peace."

Monday, May 8, 1995:

After Communion, I saw myself walking with many people along a pathway. It was a winding path and gradually went uphill and into a bright light. Jesus said: ***"I come to each of you individually giving each of you an equal opportunity to enter into My Kingdom. I have even paved the way for you with My death on the cross. You have all been equally redeemed. Your duty, if you accept My love, is only to love and serve Me. I give each of you a part in My plan for humanity to grow to their potential. Everyone is welcome to heaven, but you must be committed to the struggle of life to show your attention to My love and that of your neighbor. Some are granted more graces out of My generous bounty of graces, but do not be concerned with jealousies or envy of someone else's better gifts. You are all a part of My faith community. Be joyful that you are asked to serve Me and be ready to fulfill all that you can be for Me. Your reward of eternal life awaits you as each one's cup will be filled with My glory no matter to what extent that is for each. Rejoice and be glad, the Lord has come. Life is beautiful in the eyes of those who understand My law and keep it."***

Later, at church, I saw a train station as our moment of departure from this life. Jesus said: ***"My people, many thoughts run through your mind when you think of your life on earth. You are here but a short time before you have to make an accounting for your life. When you have a quiet moment in meditation, you can realize how your loving Savior loves you. When you have My love, you are peaceful and content. For you know full well that being with Me is the same as being in the presence of the Father. The Father and I are one and we draw you to us. Seek your everlasting life with Me by remaining faithful to My word."***

Tuesday, May 9, 1995:

After Communion, I saw a shaped stone like a cornerstone. Jesus said: ***"I am your rock of faith, the cornerstone on which I built My Church. If you have faith in My love for you and follow My ways, surely you will have life in Me. As My Church was***

J.
T.

forming, there were great missionaries of My word to spread the good news of My resurrection. So, again, history repeats itself, since new missionaries are being called to evangelize the people before the tribulation comes. Listen to My servants who are revealing what is necessary for the people to come to Me. Accept Me into your hearts and your everyday lives, and your life will be made new through Me."

Later, at church, I saw people waiting and sitting around. Jesus said: *"My people, many ask Me things in prayer. I hear all your prayers and I want to bless you with an answer where it is beneficial for your soul. Keep in mind that all things must be in conformity with My will and at the proper time I deem appropriate. I welcome your faith in asking Me and know that I could help you. Many times I answer prayers but in My time and not always your time. Do not question why I do things, since many times you do not have all the facts to decide the case. Rest in the knowledge that I will do for you what is necessary to best save your soul. Be more concerned about sending your prayers to Me than just getting your way all the time."*

Wednesday, May 10, 1995:

After Communion, I could see a door in front of me and it looked like a beautiful world on the other side. Jesus said: *"My people, you are seeing a door of opportunity. Many times you are faced with decisions in your earthly life. Some prefer to go it alone and think they can solve life's problems without Me because their pride blinds their decision. It may seem hard at first to let go and sometimes to admit defeat and allow My way and My help to be sought to solve your difficulty. Do not be hasty in your decisions, for without Me you will flounder in your failure and possibly despair in your frustration. When you give yourself over to Me, I will lead you through your door of trust and you will see that My way will be better for your soul and your peace. Man does not understand My ways since He thinks on an earthly plane. But when you see that My plan is best, it is because it is on a higher spiritual plane that lets you overlook the earthly situation. This will present a new world of acceptance of My will for you. All in heaven will rejoice in your decision for Me."*

Later, at the prayer group, I saw a king on a card with some bills of money. Jesus said: ***"Place your trust in Me only, instead of in this world's goods. My love and power are endless, but your money turns worthless in time. Those things you store and buy will rot and pass away. Look for those things that will last, not those that pass away."*** I saw a man dressed in an old army uniform with a narrow brown hat. Jesus said: ***"You are commemorating the 50th anniversary of the end of World War II at a time when World War III hangs in the balance. Unless men can control their greed and anger you will be doomed to repeat a terrible war where many will be killed."*** I saw an angel and sensed it was my guardian angel, Mark. He had a message. He said: ***"You and others will be asked to serve the many. Be judged worthy to serve your Lord and follow His will to help others, without complaint. Ask the Lord to help you meet your goal."*** I then saw some little children. Jesus said: ***"I love the children very much and I ask you to protect them from abuse and help teach them the true faith by example. Bring them to Me so their souls may be united with Me."*** I saw a bridge and some houses. Jesus said: ***"You and My messengers are being called to bridge the gap of spreading My word among the people. Feed My sheep so that their desire for Me will consume them."*** I then saw an ornate closet opening. It looked like doors opening up to an icon. Jesus said: ***"I am opening My graces from My heart as I pour them on all the faithful to strengthen them for the trial. May you reverence My presence whereever you find Me."*** I saw a sword and a picture of a Japanese emperor. Jesus said: ***"Japan will be one of the powers used by the Anti-Christ from the roots of the old line of emperors. Here again you will see evil raised up again from where it once reigned. Many will be deceived by miracles to follow such leaders."***

Thursday, May 11, 1995:

After Communion, I saw some women preparing to take food and clothing together into the woods. Jesus said: ***"My people, you must prepare spiritually and physically for your coming trial. You will see events as I told you coming to a head. The evil men have been planning their hour for many years. Soon they will have their moment in time. This will be a considerably troublesome time for My faithful. It will be an extreme test of your faith. You***

must call on My help, if you are to save your soul. I will test you to see the real depth of your love and trust in Me. Many will falter since this will indeed be a harsh time compared with what you have known up to now. Know that My warning is not far off. Pray, My people, for My strength and discern in prayer how you will approach these times."

Later, at church, I saw a picture of a monk and then I saw a brother dressed as a Franciscan in brown garb. Jesus said: ***"My people, for those who want to grow closer to Me, I encourage you to look to a contemplative time in your life. You must guard your interior life which is your inner spiritual life. It is your time when you give Me your personal attention and listen to My word, that you should treasure. I pour out My love on those who accept Me. All are able to receive Me, but only a few are consistent in their pursuit of Me. I am always watchful of each of My servants and I am ready to shower you with extra graces for following My will. Those who reverence Me, especially before My Blessed Sacrament, will be wrapped firmly in My peace as I draw them closer to My heart. Be ever ready to do what pleases Me and you will continue on your road to your salvation. Love Me always as I love you and you will see a beauty and joy with Me that you cannot find anywhere else. My children, learn from Me how I share My love and your heart will have found its goal."***

Friday, May 12, 1995:

After Communion, I saw the empty opening to a tomb in the rock. Jesus said: ***"I am the Resurrection and the Life; he who believes in Me will receive eternal life. I myself am the heavenly bread come down from heaven which is given to each of you. Those who partake of My supper will be with Me in the eternal bliss of My love. Seek Me first and all else will be given you. Spread the good news of My salvation to all willing to listen. This faith is given freely to everyone, but each must accept this teaching and believe in Me to be saved. For all that would come to the Father must come through Me."***

Saturday, May 13, 1995:

In church, before the Blessed Sacrament, I saw a modern depiction of Jesus on the cross. Jesus said: ***"My people, you must not***

be so concerned with portraying My image in modern surrounds, but be content with adoring Me in the Host during adoration. This is the Bread of Life I have given you. This is My true presence by consecration of the priest. Give praise, honor and glory to Me in My Blessed Sacrament. This is your most beautiful gift I have left you. Do not be so concerned with making as much money as possible. These are worldly pursuits and are not your first priority. Be content in loving Me and your neighbor and I will bless you with enough to continue. Focus all your life on Me and how you can please Me by following My ways. This is how you should spend your time, only for Me. I am your creator who has given you all that you have. Be fruitful and multiply your blessings instead of riches. Then you will experience My peace and that will set you free from the desires of this world."

Later, at church, I saw in vision some people being married. I then saw some lights shining down from above. Jesus said: ***"My people, I am honoring you today as My Church. You are My bride and I am the groom. I have a love for you beyond that of only earthly love. My bond with you comes through My sacraments. This is why the bond of marriage is indeed blessed. For what I have joined in My sacrament is made holy and should be treated as sacred. If you could understand how glorious it is in heaven for bringing new life into the world, you would see the responsibility placed on you for the care of your children's souls. You are sharing in creation with Me in your children. Be thankful for these blessings of life and treasure each life as precious as your own. Pray, My children, to be faithful to each other as you are faithful to Me."***

Sunday, May 14, 1995:

At St. Ignatius Church, Yardley, PA, I saw a bright light in the sky close at hand with many angels all around. They were praising God and giving glory to Him. Jesus said: ***"My people, you are hearing today in the Scriptures of the new earth. For some it may seem just a vision or something not related to the here and now, but I solemnly tell you that a new heaven on earth will come after My triumph over evil. You truly will see a Garden of Eden as before the fall. This was the life I intended for man to be ever cognizant of My presence, but sin entered the world and man was cast***

out of the garden. Soon you will see this time again, for there will be an era of peace when no one will die or suffer sickness. All evil will be cast out and you will enjoy the fruits of My love. The faithful who accept Me now will be rewarded with this renewed life. You, too, along with the angels, will be praising Me and thanking Me for this gift of faith. Have hope, My friends, in Me and I will lead you home to this beautiful world of true harmony."

Later, at church, I saw some nuns praying and walking about a cloister. I had the sense to pray more in my spare time. Jesus said: ***"My children, prayer is most important in your life. It is a way of coming closer to Me and it humbles you to follow My way. For this reason, you must make proper time for prayer no matter what your activities demand. Nothing is more important than finding one hour in your day specifically for prayer. Some have committed their whole lives to Me in prayer. All I ask of you is one hour uninterrupted. My messengers require even more preparation. Even if you must excuse yourself from your company for one hour, you must make this effort. They will understand and honor you for it. This time is more for your protection from sin. It is necessary that your work be protected by having a strong spiritual life. Pray much, all My faithful, for time is drawing close for the trial."***

Monday, May 15, 1995:

After Communion, I saw a strange tracked vehicle with some kind of a new weapon like an antenna pointing out. I sensed it might be some kind of laser weapon. Jesus said: ***"Man has continued to make war on his neighbor instead of peace. He will continue to exploit science for all manner of weapons to kill his neighbor. There will come a time, though, when I will confound men in their warmaking. At the last battle I will allow My angels to show man how little power he has. All men will be laid low by one sweep of My hand and My triumph will be so complete that no one will doubt My authority. Then all will rejoice, for evil will be no more."***

Later, at church, I saw an old stone walled village and the people there were poor but joyful in faith. Jesus said: ***"My people, I bring you a message about suffering. You must see how suffering for Me will gain you many merits in heaven. It is an earthly desire to avoid suffering, yet, if you offer it up as a prayer, it can***

be applied to the remission of anyone's sins. It is easy to be faithful when all is calm and undisturbed, yet, it is meritorious for those souls who endure suffering for My sake and do not complain. If you truly love Me as I suffered for you, you would even look for an opportunity to offer up suffering for Me. See the beauty of a life where no stress disturbs the peace of a true faithful soul. This will of itself make you humble to live a life of service no matter what the cost. Come to Me, all you penitent sinners, and I will bestow My love and forgiveness on you. Then renewed in My love you will long for that precious moment when I accept you into heaven with Me."

Tuesday, May 16, 1995:

After Communion, I kept seeing an image of the Statue of Liberty from different directions. Jesus said: ***"Those who are in sin are under the bondage of sin with its stifling of the spirit away from God. Indeed, sin becomes a habit wherein the body's cravings holds the spirit a prisoner to their whims. Come to Me, My people, and My grace and peace will set you free of your bondage of sin. Ask My forgiveness and your spirit will revel in My company as a child seeks its parent. For you are My children and your soul ever seeks to be with Me. Free your spirit from the attraction of sin and do not listen to the worldly cravings of the body. By constant prayer you can purge your body and humble it into submission to the spirit."***

Later, at the Mercy Motherhouse after Communion, I saw a very clear picture of Our Lady dressed in black and wearing a crown. Mary said: ***"My son, I am your sorrowful Mother who watches over her children. I am crying for my children who have failed to heed my many messages. Men are too taken up with themselves and are not praying enough to make reparation for the sins of the world. Many times I have preached to you that my Rosary and your prayers are your weapons against evil. There is a great foreshadowing of the tribulation which is almost upon you. I am sending you this message of warning to prepare for this trial. Many souls will be lost because there are not enough prayer warriors to pray for them. You must pray much, my children, while you have time. For when the evil one comes, only those who pray to my Son for help will be saved. This will be a most severe test,***

but one I cannot hold back, my son, from purifying the world. My hope for you is that soon after that you will witness my triumph with my Son. It is for this day you will be most joyous. Continue now, my children, and hold fast to me and my Son for strength during this trial."

Wednesday, May 17, 1995:

After Communion, I saw a scene outside of some trees and a church. In another scene, I saw some nuns. Jesus said: ***"I am giving you a message of the coming tribulation. You will see many events similar to those of the Exodus. There will be many testings of the people to show them My presence and a confounding of man's desire to make himself a god. There will be times of various plagues and diseases to humble man and discourage his fighting. These things will show that I am in control and man is more vulnerable to weakness without Me. Pray, My people, that you stay close to Me in prayer no matter what befalls you."***

Thursday, May 18, 1995:

After Communion, I could see a lantern and behind was a map of what looked like the Tigris and Euphrates where the Garden of Eden was thought to be. Jesus said: ***"You are to be a light to the people in bringing My message of love. Show them in vision how beautiful their lives will be after the earth's renewal. You will see My glory manifested on earth, beyond all your earthly expectations. For those who believe in Me and give themselves over to Me in body and spirit, there will be a reward for which they will be eternally grateful. See your goal for being with Me should be inspiring from any point of view. Set aside any doubts or earthly fears and come to Me in love. For My yoke is easy and My burden light."***

Friday, May 19, 1995:

After Communion, I saw many buildings and there were faces or sculptures at the top of each of them. It appeared as if the Anti-Christ during his brief reign would have monuments to acknowledge himself like a god. Jesus said: ***"During the time of the tribulation you will see the Anti-Christ make his importance felt all over the world. You will see his likeness before you on many build-***

ings and billboards honoring himself as a god. You already have witnessed this behavior with many older and current rulers. Hold fast to your faith in Me no matter who claims to be god or demonstrates miracles. Only I am your God. Take no heed of any other false witnesses who may come forth in these end times. Believe in Me and pray for strength to endure this test. Then your reward with Me will be worth more than any earthly promise."

Later, after Communion, at the Betania Reunion, I saw Maria holding up her arms to greet us. She said: ***"Welcome, my people, I am happy to see you gathered together with Jesus."*** I then felt Mary's presence and I saw her briefly. I then saw some pictures of women praying as at Betania. Mary said: ***"Look for me and my Son in the people at my shrine in Betania. Even look for my Son in all the faces you meet since He is there, also. You have come in pilgrimage to celebrate your joy and faith in me and my Son. We welcome all of you as part of that faithful remnant who have accepted my Son's wish that you spread the Gospel message with all the nations. We also are sharing your joy and love as you come together at my Son's banquet. Continue sharing with others and pray for sinners in this troubled time. Keep close in prayer and you will truly love us and one another as in the Gospel. Let the people know you are members of the true faith by your love and your good works."***

Saturday, May 20, 1995:

After Communion, I saw the inside of a church with a big cross in front of it and I was looking at some stained glass windows. Jesus said: ***"My people, why do I see so much division in My Church? I see the hand of the evil one stirring up errors in My priest sons. I am asking all My faithful to hold on to their precious instruction as received from My apostles. Do not twist My laws and traditions for your own convenience. Be true to your conscience and do not let the false teachers lead you astray. My commands are forever and My laws changeless. Being modern does not mean you can do as you please. Live by My instruction in the Scriptures and by My love in your heart and you will not be misled. Again, a person of prayer will be led to follow My ways and stay close to My heart. Avoid those who teach heresy and stay true to My faithful remnant led by My Pope, John Paul II."***

Later, at Nocturnal Hour, I saw some houses and then I saw some open fields with only grass and no crops. Jesus said: ***"My people, a time of famine and pestilence will come upon you after a time of plenty. You will indeed be humbled by unfavorable weather and events which will cause food shortages. Many will die of starvation and some will fight over what little is left. Many of the rich will have plenty of this world's goods, but will be poor in spiritual riches. In the end, it is only your heavenly deposits which will have any value. Have hope, My friends, for in only a short time you will share in My bounteous gifts on a renewed earth. Your greatest concern will be the spiritual famine and not earthly food."***

Sunday, May 21, 1995:

After Communion, I saw the skies open and there was a great gold light that shone forth. I sensed it was both a preparation for the Ascension and Pentecost. The Holy Spirit said: ***"I am the Spirit of Love and you are seeing how heaven makes ready for the bestowing of My gifts. You will be a part of this touching of My spirit on those to be confirmed. Let the fire of My love inspire all of you in readiness for this gift. For your own preparation, make a point of getting to Confession before this feast. Then all will have on the proper wedding garments of a purified soul. Then you will be in full harmony with Me as I greet you with the graces to strengthen your spirit. You have My indwelling within you and you can help it to come forth in glory the more you are in conformity with the will of God. Follow My ways and you will be ready with all the faithful to celebrate these glorious feasts."***

Later, at church, I saw a city and in the sky I could see five green rays shooting down. I then saw a picture of an eagle, and I sensed this country would fall to the one world government making it ripe for the Anti-Christ to control. Jesus said: ***"My people, I have told you many times you will have to suffer much persecution. This will be a time so severe that you will need My help in prayer to bear this burden. Many souls will be lost to the evil one since few have heeded My warnings. If you do not convert before the tribulation, you will have little hope to survive this spiritual onslaught. My graces and help are ever present to lead you safely to avoid these evil men. With prayer I will confound their search-***

ing for you, so you will escape their plottings. My people, listen to My instructions and prepare spiritually with your Rosaries, crosses and holy water. Ask your angels to help you since you will be in a deadly spiritual battle with the demons. With My help I will give you hope to conquer this evil, so you may live forever in My glory."

Monday, May 22, 1995:

After Communion, I saw the picture of the broken Host bleeding. Jesus said: ***"You see Me broken hearted over the disunity among My people. Many have not taken Me seriously in their lives to let Me lead them. You and My elect must tell the people life can be so much easier if they would give their will over to Me. Again, I am bleeding for the suffering that continues. Man is still killing his neighbor instead of helping him. Abortions are still going on without much remorse. How long do you expect I will let this go on? I tell you this injustice will be paid for in bitter anguish, for you will be bringing great destruction upon yourselves by rejecting Me. Pray, My faithful, for there is much need of repentance."***

Later, at church, I saw a young nun and it was confirmed to be St. Therese the Little Flower. She was sitting at a bay window with sunshine behind her. (I smelled roses on entering the chapel.) She said: ***"I have come to celebrate with you at your anniversary Mass. You must see I come out of love for you and more than just to advise you. It is glorious to be called by God to serve Him. All of you are called in your own little way to do His will and carry your own crosses. You must see my life as an example to be always humble in what you do. You have seen how when men seek fame and riches, it comes to nothing. Let the Lord's little chastisements show you that His way is the most perfect way to live. Give yourself over to my Jesus and He will lead you to the proper spiritual priorities. You must show by your own example to others that to live a humble life is much more rewarding than to live only for your own gain and acknowledgment from men. Such earthly desires are vain and lead you away from your Savior. Live a life of prayer and frequent Confession and you will see a real beauty in simply following my Jesus."***

Tuesday, May 23, 1995:

After Communion, I saw some people sitting down on a train as if it was their time to go. Jesus said: ***"At times it is good to take stock of your life and where you are going. You have all been placed here to love and serve Me. One day you will have to render an account of what you have done in your life, at your judgment. See to it now, My friends, that you do not come to Me with empty***

hands. Remember during life to help others both by prayer and deed. Remember Me, also, that you ask My help each day and honor and praise Me in prayer. By acknowledging Me before men, I will acknowledge you before My Father and I will welcome you into heaven with Me."

Later, at church, I saw Jesus on the cross from the front at first. Then I saw Him suffering from just behind Him looking down. Jesus said: ***"You are seeing Me suffer for the many sins of mankind. I have been suffering this way since I was on earth even until now. I will continue suffering until the last sin occurs before the judgment. This is how much I love each of you that I would suffer for you to be saved. If men could see how their sin makes Me suffer, maybe they could appreciate how serious it is to sever the ties of love with Me by their sin. Sin destroys the spiritual life of the soul and makes it hideous before God. It is up to each of you to ask for forgiveness for your sins in Confession in order to bring back that vibrant life of grace to your souls. Be conscious then that the battle of good and evil has many souls at stake. Those willing to accept Me and follow My way will see eternal life. On the other hand, those who do not admit to being sinners and do not have contrite hearts, will turn from Me and find eternal punishment in hell."***

Wednesday, May 24, 1995:

After Communion, I saw Jesus walking on the water. Jesus said: ***"My people of America, how many signs will you need to understand My visitation? You have witnessed many floods, fires and other disasters and still you have not reformed your lives. It is as if you do not want to believe there is a connection between your sin and these chastisements. No matter how you evaluate these happenings, they are more than normal. My messages to reform your lives have fallen on many deaf ears and cold hearts. Pray for sinners in earnest to change their lives before My judgment comes and it will be too late. These events are warnings to you of your impending fate. Reform your lives, for My love goes out to you and seeks your return."***

Later, after Communion, I saw a colonial soldier and later realized the connection to soldier of Christ for confirmation. I also saw a ring of desks and understood an analogy to counsel as representing the gifts of the Holy Spirit. The Holy Spirit said: ***"I am the Spirit of Love. Have no other gods before Me. Look to do the will of God and all else will be given you. It is good to give example to those learning the faith. They will see your dedication to following My spirit and religion will have more meaning in their lives. Truly you must think of yourselves as prayer warriors as I send you the armor in which to fight the demons. For those who are open to My gifts, they will gladly be given to you to fortify yourself for the coming battle with evil. Be more open to God and do not let your distractions sway your determination to follow the will of God. Prayer will help in this work and show you the way."***

Thursday, May 25, 1995: (Ascension Thursday)

After Communion, I saw Maria as she said: ***"All praise Jesus on His Ascension."*** I then had a vision of Jesus preaching in a synagogue. Jesus said: ***"My words to My apostles were to go and preach My Gospel to all nations. I tell all of My faithful disciples the same message. If you know of the glory of My Resurrection and the promise of salvation over evil, why would you not proclaim Me from the rooftops? Do not let your pride or embarrassment stand in your way to proclaim My word. You are all called to be My ambassadors and evangelize as many souls to the faith that will listen. Bringing men back to Me has been your mission from the day I first taught each of you from someone else's hand. You are to carry on the faith to others as you yourself have received instruction."***

Later, at the prayer group, I saw a single large flame burning as an eternal flame indicating Jesus' eternal presence with us. Jesus said: ***"Keep your heart lit with My flame of love. Never let it grow cold and ever nourish that love to keep it alive. You have been graced with a gift of faith to know Me. Keep My link of prayer ever before you."*** I then saw some hanging metal lanterns as in the Orthodox rite and there was an empty chair. Jesus said: ***"You should treasure each life that comes into your life since they are all special. Appreciate each gift of life before you realize how valuable they were when they are gone."*** I saw a skylight sending in a bright light. This indicated the light of Christ in our life. Jesus said: ***"As you commemorate My Ascension, remember how I said I would send My Holy Spirit among you. You are not alone since the Holy***

Spirit is within you and you have My presence as well in My Blessed Sacrament." I then saw a dark rotating music turntable which indicated how short our life was and how we will view it at the warning. Jesus said: ***"Prepare, My people, for your lives will soon be revealed to you in a depth of knowledge you have yet to realize. For a brief time, you will see your life as I see it and you will sense how unworthy you are save for My death on the cross."*** I had a beautiful vision of Christ in gold ascending into heaven with a dove over His head. Jesus said: ***"As you see Me rising into heaven, so you shall see Me come again in judgment. As this time draws near, you will see that the messages will not last much longer. Be firm in faith and strong in prayer."*** I then saw a gold light and St. Michael the Archangel was standing with his sword ready to do battle with the demons. St. Michael said: ***"Fear not, men of My Lord, for your time of testing is almost upon you. I have been sent by God to lead the battle against the evil one. There will be one great battle at Armageddon as told in the Book of Revelation. After the Lord conquers evil once again, you will see an era of peace reign over the earth."*** Finally, I had a vision of the two hearts of Mary and Jesus joined together with a flame above them. Mary said: ***"I have been blessed to be one with my Son and I am forever grateful that I could be the bearer of my God. See these months of May and June joined together as our hearts, only more divinely. When you witness our love, you can have a sense of how you will be consumed in my Son's love as well. He awaits the day when you all can be a part of Him in heaven."***

Friday, May 26, 1995:

After Communion, I saw a tremendous churning and swirling of water. In the next scene I saw a tremendous fire burning over an entire landscape. I sensed there were strong winds of distress and disharmony between man and nature. Jesus said: ***"The winds of war are forever moving about your world. Since the day of the fall, the evil one has stirred up hate among men. Even in your world today many are still craving power by force. I tell you, My people, unless more people return to Me in prayer instead of turning to war, there will continue to be strife and suffering. Know also that as you see a crescendo of chaos and fighting occur, it will gradually create an opportunity for the Anti-Christ***

to come as a man of false peace to appease the people. Be assured though that his reign will be short but painful, especially for My faithful. Be united with Me in this time and I will bring you to My eternal glory after this trial."

At church, I saw some stones with water running over them causing a rapids to flow. Jesus said: ***"My people, many times you are caught up in all of your daily activities such that you lose sight of what your priorities should be. Always remember Me through each day in your prayers and in your thoughts. I am by your side to ask Me for help in your troubles. I am here also to keep you close to Me in My sacraments. Never lose sight of your goal to be with Me. Do not let your distractions keep Me distant. If you do everything for love of Me, you will not seek riches and pride in your deeds. See that loving Me and pleasing Me is enough to accomplish in one lifetime. By concentrating on My will, this will make all your work more worthwhile in My sight. Focus on Me and no amount of riches will be desired any more. For in Me is plenteous redemption and My gifts are enough to satisfy anyone in this life."***

Saturday, May 27, 1995:

After Communion, I could see the sunlight coming through the trees. I then saw Jesus as an ethereal white image in the sky which I assumed was as in His Ascension. Jesus said: ***"My dear people, heaven is not far from you. The spirit world is in another dimension from you unrestricted by time and space. This will be the life you will be called to. It is a life with Me when you will have full knowledge of Me without any further temptations of the body or the evil one. Right now you can only come to Me in prayer or My sacraments, but after the trial, you will see Me face to face and those faithful to My word will see My glory in heaven and on earth. Keep guard over your soul so that you will direct yourself only to Me. I will provide everything for you, if you just ask in My name and walk in My will."***

Later, at church, I saw a truck and it looked like it was carrying a large missile. Jesus said: ***"My people, many conflicts abound in your world. If they continue to take unnecessary risks, you could see this involve a wider conflict. If men refuse to settle their dif-***

ferences, they will cause more unnecessary bloodshed and possibly bring on World War III. Many prayers for peace should be offered now to head off this possibility. Without peace being sought, only war and destruction will result. Keep together in your prayer cells and hold fast to My teachings. Many will come in My name to try and mislead even My elect. So pray for My help and I will lead you safely through this trial."

Sunday, May 28, 1995:

After Communion, I saw a bunch of pink roses. As the scene backed up. I could see it was part of a bride's bouquet and I could see a bride and groom. Jesus said: ***"As you see My Church, I watch over it as a father protects his family. I have an all-consuming love for all of you. When you worship together, it is indeed a loving family joined together with Me. I call on you to walk with Me each day during the week as well as on Sunday. My messengers need to be even closer to Me both for strength and good example. Prayer should be foremost in your lives. Your free time should be used in pleasing Me as much as possible. When you are a part of Me, you cannot forget Me for a minute. You need to direct your lives in conformity with My will, if you intend to be perfected. Pray for discernment in how you are to lead your lives and share with others."***

Later, at church, I saw a pinwheel circling and sparkles were coming from it like fireworks. I sensed a major event of great significance was coming. Jesus said: ***"My people, I have sent you many messages and you do not heed them. I have sent you many signs and again you do not change your ways. You will see more signs of death and destruction to get your attention, but most will not understand. There is one event still coming which will let all of you know of My intervention. This will be man's turning point. If, still, he does not repent of his sin, you will see a fiery chastisement which will punish the unbelievers and purify the earth. I will then renew the earth and those worthy will inherit My peace on earth. Those who continue to love and serve Me during this tribulation will receive a just reward. The others will curse the darkness where they will be sent. Pray much now, My faithful, for this is your only hope—to follow Me in faith."***

Monday, May 29, 1995: (Memorial Day)

After Communion, I saw a hat drifting on the water as a representation of those who died in the wars. Jesus said: ***"You have seen many brave men fight for their country over the years, but you have not always understood the reason for all these conflicts. At the base of them is pride and greed from the leaders. I tell you, pray for your leaders, for they are the ones fanning the fires of war. Also, it is of more spiritual value to stand firm and defend your faith. To die and hold fast to your belief in Me is the new soldier who uses spiritual armor and defenses of prayer. This battle of good and evil is the real struggle for souls which heaven is watching over. Things won in war later disappear. Souls won for Me last forever and are much more prized by any comparison. Save souls."***

Later, at church, I saw a nun teaching school as at the time I went to school. Jesus said: ***"My many people are waiting to receive My message, but there are few workers to help. Some teachers of My word are not always following My faithful remnant. It is better to teach the traditional faith than all your modern approaches. Without a sincere and humble heart you cannot pass on the spirit of faith that is needed. You must spread My message as faithfully as possible. For there is not much time left to reach those sinners willing to repent. At the time of the trial, I will help you in spreading My word, but you must take some positive action to teach what you can. Show My love by example, so they can understand Me through your sincere heart."***

Tuesday, May 30, 1995:

After Communion, I saw some beautiful angels before a light shining down from heaven. Jesus said: ***"As you have heard of the angels at My Ascension, so you shall see them come to make preparation for My return. These are the most beautiful beings who assist Me in My work. They are guardians and messengers of My word. Soon they will be lining up as My army to conquer the evil one in his last hour. This victory over evil will usher in My full peace and love as it was intended for man. You will be most gracious to My angels, for they will help and guide you throughout the tribulation. Give praise and honor to Me for the***

great plan of salvation I have given you. By remaining faithful to My word you will win eternal life."

Later, after Communion, I saw darkness trying to cover over a monstrance. Gradually, I saw a monstrance appear and it was now heart shaped with rays of light dispelling the darkness. Jesus said: ***"You are seeing how much the evil one wants to cover up the power of My Blessed Sacrament. He is doing everything to get people to give Me less reverence and even have the faithful believe I am not present at all in the Host. This should be a verification in itself of how much Satan feels threatened by My Blessed Sacrament. The evil one also is trying to make people feel they can receive My sacrament even in the state of mortal sin, thus having them commit sacrilege. But as you see, My heart of love sheds light on My faithful and gives them understanding to know Me better. Give praise and glory in adoration for this wonderful gift I have bestowed on you."***

Wednesday, May 31, 1995: (Visitation)

After Communion, I saw a window frame and the window was being opened by the glass turning outside from the top. I did not see Mary, but I had feelings and indications of her presence. Mary said: ***"My children, this is a sign to you this morning to be more open to understand other people's feelings. Be willing to break down your exterior protection which keeps you distant from other's problems. Seek to open your heart more and look more to help others in their need, instead of your own selfish desires. Look for opportunities to help others and do not complain when others offer help or are helping others. In a word, be loving as my Son is to all you meet. Show more your love than your own cravings. Pour out your love on others and you will be sharing your faith as well."***

Later, at the prayer group I first saw a 1996 calendar. Jesus said: ***"Many omens of things to come have been given you through signs. I tell you now to pray especially for the events in this year of 1996. I will give you further warnings as this time approaches."*** I then saw a British flag and an insignia representing NATO. Jesus said: ***"Beware of the actions taken by this group. They are bordering on widening a war which may not be stopped without much bloodshed."*** I saw a great cloud come over the land. I then saw an eagle and President Clinton. Jesus said: ***"Your president will be visiting many sites of disasters during his term in office. Your chastisements will be so continuous that your banking system will be stretched to the breaking point. When you will have been brought to your knees by the loss of your things, then you will realize that I have given you everything and I can take it away as well. Focus on heavenly things which will last forever."*** I saw a long line with many lights along it. I was looking at a time continuum and I was speeding through to the end. Jesus said: ***"Prepare, My children, for My spiritual intervention is not far off. You will be given a time for decision to either choose Me or the world. For a moment, you will have complete knowledge of your whole life to the smallest detail."*** I then saw Mary again dressed in black. Mary said: ***"I ask all my children to pray much, for my Son's visitation is coming. He will judge all men according to their deeds. Reform your lives and hold close to my Rosary since it is your spiritual weapon against evil."*** I saw a huge orange and red flame and it broke up into smaller flames and descended upon all who were present. The Holy Spirit said: ***"I am the Spirit of Love. Receive a portion of My spirit which I am pouring out on all of you. Go and spread the Lord's message of love to all nations."*** Finally, I saw an outline of God the Father. He said: ***"I have sent you my Son and you killed Him and ridiculed Him. I have sent the Holy Spirit to instill love in your heart. In order to receive these gifts, you must be willing to open your heart and receive us. If you reject this calling, you cannot be saved. So cast aside your worldly cares and dedicate your lives to following My will. Then the graces of these gifts can be effective in your souls."***

Thursday, June 1, 1995:

After Communion, I saw Maria and she said: ***"I offer up all your prayers."*** I then saw some kind of an electrical box covered with glass on the roadside. Jesus said: ***"Evil men are putting in place devices to monitor your travel. This will all be directed toward the coming persecution in the tribulation. You are seeing many signs of this time as it quickly approaches. Pray for strength, My people. You may have to travel without your cars to avoid detection in the future."***

Friday, June 2, 1995:

After Communion, I could see a large door in the heavens. It gradually opened of itself and a great light shone forth. There was a sense of peace and love all at once. Jesus said: ***"I am giving you a glimpse of My glory much like in My Transfiguration, so that you may have hope amongst all these events. You know how much I love you all and I am always watching over you, but you must realize all people have to struggle with their own lives and their own troubles. Each of My people has to go through a test of suffering to follow how I took up My own cross on earth. In time, with your following My will, you will indeed see that your reward will be well worth your temporary trial. Have faith in My love and know I am with you."***

Later, at church, I saw at first a tall narrow cross. Then I saw a scene of a large city from a high vantage point. I sensed a situation where the devil was offering his kingdom for Christ's adoration. Jesus said: ***"The evil one will become so drunk with power and pride, that he will think he is invincible against man. He will indeed have a short reign of power where he will control much of men's lives, but I have warned you of this time to remain in prayer and avoid his presence. Just as he thinks he will win the battle, My angels and My intervention will steal away his prize of controlling the earth. I will suspend time for awhile for the sake of the elect. Then I will renew the earth and all the evil spirits will be chained in hell. No longer will he be allowed to roam the earth in search of souls to destroy. At that time peace and My love will rule the earth and all My faithful will inherit a heaven on earth. Pray, My people, to endure this trial and hold fast to the hope of My promise."***

Saturday, June 3, 1995:

After Communion, I saw some praying hands and then someone kneeling. Jesus said: ***"You must be united with Me in prayer, if you wish to converse with Me. Those who recollect themselves in the peace of My contemplation, are giving example to what I desire from all of My creatures. I have given you life and much time in order to give Me some time back in thanksgiving. Many of you have received many blessings and faith alone is your most precious gift. Take advantage of praying with Me before My***

Blessed Sacrament where I am closest to you. Give praise and adoration, as well as thanksgiving and petition in your prayer, to make it complete. Those with a good prayer life will never want for My help."

Later, at church, I saw several black tombstones but there was a covered shroud with four posts covering them. Jesus said: ***"Unless you die to self, you cannot be My disciple. You must take up your cross and endure life's troubles for My sake. For if you accept your life's problems and follow My way on earth, you will be prepared to receive your reward. For as you have seen Me suffer, I have given you an example. By accepting this life and offering it up to Me, you are now ready to receive the gifts of the Holy Spirit as you commemorate them on Pentecost. Look to the Holy Spirit for sharing My love and receive graces from Him to strengthen you for your tasks. Once you have fought the race of life and have followed My will, I await to receive you at your resurrection in the life hereafter. Receive the Holy Spirit as He breathes on you for you are His temple—He resides in you. Protect your soul with prayer so you can be more worthy as you carry My spirit. Encourage each other with a Christian love which others will recognize in you."***

Sunday, June 4, 1995: (Pentecost)

After Communion, I saw a picture of Christ in the Jordan at His Baptism. In another scene I saw the apostles in the upper room with the tongues of fire. Lastly, I saw a graduation class in caps and gowns. The Holy Spirit came and said: ***"I am the Spirit of Love. You have received My indwelling at both Baptism and Confirmation. My gifts have been given you and are renewed whenever you receive any of the sacraments. My gifts have been bestowed on each of you so you can carry out your mission of evangelism as the apostles did. You, too, have the grace for healing and teaching, if you would ask My help. Do not think any task is impossible. With My help you can have the strength to bring the Lord's message to all His people. Remember to invoke Me in your prayers."***

Later, at church, I saw some beautiful faces and they were laughing. These beings seemed angelic in their appearance and I could see their wings. I asked Jesus' permission for Mark, my guardian angel, to help me understand this vision. Mark said: ***"These angels are sharing their joy at the celebration of the Feast of Pentecost. There also seems to be a little supernatural humor in that they think man is not that serious in trying to understand the Holy Spirit. For most people and even some faithful, He is a silent witness whom some do not recognize as present in their lives. If they only knew that it is because of the Holy Spirit's presence that they have their being. The Holy Spirit gives the breath of life in all living things. You all should recognize Him as the Third Person in the Blessed Trinity. Much like Jesus, you can call on Him in prayer to help you. Ask Him for the grace of His gifts to help you live a more perfect Christian life. As you pray for understanding of the Holy Spirit in your life, you will then see why the angels are wondering if you recognize the importance of this feast. Invoke the Holy Spirit more in your life and you will see how helpful He can be for you."***

Monday, June 5, 1995:

After Communion, I saw lush farmlands with many crops. Jesus said: ***"Be thankful now for your bounty of crops. There will come some years in the future when you will wish for these years again. Many things you have taken for granted and you do not realize how blessed you are. You will see when these things are taken from you how blessed you were. So give thanks and praise to God for all you have so you can better appreciate your gifts from above. Be even more thankful for your bounty of spiritual gifts as well."***

Later, at church, I saw a large building with steps going up. This looked like a Jewish temple. Mary came and said: ***"My children, remember that you all are temples of the Holy Spirit. As you have read in Scripture, I conceived my Son by the power of the Holy Spirit. As you have been told, all life is conceived by the breath of life from the Holy Spirit. He is the Spirit of Love and the spirit of life in all of you. Your body and soul is maintained in its life through Him. You do not all realize how intimately He is associated with your being alive; therefore, my children, you should realize how precious each life is. Those who murder and abort lives are sending that person's soul and the Holy Spirit out***

of that body prematurely. Each soul has a plan for its life consecrated by the will of the Father. Treat life more sacredly and do everything in your power to discourage murder, abortion and wars. By your prayers for peace, my Son's peace may prevail over those who would make war. Keep up your daily prayers as much as possible to preserve that gift of life among you."

Tuesday, June 6, 1995:

After Communion, I saw a little eight sided object in the ground. Later, I saw a large dugout hole in the ground and sensed that we would make our home in the ground. Jesus said: ***"You worry much, My people, of what is in your future. Yet you should trust more since I am with you and protecting you. When you pray, open your ears of faith and listen to My word in your hearts. Let Me lead you in your life and give everything over to Me. Then you can trust that I will show you the way you are to go. If I should give you warnings, do not be anxious about what you are to do. These things will happen, but I will instruct you what you are to do and where you are to go."***

Later, at church, I saw a large ship with three stacks and it was heading out to sea. Jesus said: ***"You must see, My people, how life is very much like a ship heading out into the unknown. There are many tests in your life and it is up to you to live by your faith through everything. As I have told you many times, when you are not troubled or tempted, you are experiencing a lull in the storm of life. It is easy when things go well to be prayerful, but when life turns rough, either by sickness or tragedy, this becomes a real test of your faith in how to deal with each event. Keep My peace through all your trials and you will find it easier to endure them. When there are problems with your friends or relatives, be willing to come to their aid in their time of need either by deed or even comfort. When you yourself are being tested with either sickness or hard times, remember to call on any person of the Trinity, My Mother, the saints, or your guardian angel. You are not alone on life's pilgrimage, so do not be afraid to ask for help. Again, keep a continuous prayer life so you are always open to follow My will. In this way, you can go through life with a proper purpose and love of Me and your neighbor."***

Wednesday, June 7, 1995:

After Communion, I saw a window and the day's light was shining in towards the floor. Jesus said: ***"Many people do not realize the blessings I pour out on all of you each day. I provide you light, the air you breathe and many other earthly gifts, but most of all I pour out My love for you in offering Myself each day to you in Communion. You have the opportunity each day to walk in My will, as we have a partnership in spirit. So, too, you have seen the gifts of the Holy Spirit which have been bestowed on you. With all of these joyful reasons for enjoying your life, then, lift up your spirits in praise and thanksgiving to God. Do not be downcast, but be filled with a Christian's joy of hope in God."***

Later, at the prayer group, I first saw a table knife and a box of crackers. Jesus said: ***"As you need to feed your body with food to survive, so also you need to feed your soul with My heavenly food for your soul to survive. I am here at every Mass ready to feed you with My Eucharist in Communion. You can receive Me physically into your body where I can strengthen your spiritual life."*** I then saw some lettering on a baby book. I also saw a little boy. I asked my angel to communicate with David, my son. He said: ***"When you are spiritually led to me as you are led to say your Rosary, I am happy for you. I want to thank you for remembering me. Remember, I am with God's saints and pray to me for any help you need."*** I saw a light shining on some people's faces. It was a light from either a TV or some device which was hypnotizing the people. Jesus said: ***"The Anti-Christ will have powers especially over those without God to control their lives. He will direct them to worship him and give him allegiance instead of God. Those who give in to the evil one will go along with him to hell at the judgment. Keep close to Me and do not let anyone deceive you. I alone am to be worshipped."*** I was on a bus or a van and all the people were looking at a bright light in the front window amongst the darkness. Jesus said: ***"I am the Light of the World and I will lead you through the darkness of the tribulation. Keep heart and have faith in Me that I will take care of you. My beacon of love will lead you in many trying times."*** I then saw some machines like slot machines. Jesus said: ***"In the future you will need to avoid all electrical devices which the evil one can manipulate. You will have to lead a much more simple life without your conveniences."***

I saw St. Therese and she said: ***"I want to thank you for this remembrance of me. I am here to help anyone in your prayer group who wants to call on me. I enjoyed your flowers."*** I finally saw an aura in bright yellow around a person. Jesus said: ***"You are seeing how the soul's spirit overshadows the outline of the body. Each soul gives off a radiance which is a measure of its spiritual graces. This is why some people who have lost limbs of the body still can sense a presence, since their spiritual body is still fully there."***

Thursday, June 8, 1995:

After Communion, I saw an impressive angel who acknowledged Himself as Raphael. He said: ***"I am Raphael the Archangel who stands before God. You are seeing today in the Scriptures how I protected Tobiah against the evil spirit who killed Sarah's previous seven husbands. Understand, I protect all married people who pray for My intercession. It is good that all married people pray over their marriages and unite with God throughout their lives. See to it, also, that each is obedient to your marriage vows and works to maintain your bond of love with each other."***

Friday, June 9, 1995:

After Communion, I saw some trees. Jesus said: ***"As you have seen, the pilot shot down in Bosnia avoid detection in the woods, so you also will need to do it. Your best cover will be underground where you cannot be seen from above or by those searching for you. I will lead you at the proper time where to hide and how to eat and drink for your survival. Avoiding the evil men and the beast will be your best plan. Do not worry. This trial of the tribulation will not last long. For those who continue to be faithful to Me in prayer, I will raise them up and they shall witness My glory before all men."***

Later, at church, I saw an owl perched in a tree. Then I saw another scene from up high in a pine woods. Jesus said: ***"My people, during the tribulation you will have to be resourceful to use what little you will have. Remember to take into hiding your spiritual weapons and a few earthly helps as I have mentioned. Many people may find in or near the parklands to be the easiest to access. Your trial may seem harsh but look what I had to go through for you. At that time it will be easy to distinguish the faithful***

from those in league with the evil one. By your love and the signs on the forehead, you will recognize whom you can trust. This will be a time of deep prayer to keep concentrated on your mission of following Me at all costs. Do not worry so much about earthly things and strive to search only to be with Me in prayer. The faithful will be severely tested but in the end your being with Me will make it all worth this purification. Keep close to Me no matter what happens."

Saturday, June 10, 1995:

After Communion, I saw a crypt in a Church and there was a nun present at the side of the altar. The tabernacle was open and empty. Jesus said: ***"Many of you are appalled by the lack of vocations both to the priesthood and for nuns as well. I would call your attention to how you teach the faith both to the laity and in your seminaries. The evil one has attacked this area over the years and your prayers for this concern have been lacking. Many now seek worldly things instead of religious vocations. There is a poor environment in your world to nurture and inspire young people to the religious life. Some of your seminaries actually do more harm than good in what they are teaching. This is why the few vocations present are being stifled. Vocations are blessings and until there is enough prayer and proper teaching, their number will remain few. This should be a sign to you how serious the battle of good and evil has come to. It is why I tell you your people need much prayer now to protect My faithful. See to it also that the true faith be propagated or there will be even fewer priests to give My Sacraments."***

Later, at church, I saw several small children being held by their parents. Jesus said: ***"I have told you much of the value of each life. Now, even more, it is important that you help the little children to learn the true faith. These little lives can be formed around Me or can be misled to follow the things of earth. It is important by your example to show them the need for God in their lives. It becomes more imperative to show them before the time when the evil one's influence will spread. Pray much, My children, and let the children pray with you. You are indirectly responsible for their souls especially those you can influence."***

Sunday, June 11, 1995: (Trinity Sunday)

After Communion, I saw a bright gold light and had a sense of all three persons of the Blessed Trinity present. Jesus said: ***"We all are one in the same Spirit. It is a mystery for you to fully understand Our presence. All of creation answers to the Father, as all of the universe is held in place. I am at your beck and call as your spiritual food to give you strength to endure life's trials. The Holy Spirit is the spirit of life which enables all life. In every attribute, you can think of Us as infinitely perfect and all knowing. You will never be able to fully comprehend Us, but by reading the Scriptures, you can come to know us more closely. Suffice it to say that seeking Us is your soul's desire and goal. Without Us you can have no peace, light or direction. Do not let the evil one try to deceive you. His powers are nothing compared to Ours. He is only being allowed to test your faith. You have been given free will as in Our image and it is your choice to choose God or not. We do not force Our love on you but welcome your acceptance. Once you give your will over to Us, your plan of perfection will be given you to stand the test."***

Later, at church, I saw a large picture of what looked like Padre Pio raising His hand with bandages on it. At the same time there was a very bright light shining on the picture to the left which had a picture of Jesus in the middle. Jesus said: ***"You have seen the stories of those who received My stigmata. You know also of that experience with Padre Pio and others. This is a grace I have bestowed on those who requested this sign and were willing to offer up their suffering to Me for others. The pain of My wounds I suffered for all men that you may be open to receive heaven. Salvation is waiting for each of you reaching out to Me in faith. My love for all of you was and still is going on when I suffer for your sins. This is the joining of all men into My one body which you only partially understand. As you give your will over to Me, you become more consumed into Me where I can more perfect your soul and make it pleasing to My Father. The more perfect you become, the closer you will be to going straight to heaven without purification. This is why the more pain you suffer for Me on earth, the more merits will be given you as your heavenly treasure."***

Monday, June 12, 1995:

After Communion, I saw some stone walls. Later, I saw parapets as to a prison. Jesus said: ***"My people, you have heard Me describe to My apostles how I told them they will be held fast by others against their will. Also, that they would be persecuted for the sake of My name. I tell you there will be an evil time when the evil one will lead men against you and you, too, will be tested because of Me. They will cast you in prison and will torture you and some may even be martyred as examples. But fear not, My people, for My victory is a few moments away and then you will taste of the sweetness of My glory. You will share in the peace and love of heaven."***

Later, at church, I saw an altar of three to five steps and there were black figures of animals that looked Egyptian in origin. One looked like a crocodile and another had a large man-like body. Jesus said: ***"You will see. The evil one will encourage the people to worship these idols as gods. The evil men will threaten the people to worship the Anti-Christ and these gods, or they will take away the mark to buy and sell. You could even see that the electrical devices to buy and sell would give little electrical jolts to perform certain actions desired by the Anti-Christ. You will see during the tribulation that the evil one will have great power over those who do not get help from God. This, again, is why I will direct you away from these evil men and help you to avoid detection as well as provide for your needs. Fear not this power which will test you but a short time. Pray fervently to Me and I will strengthen you to resist them."***

Tuesday, June 13, 1995: (St. Anthony feast day)

After Communion, I saw our tapestry representing prayer next to the tabernacle and it was all overshadowed with the sunlight falling on me. Jesus said: ***"I am showing you this vision that you may be directed to Me in prayer. When you receive Me in My most Blessed Sacrament, you should prepare yourself by making reparation for your sins. Remember, also, if you should have serious sin, that you go to Confession to the priest before receiving Me in Communion. This is only right that you prepare a place of holiness to receive Me. Do not take Communion for granted or take it lightly that your God of the universe comes to stay with***

you. I make few requests of My servants, but I am a jealous God in that there be no other concerns or gods before Me. I am not just another one of your fancies, but I am your Creator, the one whom your soul is drawn to. Take time and give Me reverence and I will witness your love before My Father."

Later, at church, I could see a stained-glass window with a man in brown robes. It appeared to be St. Anthony of Padua. I asked St. Anthony for a message. He said: ***"Many have asked me to intercede for them in finding things. Still, there are some who do not always remember me. It is for this reason I come to tell all of my help in your problems. I find it much more meaningful if people would pray for heavenly gifts instead of earthly gifts. Many of your concerns after a few years will mean nothing, but the heavenly graces will last forever. Seek the Lord in all of your desires and be faithful to all His commandments. He will see your faith and reward you accordingly."***

Wednesday, June 14, 1995:

After Communion, I saw a five-pointed glass star rising. At the side of it I saw a Jewish glass star of David also rising. Jesus said: ***"I have told you to watch for the appearance of a star to signify the entrance of the evil one at the tribulation time. His time is coming and will soon be upon you. But, also, along with this you will see his kingdom fall quickly because it is not of God. Then you will see the rise of the glory of My Kingdom as it was intended. There will be a battle of the stars and I will be victorious as the earth will be purified of all the evil doers. Give praise and glory to God for the peace and love that will reign after."***

Later, at the prayer group I first saw some cars from up above and they had neon lights around the engine. Jesus said: ***"As the evil one will use electrical devices to help him, you will see men with devices to locate your car anywhere you drive it. Electrical devices will be hidden in your cars to enable anyone to locate your car. Be aware of this when you must go into hiding."*** I then saw a woman dressed in black whom I recognized as Mother Cabrini. She said: ***"I see you coming this way and I ask you to come and visit my shrine. This is holy ground on the hill and the Lord wishes you to visit here. You will see it to be a place of peace where the Lord pours out His love from His heart."*** I saw an altar and there was an eagle resting on a table. I saw a large angel like an archangel behind the altar and I sensed it could possibly be Gabriel. Jesus said: ***"I will send you My angels in your time of need to protect your souls from the demons of the trial. They will lead you and help you in the battle of good and evil. Pray to them to help you in your difficulties."*** I then saw a 3-D image of Christ on the cross as I moved around Him. Jesus said: ***"My people, I am pleading with you to pray and lead holy lives. Do your best to avoid sin and make reparation for sin in all you do. The sins of the world are pressing down on Me as I accept the pain for all of them. See, by encouraging others to follow your example, you will lessen the suffering I must endure."*** I saw a silhouette of Mary with a bright yellow light. She said: ***"All of your trips will seem like pilgrimages as you are led to share my Son's word with others. You must live my Son's message to teach all nations and evangelize those around you."*** I finally saw a silver shield and men preparing for battle. Jesus said: ***"You must see that you are in a battle with the demons for control over souls. You must first pray much to build up your spiritual armor so you will be ready to endure the tribulation. You will have to go forward with My grace to convert souls before it is too late to save them. You will be harassed since the evil one will detest your actions to take his prizes."***

Thursday, June 15, 1995:

After Communion, I saw Maria and she said: ***"I am present with you through Jesus."*** I saw a white luminous cross in the distance. It moved steadily toward me. Then it turned around and I was directed to follow it. Jesus said: ***"I come to each of you in spirit so that I may direct your lives for those willing to follow Me. For this is the message I gave to all My apostles when I called them—to follow Me. With Me at your side I will lead you and help you through all life's troubles. As I come for you at the end of the tribulation, I will lead you again into a new world without sin or evil influence. You will then lead a life much like Adam did before the fall. You will be able to converse with Me and your bodies will be radiant like Moses in the readings, for you will be transformed into resurrected bodies in My glory on earth for the millennium."***

Friday, June 16, 1995:

After Communion, I saw a man lying in a casket. He then raised upward and came alive and walked forward in a flowing robe. Jesus said: ***"You are a resurrected people and must rise to life in the spirit. You must be vibrant in love and willing to share My message of salvation. Many find time for words of the world, but those who speak of My name will be applauded most in heaven. Do not keep My word secret, but be willing to spread it by your words and your actions. As you lead a life of holiness, your actions will speak louder than your words."***

Later, at church, I saw some planes taking off from a modern aircraft carrier. Jesus said: ***"My people, through the years you have had many wars. As your technology has advanced, it is turned into weapons of war to kill men. Man has failed to understand the horrors of war and the loss of life, so some may possess some land which will pass from their hands in time, anyway. The evil one stirs up man's pride and greed to reach for what others have. Other times, there is anger over race or religion which causes conflict. I come to you offering My peace plan which is different from your peace which is only a lull between wars. You must bring My peace to others in your example. Spread My peace among those whom you meet and pray especially for My peace, that it may come soon. In addition, I ask you to pray for your own faith and for the conversion of sinners. When men are in harmony with Me in prayer, only then will My peace prevent wars. There is coming soon a total peace free from anger and wars when the demons will be chained in hell. This will be My reign of heaven on earth. This will be a new beginning for man to live in true harmony with Me and share My love intimately."***

Saturday, June 17, 1995:

After Communion, I could see a large cross with the corpus lying down on the ground. Then a veil of darkness fell over the cross for a time. Finally, I could see the cross raised with a great light shining and Jesus was rising to heaven. Jesus said: ***"You are seeing in My resurrection how it will be for you in the future. You will struggle for a time now. Then there will be a time of darkness in the tribulation, but I will protect you. Following the purification you will be raised with Me in glory. For a time you will see***

heaven on earth and then later all of My faithful will be joined with Me in heaven with My Father. This will be your true resurrection when all those judged worthy will share in My banquet."

Later, at Nocturnal Hour, I saw a great facade of lights, glass and stone on the side of a massive pyramid. It appeared to be an altar. Jesus said: ***"You must prepare to face the evil one of the tribulation. He will have strong powers and will try to get the people to adore him as a god because of his miracles. He will be a false prophet and will have many false witnesses trying to lead the people astray. This will be his last moment to grasp souls and he will fight with vengence. His power and skills will confuse even My elect. Pray to Me for help during this time and do not lose hope. When his time is over, you will see that I will be victorious. For his power will be taken from him since I will allow it only for a short time. This will be a time of testing to truly separate the sheep from the goats. Those who seek Me will be saved, while those who fall victim to the evil one will be lost forever. See, My triumph over sin gives hope to all those who seek to be with Me."***

Sunday, June 18, 1995: (Corpus Christi-Father's Day)

After Communion, I saw the Host being raised as at the Consecration. I then saw an altar in a huge building with a very large audience all around the altar. After Communion, I could see the face of Christ reflected in all the faces of the people to signify One Body in Christ. Jesus said: ***"I have made you all in My image and I share with all the fathers in the act of creating new life. Please, I plead with you to obey the commandments and use your gifts for creating new life naturally without obstructions or artificial means. Today, also, I share with you My love in the most blessed gift I can give you—My Body and Blood in the Eucharist. This Sacrament I have made for you so it can be a continual renewal of My spirit in you. It is My love I reach out to you, so you can appreciate the beauty of the graces I bestow upon you. When you experience My love in you at Communion, I draw you close to My heart. You can see the power of My Divine Love overshadows any earthly feeling or desire. When I am with you, you can be in a spiritual ecstasy beyond anything you could want. It is My gift of My real presence in this Sacrament that should overwhelm your senses and your mind in your feeble attempts to know Me.***

Since the fall, you have had a shroud cover your full understanding of Me, but, even so, it has not changed any of My glory. Give praise and glory to Me since I am your Creator and My creatures should give Me this honor. Give thanks, also, for your gift of life and My everlasting love for you, despite your imperfections. Strive in prayer and Scripture to know Me more and come before My Blessed Sacrament to adore Me and give reparation for sin."

Later, at church, I saw some beasts with three horns and they were being drawn down the banks of a pond and drowned in the water. Jesus said: ***"You are seeing in vision how the evil ones will be thrown into a pool of fire, for they have defied Me and sought only their own glory. Free will has been given to all My creatures—even the angels. For those who choose the world and its pleasures over Me, you will meet the same fate. The fires of Gehenna were prepared for the evil angels who followed Lucifer in his rebellion from heaven. You will see all creatures who do not love Me, but only themselves. They will find this same torment. If even you have fear of God, you should choose Me over such a fate for all eternity. Choosing pleasure for a short time is not worth turning from Me forever. You must see My love was instilled in every soul and you were created to love and serve Me. When you realize it is My natural plan for you to seek Me, how can you refuse My love? Many distractions take your attention, but give some time for Me each day. If you allow your body to lead you, your heart will grow cold and you will be a part of the living dead. Instead, accept My love and follow Me to your heavenly reward. You will see when all is said and done, My love is your obvious choice."***

Monday, June 19, 1995:

After Communion, I saw flashback glimpses of Bishop Sheen. Jesus said: ***"My people, you should try and understand how each life can have considerable effect on others. You can see role models in people that you admire. You can see in this way how a good faithful life can be an example and an inspiration for others to follow. So be on guard, My people, to lead good and holy lives since you may be responsible for saving souls by your good example, but your bad example could mislead others as well.***

You all have an effect on each other. Pray that effect may lead others to Me."

Later, at church, I saw almost above Me a golden monstrance with the Host and it was under a great basilica as it opened to the sky. Later, I saw a Host come into being and rested on someone's tongue. Finally, I saw no longer the Host but Jesus standing before Me as if in the Garden of Eden. Jesus said: ***"You are seeing the various forms of how I will appear to you in the remaining time***

on earth. For a while you still will have Me in the Blessed Sacrament that I have given you. Then, as the tribulation comes forward, the Mass and Communion will be hard to find. During that time, you must pray for a spiritual Communion. I will bless those in need at that time with a heavenly manna which will be shared with you to keep your spiritual strength. It will come on your tongue as the angel gave it to those at Fatima. Finally, as My victory turns the evil one aside from his power, you will no longer need Me in the Host. I will be at your call and you will see Me whenever you wish, as Adam called on Me before the fall. My love will then be spread among all My children and you all will share My joy and My peace."

Tuesday, June 20, 1995:

After Communion, I saw a tree and it had brown leaves instead of green ones. Jesus said: ***"I am reminding you, how I mentioned before, that you will be tested by extremes in the weather. Some will have too much water while others not enough. You should see in these happenings signs of your spiritual poverty. If the earthly things you treasure are lost or threatened, you will see how passing is their concern. More importantly, look to the parched earth, as many souls are barren and dry in respect to their spiritual health. Come to Me, My people. I am the living water who will refresh you. I am an oasis of graces ready to have you drink of them and bring you a renewed life in the spirit. See, by this withering without water, how you can be cut off from this life giving spirit if you refuse My love. See that you are nothing apart from Me and follow Me, so you can join in My one body of faith which will nourish all of My faithful."***

Later, at church, I saw a large government building. Toward the base of this building was a miniature building just like the large one. For added emphasis in trying to understand this vision, I saw a large goat standing on top of a mountain. This gave Me the sense of something about the evil one. Jesus said: ***"My people, you are seeing that there is a one-world government of men which controls all the major governments of the world. This group is the monied people of the world who mastermind many of the wars and great movements in the economy of the world. They use the UN as their pawn to effect their wishes. Just so, the Anti-Christ***

will exploit this one-world government to do his bidding. These things have been put in place so the evil one could grab power quickly at his appointed time. Even though these powerful influences are among you, I will confound all their plans with My own plan which surpasses any of their power. As My victory comes, all these evil men will be cleansed from the earth. My will will reign supreme and those faithful will enter My glory with Me. Keep hope and pray for your deliverance through this trial."

Wednesday, June 21, 1995:

After Communion, I saw someone wearing a hooded cloak but could not see his/her face. Jesus said: ***"My people, this cloak represents those who have many things of this world. Your lesson today is that of giving to others and at the same time to be more detached from this world's attractions and possessions. Sharing your wealth with others shows you are not selfish or seeking money for its own sake. If you are to follow a true Christian life, you are to concentrate more on heavenly things instead of earthly things. Raise your thoughts to a higher plane where you can live daily with Me and follow My will for you rather than your own desires. So be willing to throw off the cloak of this world's comforts and set yourself spiritually free so you can grow in My grace and peace."***

Later, at the prayer group I first saw a priest and He was hearing confessions. Jesus said: ***"My people. you should prepare your souls often through My Sacrament of Penance where you can keep yourself holy until I come for you. With My Sacrament of Reconciliation always available to you, why do you not take more advantage of these graces which await you?"*** I was looking down on a prayer group from above. Jesus said: ***"You must keep close to Me in your prayer groups where you will find My presence. This is a source of grace and hope where you can console each other. Your prayers and petitions reach out to Me where I can bless your intentions as it conforms to My will."*** I saw an older nun dressed in brown robes and she was looking down saddened. Jesus said: ***"Many of the clergy are finding it hard to renew their numbers. Fewer vocations are being had in areas where prayer is lacking, but some areas have many vocations where hearts are loving and seeking My help."*** I saw a knight in armor ready for battle. Jesus said: ***"You***

must be My prayer warriors because there is much sin in your world and not enough prayer being said in reparation for that sin. The result of sin is spiritual death to the soul if there is no Repentance. In order for sin to be forgiven, each person must recognize he is a sinner and ask for My forgiveness. One must reach out in love to Me and I will accept you back as the Father of the prodigal Son." St. Theresa the Little Flower came with flowers. She said: ***"You must keep yourself humble at all times and be ever vigilant in prayer. When your prayer life ceases, your love for God will grow cold. Be on guard, for the evil one will test you more with distractions as you help others. Be an example and encourage your prayer group by asking my help. You have asked me here and I will watch over you all."*** I then saw Mary standing in front of me and she directed me to look at a picture I have on my wall of the hearts of Jesus and Mary. Mary said: ***"You should see me as your model to follow so that your heart will be united with my Son's heart. It is your deep love for both of us that will draw you to us. By your consent of will we will honor you with a grace to protect your soul from the evil one."*** Finally, I saw a picture of St. Joseph and He said: ***"I want all of you to call on me to watch over and protect your families. Pray that I will help you and your members in all your difficulties. I was guardian for the Holy Family and I can be your guardian as well. And finally, when one of your family members is called from you, pray to me in earnest that their soul will be saved and that they will enjoy a happy death when their Lord receives them."***

Thursday, June 22, 1995: (S.S. John Fisher & Thomas More)

After Communion, I could see Maria E. in prayer saying: ***"Give praise to Jesus."*** I then could see a huge canopy as for dignitaries. Jesus said: ***"In life you will have to deal with principalities and powers as long as the evil one influences those here. As in My day, your rulers make their influence known and they are only concerned with their station in life and how they can lord it over their subjects. Such stubborn pride and flaunting of authority will find its end, since they give Me little less than lip service and only when it suits their purpose. Such hypocrites will receive their just chastisement. But even though such people try to influence you, never flinch from your resolve to stand up for your Chris-***

tian principles in all issues. Even if you face criticism for My name's sake, hold your ground in following the Church's teaching and you will be rewarded in secret by My Father. This is a true heroism, standing for truly holy principles."

Friday, June 23, 1995:

After Communion, I saw several faces of Jesus with a gaze of love and compassion. Jesus said: ***"This day is a celebration of My love for all My people. You know I am infinite love which is not conditional in any way. No matter how many offenses you may commit, I am always here ready to forgive you. It is you who limits our love relationship. Even though this weakened state of yours causes difficulties, see My love. Now it reaches out to everyone. You are all united to Me in this one bond of creation, so you should see how loving Me and your neighbor all fit into the divine plan. Do not let hate and jealousies steal your heart but receive My love and make it effective in the lives of those you know and meet. Keep My love before you always through constant prayer."***

Saturday, June 24, 1995:

At Marci's house in Mississauga, Canada, I was feeling a strong presence of Mary and Jesus. Mary said: ***"We are giving witness to you of the love in our hearts for all of you present. We are joined as one heart and we are happy to receive your prayers. This is holy ground and our presence you are feeling is made stronger by your prayers. Continue to pray my Rosary, dear children. I am watching over you as a loving Mother."***

Later, at St. James Church in Oaksville, I saw a large cross, then some modern architecture. Jesus said: ***"I have given you many messages on the honor you place on My position of the tabernacle. Some may think it is improper to place My repository behind the altar, yet most of the time when the Mass is not being said, I am being relegated to a place of less importance. I have given you My Blessed Sacrament to show My love for you and give substance to your churches. See that it is My presence which is most important, not any of your opinions. Again, your modernism is a problem for the people to have a true sense of the sacred. Realize, also, My crucifix is an important part of your***

worship so that you understand suffering is a part of this world. You are a resurrected people by My death on the cross, but you must share in My suffering, if you are to grow in your faith. Give honor and praise to Me in My Church, no matter how you find Me. Give thanks for all I have given you and keep yourself holy by Confession so you may receive Me with a pure heart and soul. Do not commit sins of sacrilege by receiving Me with serious sin on your souls. Believe in My One Body which will be with you until the end of time."

At St. Patrick's Church in Mississauga, after Communion, I saw an altar and a large moving picture of the all loving face of Jesus. After, I saw a maroon curtain and it gradually became very dark. Jesus said: ***"Today you are seeing Me as I came to your earth as the Messiah described in the Scriptures. Even though you were not worthy, I came to free all of you from your bondage of sin. Receive Me into your heart so your love may be complete in My oneness. My children you will also see Me return at the judgment as I promised My apostles, but, before that, I have sent My Mother to prepare the way. You also are receiving many signs and messages from those messengers I have chosen for you. You have had prophets in the Old Testament to tell of My First Coming. Now, again, I will send more minor prophets to tell of My Second Coming. They will spread My word of hope and peace among the people willing to listen to My plan of salvation. I pour out My love on you from My heart so you will be strengthened to endure the coming trial. Rejoice and be glad, for your salvation is near."***

Sunday, June 25, 1995:

After Communion, I saw a circular necklace with earthen pottery pieces all around it. This represented the One Body of Christ which all of us are a part of. Jesus said: ***"I love My people with an enduring infinite love which unites all of you in My one body of love. I give you My Eucharist as often as you wish to partake in My spiritual body as well. It is My graces I wish to shower on you like the rain from heaven. You remain in full union with Me until your sin breaks My loving bond of life. When you do things against My commandments, you are no longer following My will for you. I provide My Sacrament of Reconciliation to come to***

Me for the forgiveness of your sins. By your being sorry for your sins, I will forgive you and make you whole again in My body. Remain close to Me by avoiding sin and your happiness will truly know no bounds in My love. Apart from the vine, you are as branches which will wither and die in your spiritual life. So take your sustenance from Me and you will bear fruit in the faith forty, sixty or a hundredfold."

Later, at Mass after Communion, I saw an altar with a cross and there was a crown of thorns around the middle of the cross. Jesus said: ***"My Mother and I are happy to greet all the pilgrims of life. You all share in a common love of Myself and My Mother. You are setting a beautiful example for all the faithful at a difficult time of life. My lesson today is in conjunction with many of your petitions for healings both physical and spiritual. It is My peace, especially, which I bring to you and I ask that you share with each other and your own family members. Through your daily prayers you must continually work toward perfection in your actions and your words. You must not only try to evangelize My message of love but you must live by your deeds as well. Do not act like the hypocrites who teach one thing but live another. I am referring particularly to how you respond to your own family members. Be understanding of their problems and try to realize why they are living a certain way. Be careful not to criticize each other but work things out as if I was directing you in how to live. It is this peace in your own family which must come first since you have the biggest input to that success. If all of My families were in prayer together, peace in your families could spread to the rest of the world. When you put aside your selfish desires and think only how best to help others, you will be witnessing My love as I want you to share it with everyone."***

Monday, June 26, 1995:

After Communion, I saw some people and they were behind bars. Jesus said: ***"I have chosen you from the womb since I formed you. You have been My people since I created you. Give thanks and praise to your God for His generosity for your gift of life. Because of Adam's sin, I have come to die and suffer for you that you may be released from the shackles of your sin. Many take life and My gift of salvation for granted but these, indeed, are gifts*** *for which you should be most grateful. Come adore your God and give Him thanks after each Communion. You can listen to Me in your prayer where I can direct you how to imitate Me in life."*

Later, at church, I saw some candles and then the back of a Church with only wooden chairs, but very sterile for worship. Jesus said: ***"My people, you must come to My Church in the right spirit to carry on the teachings of My apostles. Many of your churches have lost a sense of the sacred and need to concentrate on a community of love and My peace. You must pray more for unity in your churches. Do not let the evil one bring division among you. You must keep central in your churches the altar, the tabernacle and the crucifix. These are the major elements to draw you to Me so your worship will be according to My will. You must understand to give Me praise and adoration as well as thanks for My gift of the Mass and My Blessed Sacrament. Do not allow these gifts to be desecrated or abused by changing their meaning. In all of your services you must keep close in prayer. Then your worship will be a joy to Me instead of creating division."***

Tuesday, June 27, 1995:

After Communion, I saw an older priest going into a sacristy. Jesus said: ***"My people, you should thank God when you have been blessed with a newly ordained priest. Your numbers of priests are few and all the more you should be thankful. The blessing comes even more in bringing Me to you in the Sacraments. My Baptism greets your children into the faith. My penance provides forgiveness for your sins and My Eucharist brings My presence into your heart and soul everyday. When couples are joined in marriage, My creation can continue in harmony with Me by the priest's celebration of the Sacrament of matrimony. You are receiving Me at all times during your life through the hand of the priest. Again, give praise to God for all I have given you through your priests. Also, pray for your priests that they will be sustained in their vocation."***

Later, at church, I saw some noted persons who seemed to act very prestigiously. Jesus said: ***"My Son, you must remain humble in all you do. Do not seek any fame or notoriety. Do not listen to the evil one who wants you to seek acknowledgment before men. It is My love you must hold dear to your heart. You are receiving***

My words to teach and encourage the faithful. For those who would call them 'your' messages, continue to remind them that I write them for you as in your prayer. It is important that you keep close in prayer for this will give you My peace amidst all your distractions of the world. All of My messengers are being called at this time to spread My message of hope and prepare for the coming trial. After the purification, all will see for themselves how My word comes to fruition and your joy will be complete."

Wednesday, June 28, 1995: (St. Irenaeus)

After Communion, I saw a priest in red vestments and then I saw an olive branch representing peace. Jesus said: ***"My people, I bring you My peace to your confused world much like I brought peace to My apostles. This is a spiritual peace much different from your earthly peace. With Me, you will take your rest, for I will refresh your souls with My heavenly graces. I do everything for you that you may understand the extent of My complete love for you. In return for My love to those who believe in Me, I expect your love also. You are truly free if you come to Me with open hearts ready to do My will. Give yourself wholly into My love and your heart will truly experience My peace which awaits all My children."***

Later, at the prayer group I first saw some people in a room and in front of their faces I could see the Heart of Jesus. Jesus said: ***"I bring you My love so that you may see Me in every person you meet. My Sacred Heart is overflowing with love which I want to share with each of My people. Let My love lead you to My presence in the Blessed Sacrament. Visit Me often where I can shower My graces on you."*** I then saw a fireplace and people were sharing their life's story with each other as in a family thirty years ago. Jesus said: ***"Your families were more of a focal point in your lives years ago. Now TV and many activities separate the family members. You must treasure each other in your families and make time to share with each other. This is a great faith experience to share Me with your children in prayer. Family prayer can provide My help to keep your families together and protected from the evil one."*** I saw a new shiny car that was very expensive. Jesus said: ***"Take care in your priorities to help one another. Do not be so extravagant with your spending but share your excess with those less fortunate. Remember those you help here in this life are help-***

ing Me. Do many works of mercy and you will receive heavenly treasures which are worth more than your earthly possessions." I saw someone holding a crown. Jesus said: ***"A crown in heaven awaits all My would-be saints. Strive to follow My will and you will be preparing for your life with Me in heaven. Struggle in this life to do as many good deeds for others as you have time and My blessings will gain you your prize in heaven."*** I could see a gate opening and many people entering. Jesus said: ***"I have loosed the gates of heaven by My death on the cross. What was closed since the time of Adam's sin is now open to all of you through My love. Go before the people and invite them to come to My wedding feast. You are My bride and I, the groom, bid you to enter."*** I then saw Mary. She said: ***"You are seeing my holy oil coming forth to anoint the people. Use my gift to help in healing those who believe by faith they can be healed. This is a great grace of my mercy you must share with others."*** I finally could see some people walking about. Jesus said: ***"Reach out to help your neighbor in their need. When they are hungry, provide them with food and drink. When they need clothes, freely give what you can. When they are sick, visit and pray with them for a healing. When they are in prison, comfort them. These fruits of your life's work will witness for you when I ask at the judgment if you helped Me in your neighbor. I will say to thee, 'Well done My good and trustworthy servant, come enter your master's house.' To those who were selfish and did not help their neighbor, I will say, 'Out of My sight, you evil doers, since you would not lift a finger to help Me.'"***

Thursday, June 29, 1995: (Sts. Peter & Paul)

After Communion, I saw Marie E. praying and she said: ***"Praise God and keep the faith."*** I then saw a soldier of Our Lord's day about to whip towards me and I saw chains. Jesus said: ***"As I told My apostles, you will suffer for My name's sake. Consider yourself fortunate that you are able to proclaim My message of salvation to everyone in the face of rejection by men. You may suffer in this world but by your steadfastness in the faith you will be joyful in the next world with Me. It is for love of Me that you will struggle and witness My Gospel against great odds. You will be fighting principalities and powers of the demons. Yet, fear not, for I will be at your side to win the spiritual battle. When all***

will seem hopeless, you will see My victory over evil and all the faithful will taste of My dinner as their reward. Keep faithful in prayer and remain full of hope to see Me in My splendor as you receive your reward."

Friday, June 30, 1995: (First martyrs of Rome)

After Communion, I saw a black man as a slave. Jesus said: ***"As different races have been enslaved and tortured, you also will be looked on with disdain for believing in My name. Just as these early Christians were martyred, My faithful will be at the mercy of evil men during the tribulation. Some of the early Christians were buried in the catacombs but some sought refuge underground as well. You, also, will live a life of hiding from the authorities. My love overshadows you as I will protect you spiritually, but you will suffer much for Me as I had to suffer. The humanity of man's weakened state does not always worship Me by choice. It is My gift of faith I give to those I choose that will be your salvation."***

At church, I saw a woman and some children. Jesus said: ***"You all are My children and I care for you as a Mother does for her little ones. I am here to receive your prayers of petition. I am here also to console you in your difficulties in life. I am even here to share in your sufferings and hurts from others. I am like a libation poured out to help absorb your pain and allow you to carry on. Love Me as I love you and My peace will smooth over any rough bumps in life. You will see even in your relationships with people that sharing your love with others makes people happy around you. If you complain often, people also will reflect your worries. So live life with a loving spirit helping others when you can. You will be appreciated and they will know you by your faith and love in Me."***

COME
LORD
JESUS
J.
T.

Index